WANDERING
IN
ROCK COUNTRY

STORIES BEYOND BEAUTY

Tien C. Lee

ISBN 978-1-957943-30-5 (paperback)
ISBN 978-1-957943-31-2 (hardcover)
ISBN 978-1-957943-32-9 (digital)

Rushmore Press LLC
1 800 460 9188
www.rushmorepress.com

Printed in the United States of America

PREFACE

This book shows features of rocks and tells their life stories. It is the sequel to a 2018-publication of similar nature. With a different subtitle, the current version compiles over 250 new pictures of specimens and outcrops.

Four categories of rocks are covered: silica, carbonate, hard rocks (igneous and metamorphic), and soft rocks (sedimentary) spread over six chapters. Under each chapter, the sections are written in the sequences of chance availability of specimens. My works is meant for people who appreciate rocks, and I wish my storytelling could be inspirational for readers to formulate their own narratives.

Educated as a geologist/geophysicist, I had dealt with geophysics and hydrogeology, before I retired in 2009, on projects ranging from mathematical modeling in the laboratory to hands-on practical applications in the field. On the jobs, along hiking trails, and in rural housing subdivisions in southern California, I chanced upon and picked up a variety of rocks, some of which carry fascinating geological stories. Occasionally I bought specimens from rockhounds, and I have also benefited from friends' gifts or loan of rock specimens. I feel an urge to tell rock stories before the eventual disposal of my collections.

All specimens were picked from free-standing, loose pieces in the field; none was chiseled from outcrops. Specimens have not been altered or enhanced unless they are cut to facilitate identification or display stability. All images are photographed by me and augmented with a half-dozen internet posts by others.

Not intended for systematic, scientific studies, the book is essentially a show-and-tell presentation, based mainly on observations of hand specimens. Some questions raised here could be resolved by instrumental analyses, but I prefer to limit my narration to what can be seen with the naked eye because observation of a rock's beauty is all we can do in the field and outside the laboratory. Beyond beauty, however, does a rock have an interesting story to be told?

I have visited many museums over the years to see their exhibitions of rare, magnificent mineral collections. Although I appreciate the beauty and rarity, most of us have little chance of seeing those fascinating specimens in the field. I wish to know more about specimens than the information commonly given in display name tags. What is the geological story behind each specimen? It would be beneficial if the descriptions could be more informative to visitors.

For better or worse, I attempt to set an example by stretching my imagination to make up short stories based on visual observations. Wherever possible in the stories, I have tried to tweak together some basic principles in physics, chemistry, biology, or geology. Common rock names are adopted here, which may not be conforming to the finesse for professional practices. Some pieces might be inadvertently misidentified or misinterpreted because natural staining, varnishing, or patination could have masked their true identities.

The text is written for personal collection with some daring, original thought. My claimed observations and interpretations could be provocative, contentious, or even outrageous to some readers. Now, please let us pause for a moment! Few serious geologists would tell a story solely depended on one rock specimen.

My version of each story is just a beginning for the complete narrative to be told. One must visit outcrops, examine rock samples in the context of their geologic settings, make laboratory analyses, and synthesize data by modeling to generate a convincing geological story. Obviously, I did not do what I have preached. But let us see what can be said about each individual specimen.

This new edition of book keeps the same chapter labels as its predecessor except that: Chapter 5 is now called *FANTASY* to reflect more imaginative tales, and the previously imposed one-page limitation for story of each specimen is now relaxed. All stories stay independent of one another; hence readers can flip to any section without losing continuity in context. In addition, the *MISCELLANY* as chapter 6 supplements what are left out in the earlier chapters. The *GLOSSARY* has been expanded to include *INDEX* as Chapter 7. A few figures in the earlier version that have been duplicated here are pre-fixed with I for post-publication designation of volume or series I.

To avoid jamming the text with references, very few references have been cited here. If needed, however, please search on the internet with some keywords from the text for more relevant information.

I do not have an exotic mineral or rock collection, but I hope my storytelling about commonly available rocks is educational and entertaining to some rock hobbyists and enthusiasts as well as aspiring geologists. Enjoy!

Acknowledgment

In this version of '*Wandering in Rock Country*, I rely more on specimens that were gifted or loaned to me by friends as individually acknowledged in the text. I appreciate the camaraderie among the rockhounds through Orange Belt Mineral Society (OBMS) of San Bernardino, California. My wife, Zora, has accompanied me to most of the field trips for rock collection or geological sightseeing.

Section 5-9 on *Martian Blueberries* was added at the suggestion by Emeritus Professor Chi-Yuen Wang of UC Berkeley to address any equivalent earthlings on Mars. Section 5-10 was written under the 2019-21 stay-at-home mandate to minimize person-to-person spread of viruses during the Covid-19 pandemic; it was an extension of Section 5-8 on stromatolites, the most ancient structures built by the oldest known organisms (cyanobacteria), which still strive nowadays to construct stromatolites in the extremophile niches on Earth. This section also ponders on the origin of life by way of viruses and bacteria – a farfetched fantasy.

I am particularly indebted to Emeritus Professor Lewis H. Cohen of UC Riverside, who is the first person other than myself to have painstakingly read through and commented on the first draft (except the miscellany chapter).

It has been years since I began to write something about my collection and make the display stands for the specimens. Unless otherwise noted, all photos were taken under the shade of normal day light without filtering. I hereby relinquish my mental burden of collecting rock specimens by releasing two unorthodox rock books. Thanks for browsing through it and please send any comment to tien.lee@ucr.edu.

Cover Page

See Figure 3-19, *suiseki gneiss*, for the narrative of the cover picture.

INTRODUCTION

I wander in the deserts, hills, valleys, and beaches.

Stand the rocks in solitude with beauty. Born differently,
nurtured distinctly, rocks live transitorily but stay eternally.
I try to speak for the rocks, but they do not talk back.

Will you voice for them?

Tien C. Lee is an Emeritus Professor of Geophysics/Hydrogeology at the
University of California at Riverside, California. He grew up in Taiwan and is
professionally cultivated in the USA. He has published peer-reviewed journal
articles on seismology, geoelectricity, hydrogeology, potential field, and
terrestrial heat flow. He has also authored three books: *Applied Mathematics
in Hydrogeology* (1998), *Thus I Came* (2017; 2020), and *Wandering in Rock
Country* (2018; 2022).

Chapters

Chapter 1: SILICA WORLD

Chapter 1: SILICA WORLD

Solid silica (SiO_2) occurs commonly in two forms near the Earth's surface: crystalline quartz and cryptocrystalline (amorphous) chalcedony.

Macroscopically, crystalline quartz occurs in two categories: common quartz (opaque, milky white) and quartz crystal (transparent). The latter includes rock crystal (clear), amethyst (purple, violet), smoky (black, dark), citrine (yellow), rosy (pink), druse quartz (tiny crystals in crevices or vugs) and many other uncommon names, e.g., prasiolite (green). One can easily find pieces of common quartz without crystal form on trails in granitic terrain but nowadays, the chance of finding quartz crystals is very slim (except druse quartz) in areas frequented by the public.

Amorphous chalcedony usually appears milky white but sometimes tinted with grayish, brownish, reddish, or even bluish hues. There are many varieties of chalcedony. Well-known are agate (translucent, curved & color-banded, typically found with geode), onyx (flat, parallel, and color-banded), and jasper (opaque, reddish brown, irregularly shaped). Those are usually associated with volcanic rocks through deposition from or replacement by hydrothermal fluids in the rocks' crevices or former gas-bubble chambers (cavities); and sometimes they can also occur in sedimentary rocks as replacement products. Some silicas can precipitate by incorporating water molecules as opal – a hydrated chalcedony or mineraloid.

Chalcedony can also originate directly from deposits of silica-bearing organism such as single-cell diatoms and radiolarians, but those organic debris usually end up as sedimentary chert. Besides, silica can congregate as nodules, aggregates, or even layers in sediments as gray chert or in limestone as black flint. Silica-bearing fluid can transform buried wood to become petrified wood, replace carbonate in seashells as chalcedony-shell fossils, or lithify animal excrement as rarely found silicified coprolite. In short, silica can preserve dead organism or its debris as chalcedony fossil.

Sometimes it could be challenging to tell different varieties of chalcedony apart with the unaided eye, especially for small-sized samples. The first step is to get oneself familiar with different varieties that have already been named by others. But the key is still to name it by mineral association or in the context of field observation.

1-1. Biogenic Chalcedony

Figure 1-1A: Chalcedony fossils – three sea clams and two deformed clams. LD = Long Dimension of specimen = 4 cm.

We have talked about various inorganic processes that lead to the formation of different varieties of chalcedony. Silica-bearing organisms can also turn into chalcedony (chert) after their dead bodies are buried. Conversely, can some living organisms extract silica from solution and excrete silica to form solid chalcedony? In other words, is there any biogenic chalcedony? Based on observations of a suite of chalcedony nodules, following are my arguments for its occurrence in the past. No proof is here shown because traces of micro-organisms, if they still exist at all, are visible only through high-power microscopes, or electronic microscopes. We see the products of silica discharging organisms with the naked eye only, not the dead organisms themselves, nor the organisms of which the skeleton are made of silica such as diatoms or radiolarians.

My collection includes 60 specimens of chalcedony. All are neat, clean, solitary specimens. The absence of visual trace or residual of their host rocks implies that those specimens have been easily retrieved from their host formation. A few splinters (less than 3 mm across) have resulted from damage during sample handling, rather than forced 'cord-cutting' off their sites of genesis. The ease of retrieval suggests that those chalcedony samples were incubated in cold, soft sediments, not in association with volcanic hydrothermal activities.

FOSSIL CHALCEDONY: Three of the five pieces of chalcedony in **Figure 1-1A** are clearly clam fossils of which some features are further revealed by their mirror images. It is ambiguous, however, whether the other two could have originated from sea clams. If so, the two clams were highly deformed before fossilization. By association of occurrence, we can claim that all five pieces stem from the same environment – coastal seafloor. Shallow seafloor is a fertile ground where micro-organisms flourish, but favorable environment does not guarantee chalcedony can be produced biologically.

Those clam fossils in Figure 1-1A are silica replacement of former calcareous clam shells, not fossilized biogenic product of dead organisms. The replacement is post-depositional, either prior to or post burial. Putting aside the five specimens as replacement chalcedony, my idea of biogenic origin of chalcedony mostly pertains to other specimens in the following pictures.

BLACK/WHITE CHALCEDONY NODULES: All chalcedony is featured in black or light tan and sometimes a hybrid of the two colors. (Light tan is here referred as white for short.) All appear translucent; and all can be well polished as proven with a few trial specimens.

The exterior of the white chalcedony is grainy, rough, like the skin or rind of a litchi fruit; while the black's exterior is smooth, without litchi-like protuberances, but marked with subtle lineation, like the longitudinal ridges on our fingernails. And of course, the hybrid displays a texture that straddles in between. Common to most are the presences of small sub-nodules to individual 'master' nodules.

Two stand-alone pieces of ball-shaped black chalcedony (no sub-nodule) are presented in **Figure 1-1B**. There is no equivalent, sub-nodule-free, white chalcedony.

Figure 1-1B: Ball chalcedony. Largest LD = 4.5 cm.

Note that the white chalcedony in the center entraps one black sub-nodule; and the white and black together look like a partially peeled litchi, revealing its inner black nut. The partial exposure of the enclosed black is not caused by peeling off the white because the white band around the 'black nut' resembles the rest of the white rind in its grainy external texture. The white somehow stopped growing and only partially encloses the black sub-nodule nut. Note also that the white and the black are seamlessly 'welded' together such that there is no visible hairline-fissure between them.

The remaining two in Figure 1-1B are hybrids. One of them is topped-off with a small dark bead (a small sub-nodule) and the other is necked with a white scarf between the black head and body. Note the transition between black and white is also brisk, not gradational.

Figure 1-1C: Chalcedony with white coating of opal? Largest LD = 6 cm.

SUB-NODULES: Three of the five nodules in **Figure 1-1C** are infused with multi sub-nodules; the central spherical piece is coated white, but it is free of any sub-nodule; while the frontal piece is splattered with patches of white coat, and it consists of triple lobes and one small sub-nodule.

The central spherical nodule is wrapped in a white coat; inside the thin coat is a ball of pitch-black chalcedony, as revealed by black dots and a small cut at the base. (See the cut face in Figure 5-3A.)

The nodule north of the white ball in Figure 1-1C is spheroidal and is paler than others; on its exterior sprout several small 'cancerous' sub-nodules. On the left (west), a black nodule is topped with two stacked sub-nodules. And to the right (east), several sub-nodules cluster atop the main base nodule body; those sub-nodules stack up to make this specimen, about 6 cm in height, among the largest in my suite of collections.

The profusion of sub-nodules and their stacking suggest that these nodules were secreted meticulously by ancient silica consuming and excreting organisms. Precipitation of and replacement by silica in groundwater or hydrothermal fluids cannot yield such 'growing' textural intricacy. Barring the possibility that the two nodules with white coat in Figure 1-1C were doped by a rock dealer into the pile of chalcedony specimens, the coating is also inferred here to be biogenic by reason of association. If true, the white coat is opal although it lacks the telltale opalescence.

OPAL COATING: This claim of opal occurrence is substantiated by two white veinlets which join as a 'longitude-and-latitude T-junction' on the central ball (lying, respectively, between and north of two dark black

Figure 1-1D: Intertwining of black and white chalcedony. Largest LD = 6 cm.

specks). Each veinlet is less than one millimeter wide. The 'partial latitude of the T' spans 5 centimeters in arc length with a lengthwise hairline fissure in the mid-line, while the 2-centimeter arc segment along the 'longitude of the T' is intact with a distinctive white hue. The presence of T-veinlets symptomizes dehydration of opal because their thinness facilitates dehydration. If verified, the white coating exemplifies an event that opal could also occur at sea-water temperature although it is well known that opal can originate from diatom – a single-cell alga with silica cell wall.

BIOGENIC: **Figure 1-1D** supplements my contention of biogenic chalcedony. The white girdles around the black (gray) and spreads out. Then, later, the dark sub-nodules sprout out of the white wraps. Many sub-nodules show growth rings at the tips, like a retracted, taper-off multi-segmented rod of a car antenna or a mechanical projector pointer (not laser pointer). Deposition or precipitation cannot create such complex patterns in space and time. Instead, micro-organisms are the architects and builders who configured the fascinating oddities of these chalcedony nodules.

Figure 1-1E: Contrast in black and white chalcedony. largest LD = 5 cm.

There were two main types of bacteria (micro-organisms) that fed on the same silica from seawater but spit out distinctive white and black chalcedony. One thrived in one favorable season or for uncertain period while the other flourished in another period. The two phased or swapped in and out as the dominant actor when the respective growth season alternated. They grew together, cohabited together, during the transitory period to yield the gray hybrid of the white and black. **Figure 1-1E** shows mostly the dominant black chalcedony, except one contrasting white chalcedony at the center for comparison in the same picture-taken setting.

Somehow the nodules ceased growing beyond 6 cm. All were uplifted tectonically at unknown past time from their birthplace at shallow seafloor, along with their unknown host sediments, to become part of the present Morocco, where all the samples have originated.

Alternatively, could those specimens originate from silica-rich colloidal solution? To alleviate the uncertainty, I sliced the largest specimen in half and trimmed some sub-nodules (**Figure 1-1F**) to find any clue of biological activities, but the telltale signature of micro-organisms was not found.

Figure 1-1F: Chalcedony with shaved sub-nodules. Largest LD = 5 cm.

DIAGRESSION: Now, let me digress the arguments for biogenic origin: presence of white and black chalcedony in the same nodule with litchi-like grainy surface on the white and subtle finger-nail-like ridges on the black; profusion of sub-nodules in solitary, stacked, or taper-off forms; sprouting of black sub-nodules on white wrapping or alternatively the girdling of white over the black cores; and most critically, association of nodules with chalcedony-clam fossils.

Precipitates from colloidal solution will spread and flatten like a horizontal disk and will be dotted with botryoidal spherules, not globular or stacked sub-nodules. Even though the in-situ orientations of nodules are unknown, the axes of sub-nodules appear to orient randomly with respect to the principal trend of each master nodule. Organisms can do it randomly but, colloidal precipitates would spread over the curved surface of master nodules. Thus, such negative reasoning kills the prospect of colloidal solution as an alternative for the origin of chalcedony.

Next, let someone else prove in the future by instrumental analyses that the litchi-like protrusions on the clam fossils and on the white chalcedony are the same (i.e., all chalcedonies are of marine-origin), that white-coated chalcedony in Figure 1-1C and the rest are the same genetically (i.e., it was not doped by the rock dealer), and that the white coating is opal. These proofs will assure that the suite of chalcedony is biogenic, and that opal can form at seawater temperature.

Figure 1-1G is the rest of my collection of 'biogenic chalcedony'. It is amazing that the organisms can yield chalcedony in various hues (black, white, tanning white) and forms as well as varied sub-nodule clusters.

Finally, we may have a semantics issue. The clam fossil is a replacement product and can be properly called a nodule. However, all the nodules

Figure 1-1G: Chalcedony nodules with various shapes and sub-nodules. Largest LD = 6 cm.

which are alluded to biogenic origin are concretions in geological terminology because they used to grow or accumulate through secretion by micro-organisms. I use the term, nodule, for ease of visualization and in analogy to cancerous nodules as produced from uninhibited cell multiplications.

1-2. Desert Chalcedony

The suite of chalcedony presented here looks drastically different from the biogenic suite in Section 1-1, reflecting intrinsic contrasts in occurrences and compositions as well as extrinsic environmental impacts. All specimens in Figures 1-2A through -2E

Figure 1-2A: Three pieces of chalcedony, in transition from black to tanning white. LD = Long Dimension = 10 cm; uncut; from San Bernardino County, California.

come from a desert wash where chalcedony pieces scatters amid abundant volcanic debris and lesser amount of plutonic rock fragments.

Figure 1-2B: Chalcedony mixed with host rocks. LD = 10 cm; uncut; from San Bernardino County, California.

TRANSITION in STAIN: **Figure 1-2A** exhibits three pieces of chalcedony: black, light tan, and hybrid in the middle. Each is clean, free of extraneous attachment. The display stands for the in-situ seating posture because all undersides are slightly, reddishly tainted. All surfaces were densely dented or chipped and have pit holes. However, the uneven surfaces have since been smoothed and the visible surfaces are well polished and varnished naturally, especially so for the tan-

white piece on the right. Some pits in the tan-white piece are dappled with dull, black stuff but its ground-facing side is devoid of any black spots. The contrast between the sky- and ground-facing sides suggests the black spots could be relics of sun-light dependent organisms – implying incipient lichen genesis (symbiotic fungi and algae).

The 'purity' in composition suggests each piece originates from the central part, not peripheral, of a once much-bigger parental chalcedony body. And the hybrid piece comes from a transition zone between the black and tan chalcedony.

TUNNELING: Around the margin of the original chalcedony body, silica-bearing fluid had infiltrated into fissures (as stemmed from cavities or crevices) to result in inter-fingering locks between chalcedony and the hosting igneous rocks. A mixed chunk, after breaking loose from its hosting rock body and resurfacing in the desert wash, evolved into meticulously carved chalcedony as splendidly presented in **Figure 1-2B**. The exterior of the two pieces, volcanically originated and desert-modified, is radically different from the biogenic bunch in Figure 1-1 series.

Figure 1-2C: Chalcedony, intermediate between the former two sets. LD = 10 cm; base cut.

The host rocks, composed of quartz, feldspar, and biotite, can be easily weathered in the presence of water, especially for the latter two mineral groups. In addition to the role of chemical weathering, water is more effective to erode the rocks. The erosion is not due to mechanical abrasion by the flowing suspended particles; instead, it is done through static ice-water phase change and associated volume expansion and contraction.

Although scarcely available in the desert, moisture that condensed in cold nights or in winter from the atmosphere can seep into micro-fissures or interface between different mineral grains. If the water freezes, it expands to enlarge the fissures. As the ice thaws, the enlarged fissures can draw in more water through capillary suction, readying for the next round of freeze-thaw cycle at greater amount of moisture and in the renewed but bigger and longer fissures. The progression is

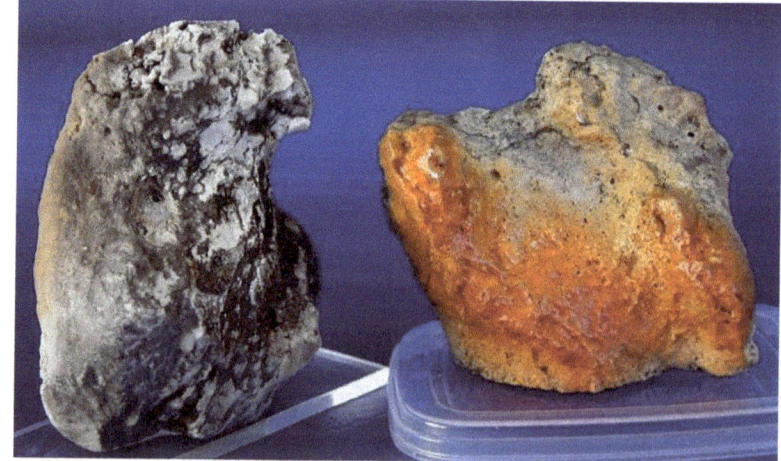

Figure 1-2D: Country rocks around ancestral chalcedony. LD = 11 cm; base cut.

imperceptibly slow; however, after countless cycles, particles are dislodged to form dents, depressions, caves, and even tunnels. The excavated was former feldspar or quartz grains or mica while the protruded is the weathering-resistive chalcedony. The mesh of residual chalcedony-veinlets is wind-smoothed and -polished, but the depressions stay unsmoothed.

Note the feldspars are dotted with black pinholes. So, the product of what we see today in Figure 1-2B has resulted from water-inflicted physical dislodging and chemical weathering as well as wind polishing and varnishing. The specimens in Figure 1-2A are visibly pure chalcedony and therefore suffer no chemical weathering to yield the rugged surface relief.

TRANSITORY: **Figure 1-2C** shows two chalcedony specimens that lie somewhere in texture and composition between the two suites in Figures 1-2A and 1-2B. The reddish front on the left piece was ground-facing, stained by ferric soil water. The right piece is well polished on its front face, but its rear is rough, signaling a recent breakage.

NEXT TO THE HOST: The set in **Figure 1-2D,** picked from the same desert wash, is a representative of country rocks that have enclosed the realm of chalcedony. The light-colored and red-tainted (right piece) is a broken piece of quartz with minor attachment of feldspar. Its underside was red stained by passing ferric soil water. The ground-facing surface is better polished than the sky-facing surface, suggesting that flash water might have flipped over this piece some time ago, or the rear is a recent breakage face.

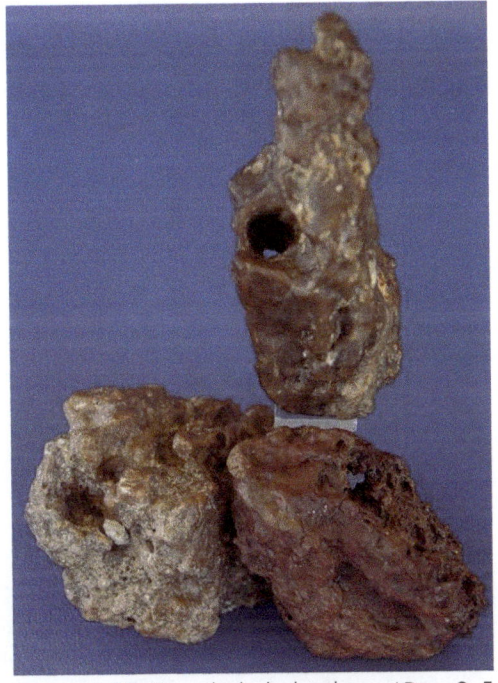

Figure 1-2E: Tunneled chalcedony; LD = 8.5 cm for center piece; one base cut; from San Bernardino County, California.

The piece on the left in Figure 1-2D is featured in three shades of darkness. The white is composed of feldspar and quartz grains, plus small blotches of chalcedony. The reddish in the rear surface is tainted by soil water. The rest is covered by dull, black patches with potential biogenic origin for its dullness. (Inorganic varnish is usually shining.) Underneath the red and black covers is the white 'framework' of this specimen. The framework is eroded to appear 'bird-beak like' because of its weathering-prone feldspar. As compared to quartz, the feldspar also tends to be easily inhabited by microbial to have the dark gray coverage.

Another set of 'clean' chalcedony is shown in **Figure 1-2E**. Other affiliated minerals have been stripped by weathering and erosion. The tunnels follow the paths of former weak minerals. Next to the wedged white grain on the lower-left piece is a hidden tunnel, which is not seen in the picture.

1-3. Sedimentary Jasper

Figure 1-3A: Volcanic jasper. LD = 13 cm; no cut; from San Bernardino County, California.

Figure 1-3B: Red jasper and yellow-red-black intermixed jasper. LD = 10 cm; multiple cuts; from San Bernardino County, California.

This section heading is a little outlandish because jasper is normally associated with volcanic activities. But let us go ahead anyway.

In association with volcanic activities, silica is one of the last components to precipitate from the residual magmatic or hydrothermal fluids, which can be mixed with influx of groundwater in contact with magma. The fluid fills the crevices, which were formed owing to cooling contraction of the newly solidified volcanic rocks or vacated by escape of gas from lava. As the temperature drops, silica precipitates as white chalcedony, or yellowish and reddish jasper if tainted with ferric iron.

VOLCANIC ORIGIN: **Figure 1-3A** displays two pieces of jasper. They were dislodged naturally from their parental volcanic rocks. As solitary pieces in the desert, they have been subject to wind abrasion and water denudation through innumerable cycles of water freezing expansion and ice thawing contraction. The two are not well polished but some of their ridges and protruding parts are. As it is, the two are suitable for small desktop suiseki – arts of rock display in Japanese.

There are many shades of jasper, depending on types and amounts of trace-element constituents. Jasper is opaque, as distinguished from translucent chalcedony. **Figure 1-3B** is an example even though we cannot qualify and quantify the iron impurity with the naked eye. The left piece can be much better polished and varnished, as compared to the right one.

Impurity in jasper is either blessed or cursed. It is blissful for a skilled craftsperson to turn a non-appealing piece into cherished jewelry. On the other hand, impurity found after cutting the stone can be a frustrating experience to a novice of jewelry making.

The top piece in **Figure 1-3C** is a banded jasper, like the left piece in Figure 1-3B. Beside color banding, we hardly see another physical interface. However, the bottom piece is clearly layered. There are four jutting jasper layers, with recessive furrows sandwiched in between. The jasper layers are well polished, but the furrows of the unknown material are not. The jasper in the bottom piece was formed episodically (or rhythmically) with intervening pauses for non-jasper material to top over before a new jasper layer was set in again. Deposition in the top piece was continuous but punctuated with periodic changes in color.

Figure 1-3C: Banded (top) and layered jasper. LD = 9 cm; uncut; San Bernardino County, California.

SEDIMENTARY SIGNATURE: **Figure 1-3D** showcases two contrasting pieces of jasper in color, texture, polishing, and varnishing. The first two attributes are intrinsic properties while the other two reflect extrinsic environmental impact by wind and water in the desert. The left piece, coined here as 'pseudo-jasper', was picked from ancient lake deposits just outside the volcanic field where the 'true' jasper specimens were collected.

The layering in the jasper on the right is poorly defined; in contrast, layering is obvious for the left piece but becomes obscure upward. The layers appear to have been welded together at gently wavy seams.

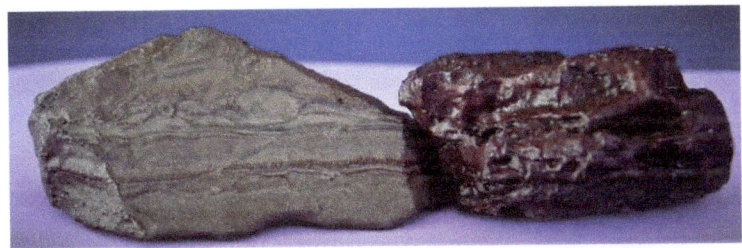

Figure 1-3D: Jasper and layered 'jasper'. LD = 11 cm; uncut.

Much better layering is featured in **Figure 1-3E**. The left piece is weakly cross bedded while the right piece displays sharp layering contrast. Both elicit the conjecture of their sedimentary origin. What is the major difference in layering between the bottom piece in Figure 1-3C and the right piece here?

Figure 1-3E: Layered 'jasper'. LD = 13 cm; uncut; San Bernardino County.

The jagged interface is due to cooling volcanic rocks while the smooth favors particles settling through a water column.

Both are softer than jasper in Mohs hardness and respond sluggishly to a neodymium magnet. They are lighter than the equivalently sized sedimentary rocks. Their individual particles or grains are not visible; other than layering features, all appear homogeneous. I found rock fragments scattered randomly atop ancient lake beds but no parental source rock.

What is the riddle here? They are relics of lacustrine deposits, originated from volcanic ash which sank to the floor of a lake next to the jasper-yielding volcanic field and had since been silicified to look like jasper for its pale reddish-brown hue. One may coin them as 'pseudo-jasper', or more properly sedimentary chert for its connotation with sedimentary origin.

Figure 1-3F: Red ventifact sandstone. LD = 15 cm; uncut; San Bernardino County, California.

SANDSTONE VENTIFACT: The contention that the pieces in Figure 1-3E are sedimentary origin is supported in **Figure 1-3F**. The two are among rock fragments found atop the same ancient lake deposits mentioned previously. The red is not surficial staining; it extends into the interior. Debris eroded and transported from the nearby volcanic rocks are the sources for the lacustrine sandstone.

The grains in the sandstone are barely discernible and appear well sorted, suggesting the fine-grained sands were deposited by low-energy (i.e., slow) running water, not by flash flood water which would have yielded debris of mixed or chaotic grain-size distribution.

If the above scenario for sandstone is acceptable, one may offer an alternative interpretation for the ultra-fine-grained rocks in Figure 1-3E. They are mud deposited far away from the lake shore, not fallout from volcanic ashes. There, the muddy water kept the site a little anaerobic and hence created a reducing environment. The product (Figure 1-3E) in the reducing environment was pale, in contrast to the bright red in Figure 1-3F.

Next, let us view the extrinsic environmental factors that have shaped the two pieces of sandstone in Figure 1-3F into what we see today since they became solitary after being fragmented from their parental bodies. The two are each bounded by faces to form the so-called ventifact that has resulted from wind abrasion with suspended particles. Each is then partially coated with white calcium carbonate as caliche, which is plentiful in alkaline water in the desert. The caliche pastes two small patches to the rear face of the tower piece but engulfs the entire lower half of the pyramidal piece. (Jay, my grandson, picked up the tower piece when he was a third grader.)

STAR-BURST JASPER: Since we are on the subject of jasper, let me duplicate an earlier Figure I5-20a (Lee, 2018) as **Figure 1-3G** for

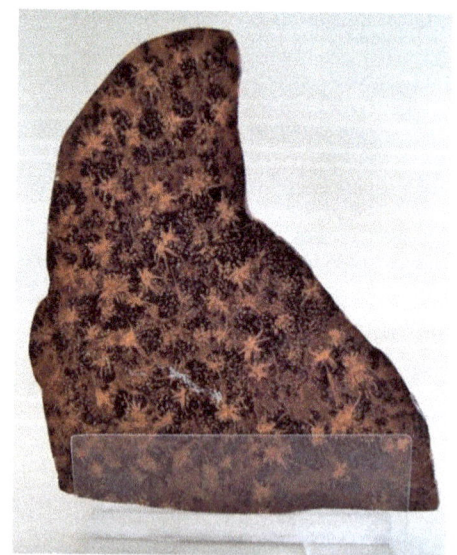

Figure 1-3G: 'star-burst jasper'. LD = 20 cm; slab; bought.

supplementary narration. Some name it star-burst jasper in trade, but a three-year-old toddler called it spider-crab rock. I viewed it as a porphyritic volcanic rock: trachytic andesite or preferably silica-deficient phonolite. The reddish orange 'crabs and their eggs' (phenocrysts) submerge and populate in the 'sea of black lava' (groundmass).

Observation: Grossly, clusters and specks align to form subtle, up-down flow lines; accretion of clusters reduces locally the speck density around each cluster; and some shoots are broken and stacked over as shady, subdued, orange-red patches. The white strip is secondary filling in fissures.

Story: Red feldspathod nucleates from the cooling, low-viscosity, moving lava, to result in flow-aligned specks of phenocrysts. Numerous specks then coagulate into shoots of tapered stripes. Moving lava sweeps the shoots into clusters, like the jammed twigs or branches as frequently observed in receding flood waters; few clusters, if any, initiate radially crystal growth. Meanwhile, volcanic gases have escaped from the fluidic lava, unlike vesicular basalt, to leave behind no visible vesicles. The final scene of those presumptive dynamics is preserved in what we enjoy seeing today when the lava has cooled sufficiently to immobilize phenocryst migration in the groundmass. As a footnote: if the phenocrysts were white, some rock collectors in China might call this porphyritic rock: a high-valued chrysanthema (or daisy) stone (see Sections 6-2 and -8).

1-4. Geodes

Geode is a globular nodule with an interior cavity. Its enclosing crust is usually white chalcedony and the crust itself is wrapped with an irregular skin cover made of its host rock. Its cavity may be partially or fully filled with crystals such as quartz, calcite, and sulfide minerals. A hollow one is more prized because it may have better crystals.

Geode nodules occur usually in limestone, volcanic ash, or pyroclastics (tephra, volcanic debris) where cavities can offer space for mineral-bearing fluids to infiltrate and grow crystals. The nodules are more resistive to weathering and erosion than the host rocks; hence, nodules often stay in solitary form amid sediments that derive from the hosts. However, it is challenging to know what are inside before you have the geode cut open unless you have prior experience with the same suite of geodes.

Figure 1-4A: A geode with three distinctive types of crystals. Picture width is about 5 cm; one cut; courtesy of Mr. Jim Wolford.

The geode in **Figure 1-4A** is unusual for its bearing of three recognizable types of minerals. Most geodes carry one type of minerals only. Notable is the thick, white chalcedony crust that encases the cavity.

Most abundant are druse quartz crystals, small but well developed. Two thin translucent plates of calcite (one to two mm thick) stand out of the cavity. The free edges of the calcite plates are serrated, signaling sequences of crystal growth. It is uncommon for calcite to occur in solitary platy state. The yellowish hue coupled with translucent plate may alternatively be suggestive of siderite (ferrous carbonate), not calcite (calcium carbonate).

Two visible clusters of black, acicular (needle-like) crystals radiate into the cavity (respectively at the upper middle and lower right). The black mineral is a sulfide yet-to-be named. Two blue specks at the left-middle are optical illusion.

See Figure 1-9 and Figures 4-10D through 4-10G for more pieces of geodes. The latter group display UV fluorescence.

Figure 1-4B is an assortment of silica products, natural or man-made. From left to right, the back row displays quartz, jasper, and jasper, while the front row registers geode, chalcedony, and chalcedony. The stacked disks on the left stand are man-made fused (amorphous) silica; while on the right stand, the disks are manufactured quartz with their C-axis of crystal structure pointing upward. The cylindrical post at the center is acrylic plastic.

Except the geode, all specimens are very well polished naturally. The two pieces of chalcedony in the front row seem to have been precipitated out of colloidal solutions of silica. The banded quartz on the left of the rear row is splintered from quartzite (metamorphosed sandstone) to inherit its black stripes.

Figure 1-4B: An assortment of silica products. LD = 10 cm; some base cuts.

The geode is not what one wishes to have: druse quartz crystals fill up the entire cavity. But one does not know it has been filled-up until the piece is cut open. The cavity is mostly stuffed with fragments (dark brown) of the hosting volcanic rocks and the rest filled with chalcedony, which shows an incipient crystallization of quartz had started but there was not enough space to wiggle around for crystal growth – a case of death on arrival. The chalcedony in the geode fluoresces in green under ultraviolet light (see Chapter 4 for more about fluorescence).

The tall jasper is a mold after former cracks into which silica fluid permeated. The grooves on the jasper are filled with unknown but silicified scrap which is grainy for holding tiny jasper fragments. Abrasion and polishing by desert wind turn the piece into a small outstanding decorator.

At the rear center is a jasper of which the origin is tough to decipher. Whatever it is, remarkably, nature somehow makes the piece into an equilateral triangular disk with a bilateral symmetry around a median line.

Figure 1-4C: Quartz in geode. LD = 23 cm; from western Texas; courtesy of CTAL.

The two sets of man-made disks are visibly indistinguishable but optically, yes; and thermal conductivity of the two is distinguishable by finger touch. Pressing one's fingertip on the disks, the quartz disk will conduct heat away rapidly to have a cool feeling, in contrast to the feel for the poorly conductive fused silica. The sets were used as reference standards for measurements of thermal conductivity.

Figure 1-4C depicts one geode that is almost filled with quartz crystals. It has a chalcedony crust or rind. The chalcedony is layered in parallel with the egg-shaped exterior rim; the quartz crystals grow perpendicularly to the chalcedony band and meet inward at the median line. See Sections 1-9 as well as 6-9, -12, and -13 for some exotic agates.

Figure 1-5A: Flat quartz crystals with tourmaline inclusions. LD = 19 cm; uncut; bought.

1-5. Quartz with Tourmaline Inclusions

Big quartz crystals occur commonly in pegmatite dikes. The crystals typically appear in hexagonal columns when there is sufficient space for growth. Both crystals in **Figure 1-5A** have inclusions of schorl (black, opaque, iron-rich tourmaline), which is the most common accessory mineral in pegmatite. The left piece is a single quartz crystal but flat or plate-like in shape. Note the characteristic striation across the column. The 'equant' schorls are more like leftover end-impressions rather than cross-sections of elongated schorls. One residual imprint shows this piece has once held some green transparent tourmaline.

Figure 1-5B: Quartz crystal. LD = 13 cm; faces polished; from San Diego County, California.

In detail, the right piece is a composite of many smaller quartz crystals covered with sericite. Sericite is scaly, flaky, shining, white fine-grained muscovite, which is an altered product of potassium aluminosilicates (e.g., orthoclase). Without the sericite coating, the quartz crystals would appear clear and transparent.

Figure 1-5B depicts an imperfect but typical quartz crystal from one pegmatite dike. It consists of one big crystal and several much smaller crystals. The reddish-brown piece is orthoclase. The top and front surfaces have been polished.

The rose quartz in **Figure 1-5C** is banded with some cloudy white seams. Like the crystal in Figure 1-5B, it comes from the same pegmatite mine for gem-quality *elbaite* [a green lithium tourmaline, see Figure I1-13b of Lee (2018)]. But specimens in Figures 1-5B and -5C do not bear any tourmaline, which is boron aluminum silicate with trace amounts of sodium, potassium, magnesium, and iron to account for a variety of colors.

Figure 1-5C: Rose quartz from San Diego County, California. LD = 27 cm; cut at both ends.

1-6. Smorgasbord of Quartz

Quartz is the most commonly observable and identifiable mineral on the Earth's surface because it is very resistive to weathering. It is one of the final products of weathering; it can be broken but cannot be further weathered. At the Earth's surface, it is the most stable mineral chemically; it cannot be altered unless its ambient physical and chemical conditions have changed substantially.

Strolling along beaches, one sees mostly sandy quartz grains. Hiking along hilly

Figure 1-6A: Quartz pebbles. LD = 11 cm; no cut; from Imperial County, California.

trails on granitic terrain, one often stumbles over small white chunks of opaque 'common quartz', not necessarily beautiful but, for sure, eye-catching for its white color in contrast to the background of grey, unattractive rock fragments or yellowish or greyish brown soil.

Quartz released from disintegration of rocks is usually not pretty from a collector's perspective. It can be a different story if a chunk of quartz is broken loose from a quartz vein or dike, like the one depicted in Figure 1-5C. You can cut, shape, and polish it to your satisfaction. Better yet if nature takes care of it to your delight. Following is an assortment that I chance-encountered in the desert three decades ago.

Figure 1-6A depicts a set of quartz pebbles. Each is slightly different in texture and in content of trace elements too. Common to all is their oval or ellipsoidal shape. The shape is indicative that transport agents (water and wind) are at work.

All pieces in Figure 1-6A have been well rounded, polished, and varnished to have shining sheen of coating but none is stained. Most came from a desert wash; some could have existed near an ancient lake shore (but I forgot which is which).

The tower one with brownish red stripes and the piece at right-front corner could be quartzite – not a vein quartz.

Three pieces of quartz breccia are pictured in **Figure 1-6B**. They keep sharp corners and edges as breccia. They are well polished and varnished. The front piece is relatively better stained.

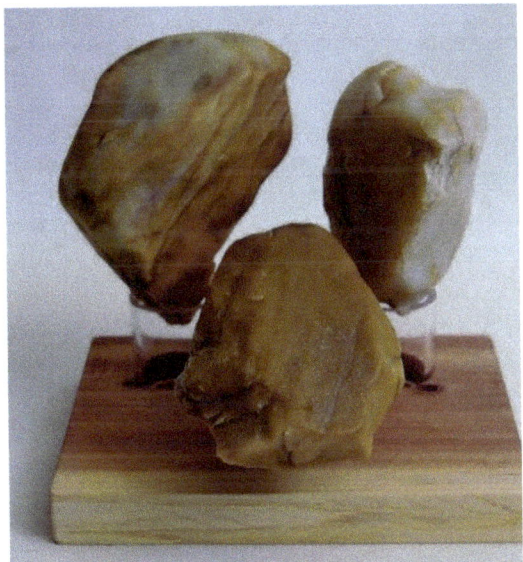

Figure 1-6B: Quartz breccia. LD = 10 cm; no cut; Imperial County, California.

Figure 1-6C: One black and two white pieces of quartz breccia. LD = 13 cm; no cut.

Figure 1-6D: Quartz cobbles. LD = 9 cm; no cut.

Figure 1-6E: Quartz and basalt cobbles. LD = 14 cm; no cut; Imperial County.

Figure 1-6C displays another set of quartz breccia: one black and two white. All come from the same desert wash. The three are better rounded as compared to the pieces in Figure 1-6B.

They do not appear to have been stained but the two white pieces are well polished and varnished. The rear face of the dark piece has a breakage scar because it has faced the ground for a long time to keep it from wind abrasion, polishing, and varnishing, as happened to the rest of the faces.

Figure 1-6D depicts one set of quartz cobbles from the desert in Imperial County. The dark green on the right piece is natural color, not stained. All are well polished and varnished.

Two pieces of different rock types are stacked together in **Figure 1-6E**. The white one is a loose piece from a quartz vein. The black one is not quartz but included here for its causal resemblance to a quartz piece. Both are well polished and varnished naturally in the desert.

The black piece is basalt. It has several strings of vesicles. Most of the vesicles are rimmed by unknown white mineral. Three white spots mark depressions filled by caliche. Note that each caliche blob is outlined by a narrow ditching or furrowing gap with the basalt, signaling re-dissolution of caliche at its edge.

Hidden amid the dark basalt are elliptical, pale white grains, which were fillers to former vesicles but are now veiled under thin black veneer to mask their identity.

Figure 1-6F: Quartz pebbles and one geode. LD = 11 cm; Imperial County.

Figure 1-7A: Chalcedony: LD = 10 cm; one base cut; from San Bernardino County.

Figure 1-6F depicts five quartz pebbles and one geode. Slightly tainted in yellow, all white pebbles come from the same desert in Imperial County, California. They are well polished and varnished.

The geode comes from Riverside County. Chalcedony fills the entire cavity enclosed by lava. Note the subtle gray ring in the chalcedony. It fluoresces under ultraviolet light.

1-7. Chalcedony versus Quartz

Chalcedony is cryptocrystalline quartz. That means it does not have any visual crystal form or structure unless it is examined under optical or electronic microscopes but macroscopically, quartz does not always appear in recognizable crystal form either. So, how do we tell them apart?

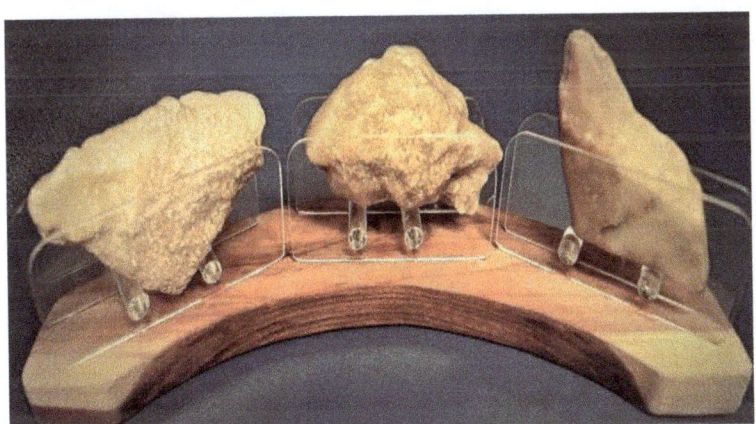

Figure 1-7B: Vein quartz. LD = 11 cm; no cut; from Imperial County, California.

Solitary pieces of quartz and chalcedony may look alike on the desert floor because of their shape modifications in response to erosion and weathering under similar environments. Both can occur in veins or dikes, but chalcedony originates from hydrothermal deposits as cavity filling while quartz comes from intrusive dikes. Loose pieces of vein quartz usually appear opaque, chunky, blocky, or massive while a piece of chalcedony seems to be porous as formed by a network of interconnected veinlets or sheets. As such, chalcedony often shows irregular outlook which mimics its housing cavity in the hosting rock; because of its low rate of silica precipitation, it can be layered or appears radiating, crisscrossing, or botryoidal. If not broken recently, most isolated pieces in the desert have peculiar shape with smoothed corners.

Note the holes on the right two pieces of chalcedony in **Figure 1-7A**. Those visible holes do not prevail in the interior (unlike vesicular basalt or lava). The holes came from sites that were once occupied by impurity or weak mineral components but have now been evacuated or unplugged through erosion and weathering. Overall, chalcedony has abundant microscopic pores and hence can be easily dyed in color, as appear in some trade shops of rocks and minerals.

The left piece in Figure 1-7A is chunky with irregular outlook. The white on the right piece is opal coated – another indicator of chalcedony.

Figure 1-7C: Bulky vein quartz. LD = 25 cm; no cut; from Imperial County, California.

See more 'porous' or 'tunneled' chalcedony in Section 1-2. Those tunnels develop along the loci of weak components.

Three small pieces of yellow, chunky, massive vein quartz are displayed in **Figure 1-7B**. They are citrine quartz. All have been shaped, polished, stained, and varnished in the desert. They show no pit hole because each is homogeneous, without any extraneous components to have been preferentially weathered to make surficial pit holes.

Figure 1-7C depicts two pieces of common, white vein quartz. The right piece had suffered a recent natural breakage. However, both are well polished and varnished but not stained. They are impervious, massive.

Similarly, **Figure 1-7D** depicts another pair of bulky, massive vein quartz. The two common quartz pieces differ in zoning and color, but both are well polished and varnished. Unlike chalcedony, all the nonporous vein quartz cannot be easily dyed artificially.

Figure 1-7D: Massive vein quartz. LD = 16 cm; one base cut; from Imperial County, California.

Figure 1-7E: Partially encrusted vein quartz. LD = 21 cm; from Arizona; gifted by Mr. Tony Gilham.

Figure 1-7F: Chalcedony. LD = 21 cm; from San Bernardino County, California; My wife made the display plates.

Figure 1-7E is another chunk of white vein quartz. It has been partially coated with thin, reddish-brown crust. **Figure 1-7F** depicts one more piece of porous chalcedony. The two have drastically different surfaces. The former is bulky with erosional features and with harsh edges as dislocated from its parental quartz vein; while the latter has an outlook of spillover cast and its right side, which used to be ground facing, was stained reddish brown by soil water.

Figure 1-7G exhibits an odd piece of brownish chalcedony. The peel-off spots show it is a white chalcedony covered naturally with thin brownish coat. It has a harmonious outlook, dotted with minute protuberances.

Figure 1-7G: Brownish coated chalcedony. LD = 11 cm; source unknown; gifted by Tony Gilham.

1-8. Rutilated Quartz

Figure 1-8 depicts one clear quartz crystal with rutile and ilmenite inclusions. The acicular rutile is so abundant in this quartz crystal that rutile needles appear everywhere. Its color ranges from golden yellow to white. The latter has bundled into fibrous-like stripes while the former stays as solitary needles although all are individually acicular and straight. (The specimen has been slightly polished at the edge.)

Accompanied with the inclusion of rutile (TiO_2) is another inclusion of grey titanium-bearing ilmenite ($FeTiO_3$). Also, by differences in color or reflection, some small quartz crystals are recognized, and they have grown inside the much bigger enclosing quartz crystal.

Here we notice the similarity in chemical formula between silica or quartz (SiO_2) and rutile (TiO_2); and note ilmenite as a compound of ferrous iron oxide (FeO) and titanium dioxide (TiO_2). Following is speculation on sequence of events.

As judged by the observation that white rutile radiates from one cluster of grey ilmenites at the lower right corner, ilmenite is the first mineral crystalized. And rutile comes next. Meanwhile, incipient quartz crystallization comes along. But

Figure 1-8: Quartz with inclusions of rutile and ilmenite. LD = 5 cm. Forgotten source location; polished.

before those small quartz crystals grow fully, all (ilmenite, rutile, and tiny quartz crystals) are engulfed later by rapidly crystallizing silica fluid.

It is amazing that the rutile can keep its needles straight under the imposing stress associated with quartz crystallization. A likely cause: the slenderness of the rutile needles can diffuse the imposing stress, like using a needle to pierce resistless into soft material without seriously distorting itself and the shape of the material being punctured. A minor note: the rutile was enclosed by the growing quartz, not the other way around that the rutile had pierced into a growing quartz crystal. In short, all crystals have grown from viscous, stagnant fluid, unlike the precipitation of feldspathoid from moving, low-viscosity lava narrated for Figure 1-3H.

1-9. Geode with Bird's Eye

Like many other geodes, the piece in **Figure 1-9A** is encrusted with thin, banded chalcedony (agate) – a rind of curvy, twirl, dark or bluish gray laminae. Inward to the cavity, white, druse quartz grows perpendicularly from the chalcedony or agate rind. Those quartz crystals sprouted or nucleated at closely spaced points around the inner rind simultaneously but did not have enough space to grow into well-defined crystal forms. As a result, the crystals jammed one another to squeeze out a columnar-like structure. However, near their growth termination tips, somehow purple or violet, semi-transparent, hexagonal crystal forms appear – the amethyst.

Most noticeable and unusual feature in this cut-face of geode is one "bird's eye". The eye consists of one dark pupil (core) and four concentric circular rings which are similar in shades of color to the rind of geode. Comparable growth patterns of white quartz and violet amethyst also appear around the eye. The crystals grow radially outward from the circular eye. However, the growth in the lower part, where the 'eye-crystals' meet the 'rind-crystals', is free of purple amethyst tips between them.

Figure 1-9A: Geode with bird's eye. LD = 28 cm; unknown source location; courtesy of Ms. Mary Hedden.

Amethyst is also absent where two sets of white quartz crystals, grown from opposite-facing segments of rind, juxtapose against each other, for example, at the lower-right bay of the geode. Hence, the juxtaposition happened before the amethyst appeared.

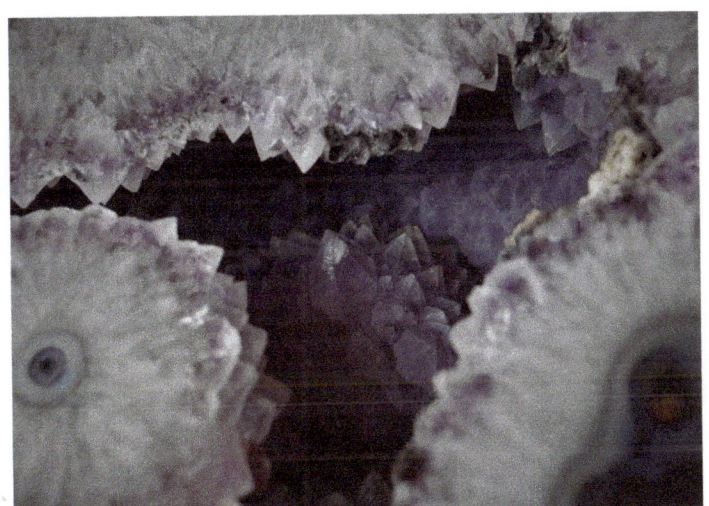

Figure 1-9B: An interior view of the geode in Figure 1-9A.

How did the bird's eye occur? One clue can be seen at the bright but out-of-focus spot in the cavity. An enlarged in-focus image around that spot is presented in **Figure 1-9B,** which also reveals more amethyst crystals. In the mid-background, there appears one dome-shaped knoll of crystals, of which the largest piece sticks out as the apex. If the knoll were cut, a second bird's eye would appear under the apex. The pedestal or apron of amethyst around the bird's eye exemplifies the radial growth of crystals from a central core and the termination with amethyst tips.

The violet color of amethyst results from minor impurity in iron or other transitory elements. Greater amount of impurity may turn it into a dark-black smoky quartz. If heated artificially, the amethyst's color may change too. Also, the rim of this geode turns green under ultraviolet light, but the rest does not fluoresce. See Figures 1-4 and 4-10D through 4-10G as well as Sections 6-9, -12, and -13 for more geodes.

Figure 1-10A: Vein quartz. LD = 13 cm (left); no cut; from Imperial County, California.

1-10. Crystal, Chalcedony, and Slickenside

Figure 1-10B: Vein quartz. LD = 15 cm (left, base cut); from Imperial County, California.

By now, the readers have seen a few common varieties of solid silica. Here are short narratives and pictures of more specimens.

The specimens in **Figures 1-10A** and **B** came from four different quartz veins. The former two are slightly translucent. After their detachment from parental veins, both have been tumbled around in the desert to have sharp corners rounded. Their surfaces are well polished: one is stained reddish yellow but the other keeps its white color except streaks along fissures. Can the colored piece have original or intrinsic hue? One cut to the rock will have the answer.

The two specimens in Figure 1-10B are opaque and both are not stained. The left piece is polished naturally while the right piece has been well eroded in the desert to yield bumps (mesas) and depressions (holes).

Figure 1-10C exhibits one half-disk of agate. Its base was slightly sliced off for stability on the stand. The piece is 3 cm thick at midway of its base and from there, it tapers to the peripheral; and the sharp

Figure 1-10C: Half-disk agate: LD = 14 cm; from San Bernardino County, California.

Figure 1-10D: Chalcedony and feldspar. LD = 12 cm (right); from San Bernardino County, California.

edge was rounded off artificially. The white coating is believed to be opal – dehydrated chalcedony, but it does not fluoresce.

Specimens with mixed components of chalcedony and feldspar are presented in **Figure 1-10D**. The surface of the chalcedony (left piece) is full of protuberances and pits because most feldspar was extracted naturally; it still bears minor residual feldspar. In contrast, the piece on the right is dominated by feldspar; a few bits of chalcedony dot the rear side. In natural setting, the fronts of both pieces faced the ground and thus sustained a reddish stain from soil waters.

Figure 1-10E depicts a chalcedony with one dozen grains of olive-green quartz. It is the only quartz-bearing chalcedony specimen that I have seen in Mojave Desert. Prasiolite as green quartz was first discovered in Brazil. If the well-polished olive-green grains are indeed prasiolite, this piece would be a rare occurrence here.

Figure 1-10E: Green quartz in chalcedony. LD = 15 cm; base cut.

Figure 1-10F: Quartz crystals. LD = 8 cm. All crystals are local but the tallest one.

All quartz crystals in **Figure 1-10F** are clear or transparent except the central piece with brown strips of natural coating (which is duplicated from Figure I1-18b of Lee, 2018). All crystals are characterized with striations across the columns. The striations in each crystal are birth marks, stacked toward a hexagonal pyramid end. The frontal,

horizontal piece is unusual for its bi-pyramidal growth.

Figure 1-10G depicts slickenside on a piece of quartzite. Slickenside marks the relative movement of past faulting.

With respect to the overlying but missing piece, this piece slipped southeast. On the slip surface, one can also feel with fingers that it is easier for the overlying piece to glide toward northwest.

Figure 1-10G: Slickenside. Riverside County, California. Gifted by CTAL.

1-11. Brecciated Yellow Jasper

The specimen in **Figure 1-11** came from a small ridge of volcanic rocks. As usual, the lava is highly fractured and brecciated. Innumerable blocks, big or small, scatter on the desert floor. Some are jasper and fewer are agate, but more are lava. All are opaque yellow, black, brown, or red. Here is one piece of brecciated brownish-yellow jasper, which is dotted with specks of red and black agate. It also bears some remnants of untransformed

Figure 1-11: Brecciated yellow jasper. LD = 14 cm; uncut; from San Bernardino County, California.

Figure 1-12: Onyx and geode. Upper, LD = 11 cm; courtesy of Mr. Jim Wolford.

black lava and veinlet-like fillings of caliche; some black lines, however, are cracks without filling of secondary minerals. Hence, the filled and unfilled fissures reminisce different stages in brecciation.

The transformation of lava by silica into jasper happened before the rocks were brecciated. Some streaks or sutures in the jasper blocks appeared during the transformation (note the big piece at the upper left corner). Those sutures can make an interesting subtle pattern if the jasper is polished and made into decorative cabochons.

1-12. Onyx and Geode

Figure 1-12 features two views of one chalcedony nodule. The cut-face shows it is an onyx with parallel banding while the natural surface hints it may be an aggregate of small agates with curved and closed banding. To a rockhound, the challenge is how to predict the internal structure from the exterior texture.

1-13. Spherical Opal

Opal is an amorphous silica mineraloid, not a crystalline mineral. Unlike chalcedony, opal is hydrous. Although opal bears a few percent of water, it is solid. Opal can dehydrate through prolonged heating.

Figure 1-13A: Spherical opal. LD = 6 cm; base cut; Gifted by Mr. Tony Gilham.

There are three major types of opal: precious, fire, and common. Precious opal, qualified for jewelry, is iridescent or opalescent (as exemplified by some soap bubbles, butterflies, and seashells). It shows 'play of color' when viewing angle is changed, light source is altered, or opal object is moved or rotated. As a gemstone, precious or fire opal can be of concern for its sensitivity to dehydration due to heating and for vulnerability to scratching due to its low Mohs hardness (less than 6).

Common opal is indeed common, appearing as low temperature deposits inside cavities or between rock crevices. To the naked eye, common opal could be confused with chalcedony. Frequently opal from the desert have subtle webs of dehydration cracks or grooves. For lack of the appealing play of color (iridescence or opalescence), common opal is not traded as gemstone.

Figure 1-13A depicts a piece of common opal. One cut face at its bottom, with milky white color, suggests this piece of opal can be polished well.

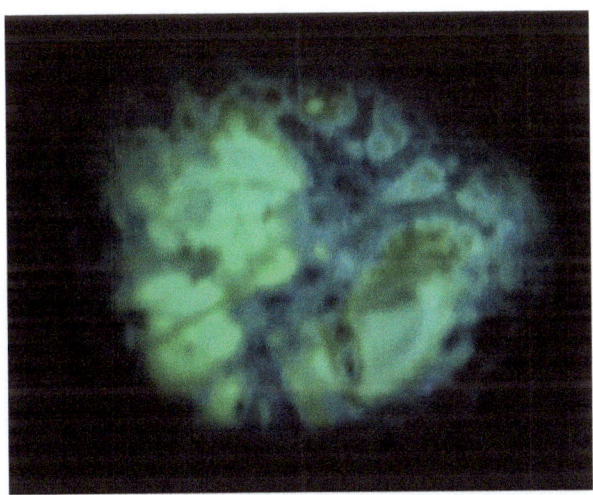

Figure 1-13B: Fluorescent opal under UV light, bottom face of Figure 1-12A.

Under ultraviolet light, the polished part of the bottom-cut face fluoresces in green (**Figure 1-13B**) while the unpolished grooves turn bluish grey. The exposed milky-white spots on the left sector of the sphere also fluoresce in green (but the picture is not shown here).

The rest of the white surface does not fluoresce even though it bears subtle dissolution pits or grooves. Likely, those dissolutions are not deep enough to expose the undehydrated interior opal. If correct, one may conjecture that the white is a veneer of dehydrated opal, and that the relic veneer does not fluoresce; only the undehydrated interior of opal will show green UV fluorescence.

Chapter 2: CARBONATE PLAY

Carbonates commonly appear in two forms: limestone or marble. Limestone is principally calcium carbonate (calcite, $CaCO_3$). Sometimes calcium carbonate can be altered to form dolomite by replacing calcium with magnesium (i.e., $CaMg(CO_3)_2$). Dolomite is both a mineral and a rock name; hence, occasionally dolostone is used as an alternative rock name. Limestone can originate from precipitation of carbonate-bearing fluid, accumulation of some calcareous organic debris, and deposition of former but fragmented limestone. It may or may not bear fossils.

Marble is limestone that has been metamorphosed at elevated temperature and pressure. It is not always devoid of any fossils, depending on the intensity of metamorphism.

Carbonatite is a rare intrusive or extrusive igneous rock, typically occurred in association with magma activities in

Figure 2-1A: Marble from riverbed. LD = Long Dimension = 18 cm; one base cut; from San Bernardino County, California.

continental rifting zones, where a continent is being pulled apart. It is not pure; its naming is qualified for igneous rocks with more than 50% carbonate.

Beside recognition by texture and mineral/chemical composition, carbonate rocks can be scratched with a pocketknife. Also, in general, calcite fizzles in weak acid like vinegar but dolomite needs stronger acid to respond effervescently.

2-1. Alluvial Carbonate

Here the section title is meant for solitary carbonate gravels that have been transported and shaped by flowing water, not something precipitated chemically from river water. A piece of rock, after being detached from its parental body and falling into river is subject to abrasion by water. Its roundness or shape depends on its composition and texture as well as power of particle-laden water flow and transport path and duration. The effects of the latter two external factors are difficult to assess for one individual piece alone. So, let us focus only on the internal factors, composition, and texture, which shape this marble piece in **Figure 2-1A** to approximate the geometry of a frustum of circular cone.

Because of its low hardness (Mohs hardness of calcite is 3 on a 1 to 10 scale), the marble cobble does not withstand well to tumbling and onslaught of particle abrasion in flowing water. However, its elongated shape or slant cylindrical surface is strongly influenced by fissure distribution. The erosion along the central, vertical fissure appears on pace to split the cobble into two halves. ('Vertical' refers here to the display stand, not the rock's natural orientation.) The upper and lower bases developed from horizontal fissures. The top-ward narrowing width (or diameter) coincides with closer spacing in fissure distribution. One may argue that the slant surface has followed, first, the breakage along vertical fractures and then, modulation by horizontal fissures. The diagonal set of fissures, being less developed, adds flavor to the overall outlook of the marble but contributes little to the general shape of this piece of marble.

Figure 2-1B: A marble cobble. LD = 28 cm. One base cut; from San Bernardino County, California.

Figure 2-1B displays another piece of marble from a riverbed. For lack of visible fissures, this piece appears to have been shaped without any preferred trend during its tumbling journey in the river. The uniformity in composition also precludes such trend from forming, other than the geometry inherited when the piece broke loose from its parental bedrock.

2-2. Silicified Marble

Naming the rock in **Figure 2-2** can be controversial. The rock is originally a piece of marble. As seen in the picture here, only a few small white patches of marble remain visible at the lower right corner, where the rock edge is off the display stand. The rest and most of the front face is covered by coarse, white caliche, elevated mesh of yellowish-brown siliceous veinlets, and a central flat area with thin, brownish yellow coating.

Simply said, the rock consists of two parts on the surface: one is knife scratch-proof, and the other is scratch-susceptible. The former includes silicified marble and chalcedony veinlets while the latter embraces the thinly yellow-coated marble, the rugged white caliche, and the remaining, uncoated white marble.

Figure 2-2: Defaced marble. LD = 20 cm. One base cut; from San Bernardino County, California.

Fissures are visible over the thinly coated marble. Most of those fissures have been infiltrated by silica-bearing solutions to form a conspicuous mesh of chalcedony veinlets. Why? The chalcedony veinlets are more resistant to erosion than the un-silicified marble outside the fissures.

Is there a boundary between the silicified and un-silicified marble? The vertical lineament (which almost bisects the front face) exposes a potential candidate boundary, but knife-scratching across it shows indifference. Nevertheless, its extension to the bottom cut-face demarcates the two. Another short lineament near the left edge of the bottom cut-face plays a similar demarcation role. Between the two lineaments lies the scratch-proof silicified marble.

The lineament is not visible in the rear side because the rear is mostly covered by hard, brown siliceous crust with a few scattered windows that glimpse into the underlying yellow coated marble. The rear is caliche free (except one tiny patch near the top) and has no exposure of the original white marble because it had faced the ground for a long time such that no caliche could have been deposited on the shaded, cold surface. Calcium carbonate is less soluble in warm water and will accordingly precipitate on the sun-facing side. Caliche manifests re-deposition of the dissolved calcite – exemplifying natural dynamics of destruction and reconstruction in the desert.

Finally, here is what I am trying to get at: the sequences of evolving events. The piece started as a white marble. It was partially silicified, and chalcedony permeated along fissures. The un-silicified parts were eroded to make the chalcedony veinlets stand out like a net of high relief in sculpture. Then, after its detachment from parental marble, yellowish iron oxides from soil water stained the entire surface. And the caliche is the latest addition as hinted by a few uncovered yellow spots in the caliche field.

Figure 2-3A: Travertine in Marble. LD = 19 cm. One cut face; from San Bernardino County, California.

2-3. Travertine in Silicified Marble

Travertine occurs typically in association with hot springs activities. Dissolved calcium carbonate in hydrothermal fluids will precipitate as calcite or aragonite when the fluids ascend from underground to vent near the ground surface as highly mineralized hot springs. The process is primarily due to drop in partial pressure of carbon dioxide rather than change in fluid temperature. **Figure 2-3A** depicts one stripe of travertine sandwiched between two pieces of white marble, as viewed from a two-dimensional perspective on the cut-face. How did it happen?

SYMMETRIC BANDING: First, the white marble cracked open. Then, hydrothermal fluids infiltrated the cracks and finally calcite (or aragonite) precipitated out of the fluids to form the banded travertine. Someone may call it Mexican onyx (real onyx is reserved for chalcedony with straight parallel banding).

Note that the banding in travertine is symmetric with respect to an axial band as marked by one blue blob near the center of the picture. Fluids flow out of hot springs will not precipitate to yield the symmetrically banded travertine; it would appear like layering in fluvial deposits (for example, see Figure I2-11b of Lee (2018) or the base of Figure 2-7).

The fracture does not lie horizontally as seemed to be in this cut face. A horizontal flow will produce asymmetric banding, layer upon layer.

The symmetric or paired banding suggests the hydrothermal fluids flow along a steep fracture vertically (up or down) or horizontally (left-to-right or right-to-left). Either vertical or lateral flow along a vertical fracture will leave a thin lamina of calcite deposit on both walls of a crack, like clogging of cholesterol in inner walls of a blood vein.

Figure 2-3B: Travertine. LD = 16 cm; multiple cuts after Figure 2-3A.

Many barely visible laminae combine to form one visible band. The bands are color-distinctive because the passing fluids have slightly different iron concentrations at different periods of time.

Banding of travertine began at both fracture edges and progressed toward the median by depositing band after band. The blue-marked axial band is the last and youngest crack-filling calcite.

ISSUES: There are some unresolved problems. Did travertine start to form right after fracturing and add more bands as the crack or fracture was widening? Or did deposition or banding of travertine begin sometime after the fracturing was completed? A more intriguing question: how did the last solid central band come into being? Hydrothermal fluids have a limited capability of carrying dissolved calcium carbonate (i.e., finite solubility of calcite). How can it fill the void with solid calcite without leaving behind some unfilled gaps amid the solid?

Some fissures developed after the formation of travertine. Those fissures, featured with dark brown hue, extend from the white marble into travertine; and the diffusion of brown stain broadened the virtual width of the fissures. The marble is also tinted yellowish at a few spots. Pick your choice: Do those spots spoil or enhance the beauty of this piece of travertine in marble?

Figure 2-3C: Two-panel view of travertine. Slabs from Figure 2-3A.

Figure 2-3B depicts a three-dimensional view of the specimen in Figure 2-3A through multiple cuts. The right face is the same as that given in Figure 2-3A. Another view of the travertine is presented by the two-slice panel in **Figure 2-3C**.

2-4. Green Marble

Figure 2-4A depicts a pale green marble from a contact metamorphic zone (formed around intrusive magma), well known for its marble with different hues. The piece was picked near one poorly maintained road toward an abandoned mine.

Notorious are black siliceous veins that jut out of marble. The strong contrast in outlook has resulted from differential resistance to wind and water erosion in the desert. This piece of marble, unlike innumerable chunks of other carbonate rock, is unusually clean; it is almost free of caliche which appears often elsewhere owing to dissolution and re-deposition of calcium carbonate.

Figure 2-4A: Pale Green Marble. LD = 18 cm. No cut; from San Bernardino County, California.

There are two differently oriented sets of black veins. The vein on the upper-right rim, extending all the way to the rear of this specimen, intercepts the other set of multiple veins. Likely, the two sets follow the paths of conjugated fractures in the marble.

The greenness of the marble is marred a little by yellowish powdery specks in the subtle depressions of the erosional relics. The depressions are bounded by remnants of crisscrossing ridges. In addition, several brownish veinlets dissect the marble.

The eye-catching black button atop the front marble face is obviously the relic of a missing vein.

Figure 2-4B illustrates another example of an erosional relic – one piece of agate stands out as an 'atoll' in the 'lagoon of marble or limestone'. The lagoon is barricaded by a broken chain of 'island' agates. All protuberances are remnants of a former agate vein (chalcedony), which occupies more than 90% in volume of this stone.

Is the patch of limestone a relic of former host rock to the agate? Or is the limestone an add-on, like caliche, to the agate after its detachment to the desert floor? The perseverance of the protuberances favors the conjecture that the limestone is a relic of former host rock.

2-5. Vein within Vein

Marbles in contact metamorphic zones near margins of igneous intrusions often show fractures that have been infiltrated by siliceous solutions to form veins. Two sets of fractured marble are displayed in **Figure 2-5A & B**. Frequently those veins stand out as ridges, jutting out of the low, depressed background marble that has been dissolved and eroded as depicted in the lower left piece.

Figure 2-4B: An 'agate atoll' in the 'lagoon' of limestone. LD = 16 cm; no cut; from San Bernardino County.

Sometimes valuable minerals may occur along those veins. But here we have no such luck. Instead, we see only zoning in veins – vein within vein because they were formed at different stages of infiltration by hydrothermal fluids with slight differences in compositions.

Of interest in pattern is one bifurcated vein in the upper left piece and several reddish suture-like curvy veinlets in the upper right piece. Unlike others, the white marble in the upper right piece is grainy because it was exposed recently and has experienced little dissolution and weathering.

2-6. Stalagmite I

Stala*c*tite and stala*g*mite are two major types of cave deposits (speleothems). If you have visited a carbonate cavern (cave), you would notice the former with a middle *c* hanging from the *c*eiling while the latter with a middle *g* rising from the *g*round. The specimen in **Figure 2-6A** came from an inactive mining dump in Mojave Desert, California. So, what is it?

Figure 2-5A & B: Fractured marble. LD = 12 cm (A), 14 (B) cm. No cut; from San Bernardino County, California.

PROCESSES: When water bearing carbon dioxide passes through limestone, it dissolves some calcium carbonate to form calcium bicarbonate. If the bicarbonate-laden water reaches a cave, the water will seep through crevices. Because the partial pressure of carbon dioxide in the water is greater than that in the cave air (i.e., greater content of carbon dioxide in the water than that in the air), the water will release carbon dioxide to the air and return calcium bicarbonate back to the insoluble calcium carbonate (calcite) to form a drip stone – stalactite hanging from cave ceiling or along the side wall.

Initially new drips are so tiny, a hollow carbonate tube forms (so-called 'soda straw tube'). The presence of such tubes is diagnostic of stalactites. But the tiny tubes can be filled up quickly. The excess water will spill over the tube to grow an inverted cone by adding downward

Figure 2-6A: Stalagmite. LD = 20 cm; no cut; from San Bernardino County, California; courtesy of Mr. Donald Alexander.

tapering cone-shells. Eventually, a stalactite appears. Its cross-section shows concentric growth rings, being younger outward.

If the drip rate exceeds the production rate of stalactite, the excess water falls to the ground to form stalagmite with upright cones, sprouting like bamboo shoots. Unlike stalactite which may grow to its own demise by adding weight, stalagmite can develop to colossal sizes if the supply is sustained. It has concentric layering in the interior too; its exterior may appear pagoda-like, with stair-step pedestals reflecting variations in seasonal water supply and deposition.

SPECIMEN: Now, consider our specimen in Figures 2-6A by assuming it had stood on the ground as displayed for this picture taken. It does not hold any 'straw tube'. The absence alone does not imply the specimen is stalagmite because the tubes are too fragile to be preserved even if they ever existed. Let us deal with the carbonate from the bottom up.

Botryoidal calcite stays at the base (B). Its precipitation might have started from a seeding grain from carbonate saturated solution (not necessarily colloidal solution); and it might be influenced by the bubbling release of carbon dioxide to shape the deposit in botryoidal form. It occurred in near-stagnate water of calcium bicarbonate.

Overlying the botryoidal is layered travertine (T, nicknamed Mexican onyx). It accumulates commonly downstream from hot springs, but hot springs is not necessary a prerequisite here. Travertine precipitates from slowly flowing water.

Next, follow the top travertine layer leftward to rear face (T, **Figure 2-6B**). Its layer thickness is reduced by half. The travertine (T) drapes and wraps around a core of limestone (C), which consists of white calcite and veinlets with mixed colors of black, grey, and reddish brown. The eye-catching reddish brown, triangular wedge (R) together with the core is the relic of fallen rock fragments. The brown relic is not accumulated at the mining dump site because both the core and wedge are rimmed with a thin bright white calcite seam (about one mm thick). The interpretation of R and C as fallen fragments assure the specimen is a piece of stalagmite.

To me, the core and wedge together acted as a barrier to the slowly flowing water under which the layered travertine on the right has formed (right T, Figure 2-6A & B). When the flow channel was

Figure 2-6B: Rear and under view of Figure 2-6A.

filled with travertine, water spilled over the barrier to form a new travertine layer that draped over the slanting surface of the core and wedge (left T, Figure 2-6B).

Then, the flow rates declined to almost stagnant, a different phase of calcite genesis ensued over the travertine layers. Dripping water from cave ceiling created stalagmitic cones (S), which rose above cave water with blunt apexes. Some cones have been beheaded accidentally to expose their underlying concentric ring texture. Piled next to the stalagmite are porous clumps of irregularly shaped calcite. Those clumps (so-called 'pop corns', P) can be a combination of fallouts from stalactite and tufa precipitated out of bicarbonate water. And more botryoidal calcite oozed out atop the earlier botryoids (B) under the ponded water. Note that this set of latest addition is demarcated from the underlying travertine with a white seam too.

My story for this piece of carbonate rock relies on some hydrogeological premises. In short, long-term variations of water supplies, being consequential to climate changes, cast their influences on the occurrences of various forms of cave calcite. The carbonate core (C) and brown wedge (R) reflected the effects of rock breakages and deformation prior to the onset of the story described above. My simplistic inferences are drawn from one specimen only. If desirable, a thorough speleological study with the context of field observations and laboratory analysis will be more definitive.

2-7. Travertine, Goethite, and Calcite Crystals

A piece of rock is an event-recording time-machine if one can unravel it and tell a good evolutionary story out of it, vis-a-vis climate change and its resulting environmental responses as recorded by varying rock compositions and texture. The specimen depicted in **Figure 2-7** offers us an interesting opportunity to explore its past. It came from an inactive mining dump in the eastern Mojave Desert, California.

The specimen reveals five major events of occurrences: Zones A to E from bottom to top or older to younger zoning.

ZONE A: Zone A is travertine, which consists of several subtle subzones with colors varying from white to light brown and gray. At the lower right corner, sandwiched in the gray is one small sliver of reddish mineral. Common to this zone is the vertical cleavages that divide this zone into many columns across all horizontal subzones.

Zone A is a downstream deposit of hot springs. Reduction in partial pressure of carbon dioxide in the venting hot waters to the atmospheric carbon dioxide pressure has caused calcium carbonate to precipitate out of the fluids as travertine, which lingers along the stream flow paths. Sub-zoning reflected slight changes in chemical composition of the source spring waters; or it could result from mixing with other surficial water masses and hence compositional variations. Later the water-soaked travertine de-watered while the hot travertine cooled down. Both de-watering and cooling induce contraction to form vertical crevices (cracks/fractures) and yield a myriad of tiny slender columns. The cooling-contraction is analogous to how columnar basalt is formed. (Note: dewatering is not dehydration, i.e., it is physical versus chemical process.)

ZONE B: Somehow the hot springs became inactive. Zone B results from later stream deposits. To the left, it has truncated its underlying Zone-A layering. Atop Zone B lies a red seam, which demarcates from its overlying Zone C with a sharp boundary. Within Zone B, there are reddish horizontal seams, slightly distorted and wavily curved. Obviously, the red seams reflected source water changes or contamination; and the waving could have resulted from normal post-depositional deformation and diffusion of red pigments.

ZONE C: Then, the activities of hot springs resumed, yielding whitish Zone C (with one intervening but incomplete grey seam). Both Zones B and C slant upward to the back in this display orientation of specimen. Visually Zone C circles backward and upward to complete its zone exposure. The plain thickening on the left is an optical distortion due to local stripping of its overlying red zone. But the activities did not last long, as compared to the duration for making Zone A. (The activities might not have been paused; the appearance of Zone B could be a diversion of springs water to somewhere else.)

RED ZONE D: Among all zones, the red Zone D is most eye-catching. Most of the lower half of this red zone is an eroded bench surface, parallel to bedding; and the bench, which makes Zone D seem visually thicker from the perspective of picture-taking. The actual thickness is more realistically represented by the bluff-like upper half, as seen on the left edge.

The red deposits are allochthonous soil. That is, they are not formed in situ because the red cannot be produced from carbonates. Zone D sediments were transported from elsewhere by stream water to overlie Zone C. On the way here, fragments of white calcite were carried and incorporated into the red bed; otherwise, the deposits are finely grained. The red is produced by goethite – hydrous ferric oxide. There is a slight chance that the red could be laterite – oxides of iron-aluminum mixtures – a weathered product in hot, humid environment. An assay for its chemical compositions can resolve the two choices.

Figure 2-7: Travertine, goethite, and calcite crystals. LD = 25 cm; broken by mining activity; no base cut; from San Bernardino County, California; gifted from Mr. Donald Alexander.

ZONE E: The red zone is capped by an aggregate of calcite crystals – white, translucent with vitreous luster, and rhombohedral – to constitute Zone E. This transition happened because the goethite-carrying water was replaced by slow moving hydrothermal fluid rich in calcium carbonate. The crystallization rates were slow enough to yield crystals up to 2 cm across but not long enough to produce large, single, solitary crystals.

On the other hand, the fluid temperature could have dropped rapidly such that crystallization happened simultaneously to yield interlocking crystals of similar sizes.

Goldilocks conditions prevail in nature. We can only guess about what might have happened.

Figure 2-8A: Stalagmite. LD = 12 cm; one base cut; from San Bernardino County, California; gifted from Mr. Don Alexander.

2-8. Stalagmite II

Here is another piece of cave limestone in **Figure 2-8A**. Overall it appears like 'popcorn' nodules, interspersed with short columns. The basic framework for this piece is travertine, as viewed from a bottom cut face. Incidental defacing at tips of some columns or 'popcorns' reveals concentric circles in cross sections, which mark episodic outward growth rings.

Because the specimen came from a mining dump with unknown *in-situ* field setting, there is no sure way to say whether it is a stalagmite or stalactite. By the same token, it might grow along the cave wall as well.

It is my guess that some secondary calcite patches (popcorns) had sit atop stalagmite on the ground rather than hanging with the stalactite under the cave ceiling. Hence, the piece is regarded as stalagmite without convincing justification. Those added patches may tarnish the beauty of stalagmite, but it is all in the eyes of beholder.

Figure 2-8B: One base slice of Figure 2-8A. LD = 12 cm, 1 cm thick; sun backlight.

CROSS SECTION: **Figure 2-8B** depicts a basal slice or slab of Figure 2-8A. The picture was taken with the sun behind the slice. Sub-horizontal wavy bands signal build-up of stalagmite, layer by layer. Diagonal, radiant beams are slender strips across travertine layering, not residual saw-cut tracks. As a note: a few OBMS rockhounds (Orange Belt Mineral Society of San Bernardino) have made beautiful cabochons out of stalagmite/stalactite for such translucent view.

Some words of caution: Unlike the horizontal layering in sediment from bottom to top, the layering in stalagmite is stacked by dripping deposition outward from a knob at downward sloping angles. The slanting strips across layering are not depositional; they have resulted from de-watering of interstitial water (not dehydration), coupled with phase change and associated volume change between calcite and aragonite.

Figure 2-9A: White marble. LD = 18 cm; base cut; from Riverside County, California.

Figure 2-9B: Blue marble. LD = 20 cm; slice; from Riverside County, California.

2-9. Marble

Marble comes in different varieties as shown in earlier Sections. Figures 2-9A through -9D depicts various pieces of marble from different parts of contact metamorphic zones next to a granitic batholith. All show aggregates of randomly orientated but interlocked calcite crystals.

Figure 2-9C: Green calcite with caliche coating. LD = 17 cm; with surface scraping.

Figure 2-9D: Marble bookend. LD = 17 cm; multi-cut.

Figure 2-9E: Marble tinted with green; LD = 10 cm; multi-cut; from Inyo County, California.

Some crystals on the exposed surface (**Figure 2-9A**) reveal two sets of rhombohedral cleavage: their traces have obviously been enhanced through slow etching by carbon-dioxide bearing moisture.

One slice (slab) of blue marble is presented in **Figure 2-9B**. Grainy crystals are visible; there is no general trend in crystal orientation. The yellowish band is intrinsic, but the light brown patches are stained by iron bearing solution.

As a footnote to the interactions between calcite and water bearing carbon dioxide, **Figure 2-9C** exemplifies the fate of a piece of green crystalline calcite that was excavated by mining activities in the early 20th century. It has well-exposed crystalline form with two sets of cleavages. Some have been tainted brownish in situ by iron oxides or perturbed by the presence of garnets but keep the characteristic rhombohedral crystal form and cleavages.

Figure 2-9F: A man-made triangular block of marble. LD = 20 cm. Courtesy of OBMS.

Calcite exposed in the semi-desert environment has been chemically altered by occasional rain drops and condensed moisture with dissolved carbon dioxide from the air. Calcite is dissolved when wet and re-deposited when dry. The rates are imperceptible but over decades, the repeated processes have weathered the crystals to hide under the visible caliche, which is puffy, rough, crumby, and porous. Here some of the powdery caliche has been scraped to keep the particles wasting from scattering on the display shelf.

The piece of marble in **Figure 2-9D** is an interlocking mosaic of calcite crystals. The crystals range in size from less than one to over three cm across. Depending on the orientation of cut with respect to crystal structure, it displays colors from translucent white, green, to blue. Some spots are stained brownish. A conjugated set of rhombohedral cleavage appears on some grains, again pending on cut-face orientation. Overall, the piece can be well polished. It does not shatter and is soft (Mohs hardness = 3); hence it is good for small but coarse carving project.

Figure 2-9E depicts a piece of white marble without perceivable grainy texture. However, the white is splashed with greenish yellow silicate minerals (tremolite?). Its fine texture makes this piece or equivalent ideal for small sculpturing endeavor. Grainy marble is not favorable for sculpturing.

The marble in **Figure 2-9F** has been saw-cut into a triangular block. Its grainless fine texture awaits an artist to finely sculpture it into a marvelous piece of art work. (Compare its fine texture with that in Figure 2-9E.)

The exposed right surface is dotted with erosional potholes and stained naturally. Two fractures had occurred in parallel to the exposed face. The fracturing was then followed by incursions of brown fluid to form veinlets. The dissolved ingradients (likely ferous ions) diffused away from the veins to form irregular, asymmetric, and curvy bands with different shades of brown.

Figure 2-9G depicts a face cut in parallel with the exposed surface (rear side of Figure 2-9F). It shows the fractures and veins are parallel to the naturally exposed surface. To what extent the color pattern has been affected by the diffusion from the vein fluids is uncertain.

2-10. Biogenic and Abiogenic Concretions

One of the marvels in some limestone is the occurrences of *concretions*. What are the concretions? And how do they come about?

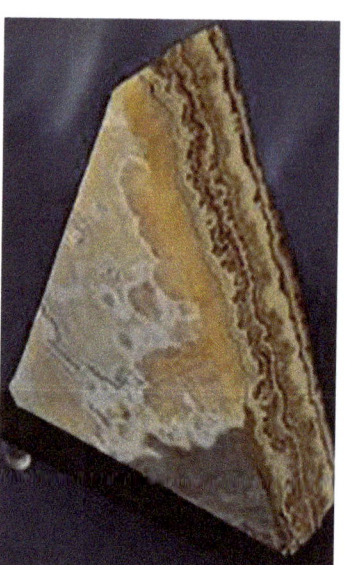

Figure 2-9G: A cut view of Figure 2-9F.

The limestone slab (0.6 cm thick) displayed in **Figure 2-10A** is silicified as inferred in part from its resistance to scratching with a pocketknife. The concretions stand out against the light brown background matrix. Due to natural impregnation of ferric oxides (limonite, goethite), the rock is tinted brown overall.

NUCLEATION: Nucleation of calcite began and evolved to light, whitish brown, circular or elliptical cores of concretions (in 2-dimensional view). Each brownish white core has faint growth rays radiated from a central nucleus (see 'Q' marking as an example) and each core is bounded by a tooth-like rim. The rim in turn is enclosed by double layers of grey and brown to complete as one concretion.

A few cores, however, are free of outer grey or brown shells. Some concretions may bear two or three cores. The rear face reveals one concretion having six cores (**Figure 2-10B**).

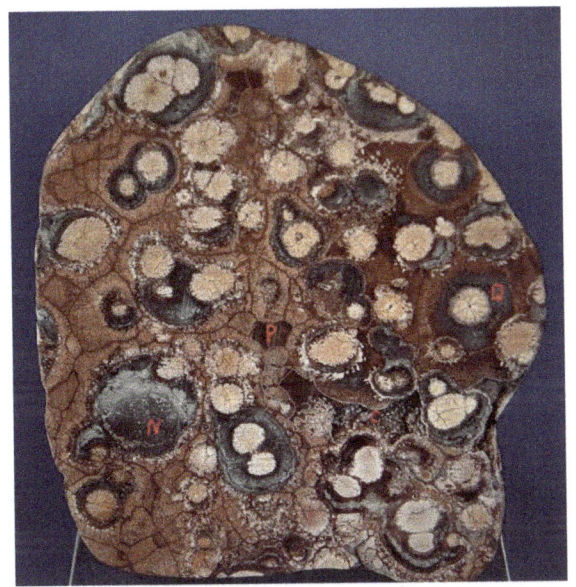

Figure 2-10A: Concretions in limestone. LD = 12 cm; slab; bought.

In general, the patterns in the front and rear faces do not correlate well, implying the 3D concretion sizes are on the order of one centimeter only. The grey circular spot marked by 'N' in Figure 2-10A does not have a light brown core because the saw cut might happen to miss it (the counterpart concretion in the rear side of the specimen marked by 'N' has 5 cores).

Note that a few dark brown polygons represented by 'P' are not concretions; and they do not have any rind. They are clay debris caught in a consolidating matrix. The area marked by 'C' is populated with tiny druse quartz in a cavity.

BIOGENIC: The brown background matrix is cracked into many polygons, which are well delineated by dark brown line segments. The whole rock is tinted brown owing to diffusion of ferric ions via those fractures.

Those observations lead to the conjecture that the inner brownish white globular cores and their associated tooth-like thin rims are biogenic while the grey and brown shells are abiotic. The abiotic inference is drawn from two facts: a few 'cores' do not have outer shells while some shells may contain multiple cores.

Figure 2-10B: Concretions in limestone (rear side of Figure 2-10A).

In short, the concretion starts from biogenic and finishes with abiogenic processes. Both products are later hardened through silicification of the entire carbonate. On the other hand, could those 'cores' be individual fossils instead of the end cluster products of micro-organism as alluded here? Alternatively, could some 'abiotic grey and brown shells' be biotic but were consumed and deleted from the records? If so, how could the 'naked tooth rings' be preserved?

2-11. Rhombohedral Calcite

Figure 2-11 depicts an often-storied rhombohedral calcite and its cleavage. The pair of rhombohedral cleavages is the telltale sign of calcite. This piece consists of many crystals, visibly definable by different orientations of cleavages. Compared to the white crystals, the bluish face signifies a recent fresh breakage.

A calcite crystal can be easily broken along one of its innumerable, rhombohedral cleavages. The newly resulted piece, although smaller in size, will resemble the old one geometrically. This is the so-called fractal breakage in self-image. By analog to biological reproduction, this would be equivalent to asexual cell division, except that calcite does not subdivide into equal parts and the subdivisions become smaller and smaller, never growing back to its former self in size. It is an irreversible process.

2-12. Orange and Green Fluorescence

Figure 2-12A is a piece of multi-mineral rock. It has plain beauty but is not impressive for storytelling. It rightly belongs to ore deposits and does not have a conventional petrographic name. I place it under this carbonate chapter for its abundance of white calcite, especially for its overwhelming orange light emission under ultraviolet (UV) light.

The milky white crystals are calcite. It has small feeble rhombohedral crystals and cleavages. It effervesces (bubbles) under weak acid, and it is knife-scratchable. The blurred white patches are blemished calcite due to abrasion during handling. Calcite is a worthless gangue mineral associated with the valuable zinc ore deposit.

Figure 2-11: Rhombohedral calcite. LD = 11 cm; no cut; from Riverside County, California.

Figure 2-12A: Calcite, willemite, and franklinite. LD = 14 cm; from New Jersey; courtesy of Mr. Danny Sweeny.

The black spots or aggregates are franklinite, of which the grain size is about 1 to 2 mm. It is a zinc-iron oxide ($ZnO·Fe_2O_3$) with a spinel crystal structure ($MgO·Al_2O_3$), which is like the isometric magnetite ($FeO·Fe_2O_3$). Franklinite is weakly responsive to a neodymium magnet. Numerous grains show sharp fractures with metallic luster and quite a few exhibit octahedral crystal form at their terminal tips.

Disseminated in the white calcite and stayed around the black franklinite are yellowish brown specks; and there is at least one apple green grain of unknown mineral. Those specks are willemite – a zinc silicate mineral ($ZnSiO_4$). Visibly absent

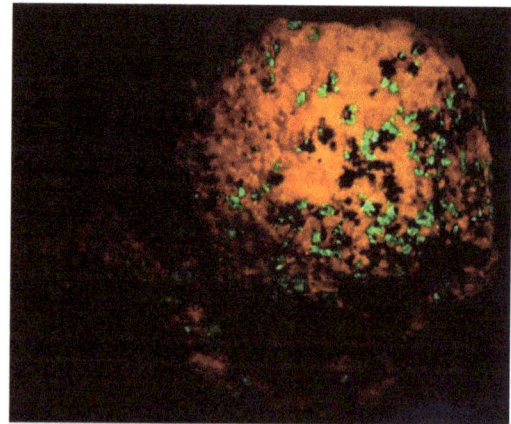

Figure 2-12B: Calcite (reddish orange), willemite (green), and franklinite (black) of zinc ore deposits under short-wavelength UV light; upper-half view of Figure 2-12A.

from the ore is another common zinc mineral, sphalerite (zinc sulfide, ZnS). Both willemite and franklinite resist scratching with a pocketknife. The two are valuable constituents of zinc ore deposits.

UV FLUORESCENCE: Under UV light, the three major minerals in Figure 2-12A can be readily recognized in **Figure 2-12B**: the reddish orange is calcite, and the green is willemite. But franklinite does not fluoresce and stays pitch black. Compare Figure 2-12B to the upper half of Figure 2-12A: some willemite is barely visible in day light but all willemite grains stand out under UV.

Figure 2-13A: Marble invaded by chalcedony. LD = 15 cm; no cut; from San Bernardino County, California.

Figure 2-13B: Rear side of Figure 2-13A.

It is noted that not all calcites will fluoresce. For example, the calcite in Figure I2-14a & b of Lee (2018) fluoresces with faint red or orange for the black rhombohedral core only; the white calcite outside the core does not respond to UV light (picture not shown here). The orange fluorescence in Figure 2-12B is caused by unknown impurity in calcite.

Figure 2-13C: Marble coupled with chalcedony. LD = 12 cm; base cut.

2-13. Chalcedony in Marble

Near contacts with magma or lava, limestone is metamorphosed to marble and is often partially silicified too. In many cases, the silica solution could invade the crevices in marble and form a mesh of chalcedony to such an extent that a loose piece in the desert may turn out to be dominated by chalcedony rather than the original host of marble (**Figure 2-13A**). The chalcedony protrudes above the low-lying marble because chalcedony is more resistive to erosion.

Also, the marble exhibits solution pits rimmed by sharp crests and ridges, more so on the rear side (**Figure 2-13B**), which faced skyward in its natural setting in the desert. The chalcedony touching the ground has been stained reddish brown by soil moisture. If so, why is the marble free of stain?

First, chalcedony bearing some microscopic air pores can be stained by easing faster diffusion in contact with moist soil over a long period of time. Second, the marble is more dissolvable in water which is colder under the shade of rock. Hence, the stain, if any, has been selectively eroded from the marble.

Why do the surficial features of the marble in the sky- and ground-facing sides differ so much? This has to do with differences between temperature and availability or retention of moisture (dew) on the sunny and shaded sides. Calcite is more soluble in cold water than in warm water. Also, the moisture will evaporate during daytime and the scarcity of water makes the dissolution more spotted in the sunny side rather than spreading out under the shade.

Figure 2-13D: Marble dotted by chalcedony protuberances. No cut; LD = 9 cm.

Figure 2-13E: Chalcedony in marble. LD = 23 cm; base cut.

Figure 2-13C depicts a specimen with a 50-to-50 volumetric apportionment between marble and chalcedony. The marble is covered with many solution pits or pinholes, some of which appear with lightly dotted shadows on an otherwise white marble picture.

Any doubt about whether the marble has hosted the chalcedony can be resolutely discarded by the protuberances or pinnacles of chalcedony over the marble in **Figure 2-13D**. The marble is covered as usual with a mosaic of tiny, surficial dissolution grooves.

A stub of white marble is presented in **Figure 2-13E**. The marble features again a network of tiny dissolution grooves and bumps, giving an impression of wrinkled skin.

The marble is also patched with reddish blobs of disjointed chalcedony. Its left side is, however, strengthened with a slender strip of chalcedony, which has resulted from silica filling in a former crevice.

On the rear, a thin sheet of chalcedony blankets over the marble but the sheet has many 'windows', revealing the white marble underneath. The incursion of silica solution into narrow cracks resulted in the precipitation of chalcedony.

Figure 2-13F: Chalcedony in marble. LD = 18 cm; base cut; from San Bernardino County, California.

Figure 2-13F is duplicated from Figure I2-15b of Lee (2018). It is added here to complete my collection in this series of chalcedony in marble. The reddish chalcedony here could be mistaken for agate with its color alone. However, the red does not extend to the bottom cut face where the chalcedony is greyish white. One chip-off spot near the top of the red strip of nuggets (aggregates) also reveals its hidden greyish white color.

The marble is wrinkled with a mesh of ruts (grooves). It is intriguing to note that those ruts enclosing the protruding red chalcedony nuggets are engraved deeper and appear more conspicuous than the grooves away from the protuberant chalcedony.

Could the difference in etching depth result from weakness around the interface between two different minerals? Could more moisture be kept in the chalcedony grains such that greater amount of calcite dissolution happens from diffusion of moisture from chalcedony over long period of time? Could the chalcedony dissipate heat faster and hence a cold rim appears around it to have greater solubility of calcite around it in the long run? None of those reasons is decisive or resolvable with visual inspection of hand specimen only. Just speculations for mental exercise.

Figure 2-13G: Marble dotted with lava blobs and protuberances. LD (right) = 11 cm; no cut; from San Bernardino County,

Again, the red coating over the chalcedony aggregates is attributable to staining by soil water, as stipulated previously for Figure 2-13A. But the reddish staining of marble is not preserved because the stained marble has been stripped by slow dissolution of calcite, as implied by the rut etching.

Figure 2-13G depicts two pieces of marble (limestone) in contact with extrusive volcanic rocks. Each is partially covered by lava. The protuberances are lava-like, not chalcedony. Again, the white marble is wrinkled with small erosional ruts. The left marble piece is coated pinkish and yellowish while the right one is equivalently coated but faintly.

A few whitish grey veinlets (less than one mm wide) crisscrossing the marble are chalcedony. The visible fissures are devoid of secondary minerals – suggesting recent cracking. The two pieces occurred in association with the extrusive lava that yields the brecciated yellow jasper in Figure 1-11.

Another piece of chalcedony protuberances on marble (**Figure 2-13H**) is added to supplement Section 2-13 on the chalcedony-marble series. Except the top surface where dissolution ruts are indicative of marble, the specimen is overwhelmingly masked by white caliche. Scaping some caliche off reveals white chalcedony and calcite, which are too intermingling to be told apart unless one goes through tedious knife-scratching tests.

Figure 2-13H: Chalcedony in marble. LD = 15 cm; one cut and some scraping; from San Bernardino County, California.

Figure 2-14: Dripstones. Top, LD = 11 cm; base; side; courtesy of Mr. Tony Gilham.

2-14. Dripstone

Without the context of field observations, sometimes it could be confusing to tell, at the first sight, what an unfamiliar specimen is. **Figure 2-14** is one case example. The sprouting, branching tubes, pillars, or columns could be mistaken as coral fossil. But there is no coral-like protuberance. It is an aggregate of dripstones dressed with a brownish grey veneer of unknown mineral. The shape of those dripstones resemble stalactites in limestone caves.

Scraping the veneer off the blunt tips of some columns reveals the white interior (top picture). Most of the white is chalcedony while the remainder appears like calcite and is knife-scratchable. A cut-face (middle picture) shows black patches that enclose irregularly shaped cavities, which are rimmed with white quartz or chalcedony. The unknown black mineral is knife-scratchable too.

The bottom picture shows the side view of dripstones. Some broken tips indicate the dripstones are partially empty, walled with chalcedony or quartz. The white circular tube at the lower left corner has one center dent (hole) which could indicate the presence of the so-called 'soda straw tube' in stalactite mentioned in Section 2.6. If correct, the dripstones are indeed stalactites.

Apparently this specimen started as dripstones (stalactites) which were partially silicified later, and finally coated with unknown brownish grey mineral.

2-15. Strawberry Onyx

All specimens in this section are scattered, man-caused fragments within a few thousand square feet on the ridge crest area of an abandoned mining site in San Bernardino County, California for the so-called strawberry onyx – a colorful carbonate onyx as distinguished from the silicious, parallel-banded onyx. Because those fragments are not restored to the original stratigraphic positions, the following narrative may sound like wishful thinking, and you can have your own stories.

Figure 2-15A: Strawberry onyx. LD = 15 cm.

Figure 2-15A illustrates an example of strawberry onyx. It lacks the telltale banding because it has been disrupted by fracturing and subsequent filling of white carbonate veins. The vertical vein on the left is exposed in the back as a thin plate dotted with small botryoids. But the piece is compact and can be well polished.

Figure 2-15B: Brecciated and recemented onyx. LD = 12 cm.

Another picture of strawberry onyx is presented in **Figure 2-15B**. Besides banding in the rear side, it has a block of brecciated but recemented onyx with vesicles which are rimmed by chalcedony and tiny druse quartz. On the northwest corner, there lies some oval concretions. The piece has been stripped off sinter covers – calcareous deposits in the crevices – as marked by the yellow residual patches. One thin sinter is still retained in the rear over the banded onyx.

These two pictures indicate the textural complexity in the onyx, missing the cherished signature of parallel, color bands.

Figure 2-15C represents a fragment with silica-and-carbonate interlayers, which are likely distal to the core of onyx. The dark brown layers are knife-scratch resistive chalcedony or agate; the rest incluing both the pink and

Figure 2-15C: Interlayering of silica and carbonate. LD = 18 cm.

Figure 2-15D: Layering of silica and carbonate. LD = 14 cm.

white layers is scratchable carbonate. Does the agate result from post-depositional replacement of carbonate by silica? The sharp interfaces between the two types of layers negate the replacement suggestion. Or, does the appearance of agate reflect changes in depositional environment? If so, the absence of carbonate occurrd during the period of cold temperature such that silica deposition dominated over carbonate because carbonate is relatively more dissolvable in cold water.

An accompanying distal fragment is presented in **Figure 2-15D**. Again, the dark brown, rugged layers are agate. In the lower half of the piece, the knife scatchable, reddish layers are deemed as carbonate. In the upper half, the white carbonate layers are distorted, twisted, and are interposed with fragmental agate segments or patches. Such interposition casts doubt whether temperature is the sole factor affecting the distribution of silica and carbonate layers.

Figure 2-15E: Layered carbonate near the desired onyx core. LD = 14 cm.

Closer to the onyx core is another piece shown in **Figure 2-15E**. All but the dark slinger of agate inside an elliptical concretion is carbonate. The carbonate is layered in different shades of color, approaching but not quite reaching the status of the brand-named colorful onyx.

Generally, the specimen in **Figure 2-15F** is a dripstone. Specifically, is it a stalactite or stalagmite? Formed by accumulation through dripping mineral water on the ground, the latter usually has a broad base or pedestal. Regardless, the piece is not a speleothem or cave deposit. It is depositional, not erosional for sure. Can it be a tufa, a depositional product of carbonate-bearing streams or springs? Unlike a puffy pile of tufa, the piece consists of distinctive columns. Like a 'carbonate forest', the 'trees' grow up to one cm high from a thin light brown sinter, which could have attached over, under, or aside a rock surface.

I may call it stalactite by naming analogy to the concrete stalactite under a leaking bridge. No matter what it is named, however, the dripstone needs water but the water is scarce atop a ridge crest in the dry desert at present. Was the area much wetter when the dripstones formed?

Figure 2-15F: Dripstone. LD = 9 cm.

Chapter 3: HARD ROCK SHOW

Hard rock is a colloquial term for igneous or metamorphic rocks, in contrast to soft rock for sedimentary rocks. Hard rock is not necessarily hard; for example, pumice, serpentinite (serpentine), graphite, and marble can be scratched with a pocketknife. Nor is it necessarily very resistive to weathering; decomposed granite is a familiar term to many southern Californians who reside over batholith (huge mass body of granitic rocks).

Igneous rocks are classified into intrusive and extrusive for plutonic and volcanic rocks, respectively. A transitional term, hypabyssal or intermediate igneous rocks (aka dike rocks which used to be feeders to volcanos), had prevailed in the older literature but such terminology is being phased out. Plutonic and volcanic rocks are distinctive in texture; the former is coarse-grained and the latter very fine-grained. A mixture of the two is a porphyritic rock with large crystals (phenocrysts) set in fine-grained groundmass (matrix). In general, rapid cooling of lava at ground surface leads to formation of fine crystals while slow cooling of magma at depth favors growth to larger crystals. Interlocking of minerals in igneous rocks, visually or microscopically, distinguish igneous from sedimentary or metamorphic rocks.

Next to textural classification (modes of occurrence) is classification according to mineral (not chemical) compositions. Rock-forming minerals are light- or dark-colored. The light-colored are felsic, including feldspar and quartz, while the dark colored are mafic and include mica, amphibole (hornblende), pyroxene, and olivine. A rock as a mixture is named for a combination of minerals at various ranges of relative abundances. For example, granite consists of orthoclase (25 to 50% by volume), plagioclase (15 to 20%), quartz (20 to 30%), mica (10 to 20%) and amphibole (~ 5%); with each within acceptable ranges, the constituents sum to 100% for one individual specimen.

A recently accepted scheme for classification of felsic igneous rocks, Streckeisen diagram, excludes the mafic minerals from consideration. It considers only relative volumetric compositions in a ternary (triangular) QAP classification scheme (Q = quartz, A = alkaline feldspar ~ orthoclase & albite, P = plagioclase or calcium silicate). If Q is greater than 20%, I use a catch-all term granite or granitic rock. If P of that rock's feldspar (A + P) content is less than 65%, I call it true 'granite'; if between 65 and 90%, granodiorite; if greater than 90%, tonalite. Some volcanic rocks are also named according to the QAP scheme, but the naming can be challenging because their mineral grains are too fine to be recognized with the naked eye only.

Why do we use volumetric ratios or percentages of minerals instead of the weight or molecular ratios? Because we cannot figure out the weight of each mineral but visually, we can estimate its relative abundance in a piece of rock; we take 'impression or perception' about volume as the observables. On a saw-cut face or thin section under microscope, if needed, one can count the grain sizes (areas) to obtain a much better estimate (with the understanding of using one 2D view for a 3D object).

Metamorphic rocks are transformed solid-to-solid from igneous and sedimentary rocks (or upgraded from other metamorphic rocks) under elevated temperature and pressure. Being crystalline and compact (no vesicle), they have strips with silky luster; some are grainy, and others show banding, foliation, or schistosity. They are named for their texture, which reflects conditions of occurrence, and sometimes prefixed with names of predominant mineral or special feature.

3-1. Granite Arch

Granite is a well-known rock for kitchen-table countertop, building material, etc. It is hard, sturdy, and beautiful if polished. Commercially it has dozens of names for different production locations, patterns, and colors. Some could be mislabeled as granite too.

Not all varieties of granite are sturdy or resistive to weathering and erosion. Most granite is not suitable for commercial use as southern Californians can attest. But the weathered or eroded granitic landscape can be spectacular sometimes. For example, Joshua Tree National Park in southern California is famous for its magnificent granite (tonalite) scenery, in addition to the splendid Joshua tree forest and elevation-zoned cacti.

Figure 3-1A: A granite (tonalite) arch. The arch is about two to three feet wide; from Riverside County, California.

Figure 3-1A is an example of granite at small outcrop scale. The rock is granite in broad sense, but a geologist would call it tonalite because its quartz content is less than 20% in volume and most of its feldspar is plagioclase (greater than 90%). It bears a couple percent of mafic minerals (biotite, and hornblende).

Both plagioclase and mafic minerals are prone to weathering. And once the rock is weathered, wind and rain at ridge top where the picture was taken will remove the debris for new exposure and perpetual renewal

of weathering. Eventually weathering and erosion together tunnel through the rock; and a natural rock bridge is born. It is a strange looking granite arch of which the picture was taken under 11:00 a.m. sun light.

Figure 3-1B: Weathered granite. LD = Long Dimension = 32 cm; no cut; from San Bernardino County, California.

Why does the mass-wasting tunnel the tonalite, instead of wearing and tearing it down from the top as commonly happens in the field? This has to do with the moisture distribution and retention in the arid region. The moisture content increases downward to the ground base surface; and pore water plays a vital role in thermal expansion and contraction to weaken the rock, respectively, as the temperature rises and declines cyclically. Hence, the rock is weaker at the base than at the top. Similar phenomena happen in the chipping of man-made retaining walls, worsening from the top toward the base. Likewise, the arches in Arches National Park have developed because of increasing moisture content downward to the ground base of the exposed sandstone formations. Once a tunnel is dug, mass wasting around the tunnel wall is accelerated simply owing to increasing surface area for chemical weathering to happen. The bridge or arch is destined to collapse eventually.

Thus, the same physical processes apply to arch making in sandstone and tonalite as well as chipping decay of man-made retaining walls despite their substantial differences in scale, structure, and material property.

Features like that in Figure 3-1A are not rare, usually seen by chance in the Southern California Batholith, especially in the semi-desert area around Riverside – my American hometown.

Figure 3-1C: Cave in granite; from foothill, eastern Sierra Nevada, Inyo County, California.

Granite arches (Spitzkoppe, pointed dome in German), on a scale comparable to sandstone arches in Arches National Park, can be found in Namib Desert of Namibia, Africa.

A good question to conclude and ponder: If the above scenario is acceptable, why don't we see more arch-like features in the field?

Now, let us shift to hand-specimen scales which dominate this book. **Figure 3-1B** is a tonalite specimen that has been weathered and eroded. It was an isolated piece in the desert, tens of miles from the outcrop shown in Figure 3-1A. In addition to two conspicuous depression pits, the specimen has a very rough surface with spotty, reddish taints. Unlike some other granitic rocks in the desert, this piece is not polished, nor varnished. The rocks in Joshua Tree National Park respond similarly, no polishing and varnishing but rough surface on the weathered and eroded remnants. Such rough surfaces have resulted from high plagioclase content in tonalite.

The surface is dotted with many juts. Each jut centers around one quartz grain with feldspar fringe, which juxtaposes to its neighboring juts. These features have resulted from differential weathering and erosion between quartz and feldspar. And such differential responses prevent uniform polishing and account for the bumpy surface.

Figure 3-1C is supplementary to Figure 3-1A. Caves like this picture are common in the foothills of eastern Sierra Nevada in Inyo County. It occurs at a batholith outcrop. This cave has one sky window opened through its ceiling, near where my four-year-old grandson stood to watch in awe his 'super grandma' poking her head out of the rock.

Dry caves are not rare. They used to be luxurious dwellings for our caveman ancestors. It is said that

Figure 3-1D: Spires in granitic terrain; eastern Sierra Nevada foothill, Inyo County, California.

our languages are developed by stay-at-home tale telling cave ladies. Cavemen are good at keeping their mouths shut, especially when they hunt as a team. Wild animals seek ground-level caves for lairs while bats hang in cave ceilings or rock crevices.

Differential erosion in granite also yields spectacular spires or crags (sharp, steep, tall rocks). The row of spires in **Figure 3-1D** stands above the ground surface of undulating, eroded blocks of granite. Note the main spires in the three groups have towered to the same elevation against the blue sky. Why?

3-2. Serpentinization

Figure 3-2 is a peridotite cobble (of which the volume is equivalent to a sphere with its diameter between 64 and 256 mm). Peridotite consists mostly of mafic minerals: olivine and pyroxene (yellowish or greenish magnesium- and iron-rich silicates). As an ultramafic rock, peridotite falls off the classification scheme of the ternary QAP diagram for felsic igneous rocks. It originates from the mantle, in contrast to the crust-originated granite. The mantle lies about 5 km below the top of oceanic crust or about 30 km below the surface of continental crust. (The Earth is structured Depth-wise as crust, mantle, liquid outer core, and solid inner core.)

Figure 3-2: Serpentinization of peridotite. LD = 15 cm; one cut; from southern California coast.

Peridotite is brought to the ground surface by tectonic uplifting and exhumation (erosional removal) of its overlying rocks; it can also appear through violent volcanic eruption as volcanic bombs, or xenoliths (i.e., alien inclusion in its enclosing host rock). This cobble does not come from volcanic eruption; it originated from a broken piece of exposed peridotite. That piece has been abraded to a well-rounded cobble by coastal seawater and altered chemically by water-rock interactions along fissures or fractures.

Noteworthy are three tones or shades of green: dark, light, and intermediate. The dark green strips or zones track a fracture network, showing transformation to serpentine from olivine and pyroxene through interactions with water, which had infiltrated along pre-existing fractures. The pale green grains are pyroxene that has been altered only slightly as inferred from the grains' irregular crystal outlines or shapes as well as size disparity. The rest with intermediate green tone signifies partial serpentinization when water permeated from fractures into surrounding rocks. Some dark green zones conform to the curving rim of cobble, suggesting those are transformed after the making of cobble; and the tone variation along the peripheral zone is indicative of varying extent of serpentinization. It is likely that some serpentinization had occurred before the piece's separation from its parental peridotite mass.

Figure 3-3A: Garnet gneiss. LD = 24 cm; uncut; from San Bernardino County, California.

After the peridotite is brought from the mantle to the ground surface, the ambient pressure and temperature (P & T) have dropped significantly below what they were when it was seated in the deep interior. Olivine and pyroxene will transform sooner or later to a new set of minerals that are stable in the new low P & T environment near the ground surface. Water accelerates the transformation as depicted in Figure 3-2.

By the same token, diamond in your ring, as harvested from kimberlite dike (porphyritic peridotite in volcanic pipe), will transform eventually to common carbon because diamond is an unstable phase of carbon in the room temperature and pressure. However, be not alarmed! Nobody has ever seen the horror of diamond-to-carbon transformation in one's ring. The decay rate is so infinitesimal that it will take thousands and thousands of generations before one sees any visible change. If you wish, you can speed up the process by heating the ring. Here is a scenario for appreciation of slow rates. If Joe accumulates his wealth at a rate of $100,000 per year (not an insignificant amount to a middle-class American), it will take him 10,000 years to become a billionaire – achievable hypothetically but a little longer than the entire period of our civilization.

3-3. Gneiss/Schist/Quartzite

Gneiss is a high-grade metamorphic rock, typically characterized by black and white layering or banding, commonly referred as foliation. **Figure 3-3A** displays one piece of gneissic cobble from a riverbed. The white is mostly feldspar, and the black is dominated by biotite. Pink garnet adds flavor to the overall black-and-white scene. Caution: the curvy appearance in banding is an optical illusion of plain layers exposed on an uneven surface owing to differential erosion among various constituents.

Figure 3-3B: Augen gneiss with quartz vein. LD = 24 cm; uncut; from Riverside County, California.

Figure 3-3B depicts another piece of foliated gneiss with a conspicuous quartz vein. The banding is not parallel to one another and varies in thickness. Noteworthy are lenticular grains of feldspar in 2D view. This type of gneiss is prefixed with an adjective as augen gneiss, where 'augen' means 'eye-shaped' in German.

Figure 3-3C exhibits one quartzite layer sandwiched between two *schist* layers, which are highly schistose (laminar or leaf-like). The top schist layer forms an overhang over the quartzite 'bluff', which is mostly stained brown beyond causal recognition; while the bottom one retreats from the cliff base and is barely visible.

3-4. Orthoclase/Amazonite

Orthoclase is a major rock-forming mineral, especially in granite with faint reddish color. It is a potassium (K) aluminosilicate, colloquially called K-feldspar or K-spar. Together with albite (sodium aluminosilicate), it is one of the two alkaline feldspars used for the 'A' of the ternary QAP scheme for classification of felsic igneous rocks.

Figure 3-3C: Schist with imbedded quartzite. LD = 19 cm; no cut; from southern California.

K-feldspar can also occur in two other crystal forms: sanidine (high temperature variety in volcanic rocks) and microcline (low temperature variety in pegmatite dikes). With the naked eye only, we can hardly tell the three apart. Hence, we will call them orthoclase collectively.

Figure 3-4A: Orthoclase and graphic granite. LD = 15 cm; multi-cut on the right, from Riverside County, California.

The big crystal in **Figure 3-4A** is an uncut orthoclase as detached naturally from a pegmatite dike that intruded into granite in the desert. (Pegmatite is a rock generated at the last evolutionary stage of residual fluids during the solidification of magma.) Its right face shows grey lineation that follows the characteristic cleavages in microcline. On the left face, there are recessive tiny grooves, which have resulted from erosion along the intrinsic micro cracks – the cleavages.

The right piece in Figure 3-4A is graphic granite. It was saw-cut to clearly show that threads of translucent grey quartz are immersed in the host of white orthoclase. The quartz grains are not phenocrysts in the groundmass of orthoclase; nor are they inclusions in orthoclase. The two are contemporary: exsolution to each other in a cooling and solidifying magma. The quartz represents excess silica when orthoclase is rapidly crystallizing, so fast that silica cannot escape from the entrapment of a solidifying orthoclase. (Usually, quartz grains lie side by side or interlock with orthoclase crystals in a normal granite.) Texturally the piece is not a typical granite but mineralogically it is a granite. It looks like a graph drawn with an ink stick; hence the name: graphic granite.

Figure 3-4B: Amazonite. LD = 23 cm. no cut; unknown source location.

As you know, Amazon.com is headquartered in Seattle, Washington State, not the Amazon jungle in Brazil. Do you know amazonite (**Figure 3-4B**) does not originate from the Amazon Basin? Amazonite occurs in many places of the world but Amazon. It was a historic misidentification of another greenish mineral from the Amazon River basin, but the name sticks.

If you see a piece of amazonite, you will not forget its green appearance because few minerals are tinted green. For a long time, the green was attributed to its bearing of trace amount of copper, by analogy to green copper-bearing minerals like chrysocolla and malachite. About two decades ago, it was found that the green comes from trace amount of lead minerals and water molecules, instead of copper minerals. (See Section 6-7 for different variety of amazonite.)

Amazonite is microcline tainted with green from bearing lead. It may be tempting to make jewelry out of it but, be aware of its brittleness and fragility as a microcline orthoclase.

3-5. T-Jointed Dike/Ring Dike

Figure 3-5A features one granitic cobble from a river deposit. The piece is stained a little brownish by soil water in its upper right quarter. Most eye-catching is an 'Inverted T' dike.

Noticeable is the presence of mafic (dark) minerals, which are less than 20 percent in total volume. The rest are telltale components of classical granite: quartz (gray translucent), orthoclase (pale pink), and albite (white).

Figure 3-5A: Granite with T-shaped dike of orthoclase. LD = 35 cm; one thin base cut; from San Bernardino County, California.

A few orthoclase crystals are large as compared to quartz, albite, and the other orthoclase grains as well. Their rectangular outlines are well defined (for example, the grain at the upper left corner), especially against mafic minerals which seem to have been smeared around the big crystals at the boundary, elsewhere the mafic minerals interlock with quartz, albite, and smaller grains of orthoclase. The texture implies that big orthoclase crystals came along late and pushed aside the earlier but smaller and still movable settlers.

The horizontal branch of the T dike, almost free of mafic minerals, consists primarily of albite and quartz. But orthoclase is exclusively present only in the vertical arm. At the T junction of the two, orthoclase prevails and overprints the horizontal, suggesting the short vertical orthoclase dike joined the horizontal albite arm at a later stage of the granitic magma evolution.

Figure 3-5B: Fine-grained granite. Width = 11 cm; one cut; from California coast.

Figure 3-5C: Granite capped by quartz dike. LD = 15 cm; uncut; from Riverside County, California.

Figure 3-5B depicts another piece of granitic cobble, which comes from a California beach. Compared to the granite in Figure 3-5A, it bears far less mafic minerals and hence appears pale in comparison. Excluding the mafic minerals from consideration, the two rocks share similar mineral compositions (orthoclase, albite, and quartz); and they are classified with the same rock name despite their difference in grain sizes and color tone.

The target-like rings are intriguing. Note the two rings: the inner ring is complete in circle but the outer one is incomplete or may have been partially worn out. Between the rings is regular granite but the core appears to have been stained yellowish brown. I do not know how to make out of their occurrences but give an outrageous misnomer – 'target dike' for short of a proper name.

One piece of dark granite capped with white quartz is displayed in **Figure 3-5C**. Both are well polished and varnished in the desert.

Usually, granite is not naturally polished and varnished. This is an exception. On the right edge, a strip of rock is foliated and heavily black-tainted. The lower-left quarter is slightly tainted; otherwise, it looks like 'typical' granite.

The white quartz cap is the remnant of a dike. Its interface with the granite is jagged, indicative of intrusive contact and hence the calling of a dike. The cap is highly fissured, as marked by thin, crisscrossing dark or red streaks.

A 'V-shaped' vestige of quartz cap (dike) covers the dark granite (lower, middle right). Some small white specks are residues of the former dike rock. The dike used to extend at least over the upper-middle one-third of the granite piece. Its stripping reveals an interface of which the surficial texture differs from the exterior of the granite.

Figure 3-6A: Volcanic bombs. LD = 11 cm; no cut; various source locations.

Figure 3-6B: Peridotite xenolith. LD = 13 cm; one cut.

3-6. Volcanic Bombs

Figure 3-6C: Peridotite xenolith. LD = 10 cm; two cuts.

Ejecta that are catapulted into the air by volcanic eruptions and that fall back to the ground are called tephra, or collectively pyroclastic deposits. According to the ranges of fragment sizes, tephra is classified as ash (less than 2 mm or 0.08 inch in diameter for an equivalent spherical volume, or smaller than a coarse sand grain), lapilli (2 to 64 mm, size between sand grain and cobble), or bomb (greater than 64 mm or bigger than a cobble). In practice, we call anything that had been airborne a bomb, other than volcanic ash.

Volcanic bombs are classified according to their shape, which depends on the fluidity of the ejected magma (lava). **Figure 3-6A** depicts five bombs, which were disrupted pieces of airborne blobs or stringers of lava rather than the spindle bombs. See Figures I3-2 and - 12c of Lee (2018) for classical spindle bombs of crustal, andesitic composition; also see Figure I3-1 for a spindle bomb which includes one peridotite xenolith from the mantle. Those ejecta spin in the air to form double-tapered ends before landing as solid spindle bombs. Sometimes the ejecta, still fluid-like (low viscosity), splash to the ground before solidification as cow pie bombs. Frequently some solid chunks with thin lava coating can be catapulted to the air and drop as volcanic blocks. Regardless of what types, those volcanic bombs pose dangerous hazards, even at miles away from an erupting volcano.

Figure 3-6D: Olivine or peridotite xenolith. Left LD = 12 cm; two cuts on the left; no cut to the right.

Not all volcanos yield bombs. Some just ooze out low-viscosity basaltic lava that spreads away to far distance from the vents. Some violent volcanic eruptions can bring rocks from the deep interior to the ground surface. Those are bombs with xenoliths from the mantle, giving us a glimpse of mantle rocks, which otherwise are hidden (**Figures 3-6B**, **-6C**, and **-6D**). Some of those peridotite xenoliths, composed mostly of olivine, are weathered.

Figure 3-7A: Pyroclastic obelisk. LD = 38 cm; base cut; from San Bernardino County, California.

3-7. Pyroclastic Obelisks

The pyroclastic obelisk (column) depicted in **Figure 3-7A** is characterized exteriorly by small blobs of brown lava and by patches of brownish white caliche. The former was primary, attached contemporarily with or shortly after the pyroclastic deposits; while the latter is secondary, added after the column's detachment from its parent and exposure on the desert floor.

The main body is brownish grey, very fine-grained pyroclastics (tephra) with faint flow lines aligned with the column. The tephra is very well cemented as to support the column's mechanical integrity under the harsh desert environment.

Figure 3-7B shows a silicified obelisk of volcanic ash. Its surface is uniformly covered with solution pits. Based on the uniform distribution

Figure 3-7B: Pyroclastic obelisk. LD = 20 cm; base cut; from San Bernardino County, California.

of pits and the observation at one base cut, this obelisk appears homogenous in composition. In contrast, the piece shown in the next figure is more heterogeneous.

Figure 3-7C is a stub of silicified volcanic ash. It is white and seems powdery, but it is not powdery because of its siliceous cementation.

The surface is blanked with solution pits and webs of relic rims between the pits. Dissolution occurs by moisture condensed from the desert air during the evening over centuries. Occasional rainfall helps but the momentary raindrops are not likely to yield such delicate solution pits in the long run.

The piece is also dotted with many small quartz grains (brownish or grayish, diameter less than 1 mm), which stand a little above the background ash surface because the quartz is more resistant to erosion or dissolution. It is not clear whether those quartz grains are contemporary with the ash. In other words, were those quartz grains inclusions in the ash when the ash was spurted out?

Figure 3-7C: Silicified volcanic ash. LD = 11 cm; base cut; from San Bernardino County, California.

Figure 3-7D: Pyroclastics: LD = 19 cm. Courtesy of Mr. Gregory Vidler; no cut; source unknown.

Alternatively, those quartz grains can be secondary. That is, they are formed during devitrification of ash after the ash deposition – a long natural process of converting glass into crystalline minerals. Volcanic glass or ash is unstable chemically or thermodynamically under atmospheric conditions; hence all will be devitrified eventually. That is why obsidian, a volcanic glass, has not been found in any pre-Cenozoic rocks or formations older than 65 million years.

An instrumental analysis of the transition between the ash and quartz grain should be able to resolve whether the quartz is primary or secondary.

One diagnostic pyroclastic rock is presented in **Figure 3-7D**. It is characterized by two contrasting components: abundant fragments of pre-existing rocks embedded in the background of volcanic ash. The rock is not porphyry because the two components were brought together by at least two distinctive volcanic eruptions and there is no large crystal.

There are three recognizable types of rock fragments. The most abundant is reddish brown, irregularly shaped specks, signaling an earlier event that yielded jasper or obsidian in volcanic rocks.

The circular dark-colored spots are eye catching. However, those are not spherule nodules or concretions. Instead, they are cross-sectional exposure of slender, cylindrical shards of dark jasper/obsidian. It is not clear why those shards occur in cylindrical form.

The remaining dark blobs of fragments are irregularly shaped; some of which may reflect unevenly exposed faces of the cylindrical shards, not a separate category.

All three types of rock fragments were engulfed by the ash jetted out during the last volcanic eruption that formed the rock shown in Figure 3-7D.

3-8. Hematite Chimney

At first sight, the jagged, pitch-black rock depicted in **Figure 3-8** could be taken as a volcanic product. The volcanic gas could have vented through the chimneys. If valid, it would be an amazing piece of volcanic rock.

Figure 3-8: Hematite chimney. LD = 12 cm; no cut; unknown source location; gifted by Ms. Kim Christensen.

The challenges are: How can a stream of flowing lava sustain straight-edged hollow cylindrical columns before the chimneys are chilled to solid form? If the black coating is the chilled skin of a wall about one to two millimeters thick, how can the grey interior of the chimney appears crystalline despite rapid cooling of such thin-walled lava? So, what is this specimen?

It is conjectured that the piece is hematite on the following arguments: 1) Streaks at various test spots are consistently brownish red, despite their black or grey surficial appearances. 2) Botryoids occur on the exterior of some chimneys. And 3) besides the cylindrical chimneys, the specimen also carries flat plates or rectangular columns.

None of the arguments alone is conclusive of hematite. Black botryoids over hematite, if present, are usually lustrous but dull here. In fact, the entire piece is dull black without any metallic luster.

The rock responds weakly to a neodymium magnet. It may bear some magnetite as to taint the expected red streak for hematite with brownish hue. Furthermore, there is unidentified white powder on some chimneys.

Collectively, those features suggest this specimen had originated from deposits around fumaroles – through venting of hot fluids and gases from a dormant volcano. It was not solidified directly from lava. Any issue could have been resolved if the setting of its sampling site were known.

3-9. Mineralization in Pegmatite

Pegmatite is a dike formed during the last stage in evolution of magma solidification. It looks like granite except the equivalent minerals are much larger in crystal size. It is often associated with hydrothermal mineralization, which may yield minerals of economic value. **Figure 3-9A** portrays such an example.

Figure 3-9A: Pink tourmaline in pegmatite. LD = 12 cm; base cut; from San Diego County, California.

It is composed of greyish semi-transparent quartz, white orthoclase, and some bluish albite. Conspicuous is the presence of pink tourmaline in columnar or blob forms – a boron-bearing silicate with trigonal cross section and striation across the column. Amid the pink tourmaline columns is inserted one grey, translucent, columnar quartz crystal (at top center).

The specimen came from a dump site for mining gem mineral, elbaite, which is a lithium-bearing tourmaline, highly valued for its clear, transparent green or pink color. The pink tourmaline here does not have any gem quality because of its fragility as resulted from hydration. But it stays with an impressive pink contrast against the light-colored feldspar and quartz.

Figure 3-9B shows another piece of pegmatite. The rock consists mostly of orthoclase and quartz. It is quite fractured.

Figure 3-9B: Multi-colored mineralization. LD = 13 cm; base cut; source location forgotten.

However, the rock is multi-colored, as resulted from hydrothermal alterations.

The left-front face is covered by waxy, lustrous, silk-like purple mineral. The purple (a smeared, lithium-bearing mica, lepidolite?) is peppered with brown streaks of weathered garnet and light-bluish green flecks of a yet-to-be identified mineral.

Figure 3-9C: Pink tourmaline. LD = 12 cm; no cut; from San Diego County, California.

On the right-front face, the quartz and orthoclase are patched with the unknown olivine-green mineral and brown garnet streaks. In the upper-left back, there appear a few specks of azurite-blue mineral (not visible in this picture view)

Figure 3-9C shows again some pink tourmaline, from the same mine as in Figure 3-9A. The tourmaline crystals are imbedded in and between white orthoclase and grey quartz crystals, suggesting all were crystallized contemporarily. The pink tourmaline against white background is for visual appreciation only, not for any jewelry making. Also, in the back of the specimen, fine grained, purple lepidolite is present.

Figure 3-9D depicts one chunk of lepidolite as a waste product from a mine near Riverside-San Diego County boundary, California. Lepidolite is a lithium-bearing mica. It is shining and flaky; on cut face, it may appear purple. The brown stain has resulted from weathering.

Figure 3-9D: Lepidolite. LD = 9 cm; no cut; from San Diego County, California.

Lithium batteries are vital for storage of electrical energy in countless electronic devices. Although lepidolite is abundant in San Diego County, it stays as a mining waste product at present because economically workable technology for extracting lithium from lepidolite is not yet available. Profitable lithium production comes mostly from some lake deposits in South America.

Another pegmatite mineral assemblage is shown in **Figure 3-9E**. It has: schorl (black tourmaline with columnar crystal), quartz (crystals in white stout column or transparent sheet or

Figure 3-9E: Pegmatite with tourmaline, quartz, feldspar, and muscovite. LD = 9 cm; no cut; unknown source location.

stab forms), feldspar (yellowish in contrast to white quartz), muscovite (scaly, white, and light blue) and other yet-to-be identified minor constituent minerals.

3-10. Native Copper

It is unusual to see native metals (free of or unbound with other elements) near the ground surface. Native gold is the familiar example for prospectors to search after. Less known is native copper, which is both an element and mineral name. Usually, the native copper occurs in blobs of irregular shapes in cavities or crevices of host rocks, deposited through hydrothermal fluids.

Figure 3-10A depicts four pieces of native copper with different modes of occurrences: nuggets (massive at the lower-left bottom but threaded at the top), 'disseminated' in basalt (lower right, greenish grey) and in-filling between breccia of basalt (reddish brown). The breccia in the last mode has been altered to reddish brown and infiltrated with small yellowish white copper speckles or threads. Each mode can be a copper ore of economic value. The green specks or patches are weathered products or natural patina (a hydrous copper carbonate), which is like patches of green scale (verdigris) seen on some household copper wares (e.g., brass faucets).

Figure 3-10A: Different modes of native copper. Big piece: LD = 19 cm, courtesy of Mr. Denny Sweeny; from Michigan.

For comparison with native copper, another copper ore mineral, malachite, is pictured in **Figure 3-10B**. Malachite is copper carbonate hydroxide in chemical composition. It often appears botryoidal in green, as seen in the lower-right quarter. But here it is mostly zoned. If properly prepared, it can be an excellent ornamental decor.

Figure 3-10B: Malachite. LD = 12 cm; unknown source location.

3-11. Actinolite and Anorthite

If you are an old timer like me before GPS days and if you lost your orientation in the greater Los Angeles area, you could reorient yourself by referencing to the east-west trending San Gabriel Mountains, which lie north of Los Angeles, Pasadena, and Pomona. The mountains make up the western branch of the Transverse

Ranges in southern California; the branch starts at the Cajon Pass, north of San Bernardino, westward to the Santa Monica Mountains in the Pacific coastal area. The Ranges separate the high desert (Mojave Desert) in the north from southern California basins or valleys. Following are two rock specimens from the San Gabriel Mountains.

Figure 3-11A: Actinolite schist. LD = 26 cm; one base cut; from the eastern San Gabriel Mountains, San Bernardino County, California.

ACTINOLITE: **Figure 3-11A** depicts one specimen of actinolite schist from the easternmost part of the San Gabriel Mountains. It is a cobble recovered from a creek. Actinolite is a member of the hydrous amphibole (hornblende) group. Actinolite and tremolite share similar chemical formulae and hence the two form a solid solution (minerals with gradational change in chemical composition between two end members). Tremolite bears more magnesium while actinolite has greater iron content and appears darker green. The group can range from highly valued translucent nephrite to hazardous fibrous asbestos. (Nephrite is tough but nicknamed soft jade, in comparison to hard jadeite jade.)

The actinolite in the schist is acicular with irregular radiating patterns; the needle-like crystals range in length from one to two centimeters. Due to weathering, some of its lustrous greenness has faded to dull whitish. The red or brown specks or stains are garnet or its weathering derivative. See Figures I5-16a and I5-19a (Lee, 2018) for other pictures of actinolite with larger crystals.

Figure 3-11B: Anorthite. LD = 18 cm; one base cut; from the central San Gabriel Mountains, Los Angeles County, California; courtesy of CTAL.

ANORTHITE: From the central part of the San Gabriel Mountains, near Pasadena, a piece of anorthite is presented in **Figure 3-11B**. Accessory to anorthite are black magnetite and green epidote or pyroxene, plus others.

Anorthite ($CaAl_2Si_2O_8$) is the calcium end member of the plagioclase solid-solution series. It is a plagioclase in mafic (dark-colored) intrusive igneous rocks (gabbro), as opposed to sodium-end member, albite ($NaAlSi_3O_8$) which occurs in felsic (light-colored) igneous rocks (granite). Anorthosite, which holds more than 90% in pure anorthite mineral, is rare near the ground surface because it solidifies from deep-seated magma and, upon exposure to the atmosphere, can be easily weathered to other minerals, such as clay.

Also, anorthite can occur in high grade metamorphic rocks, e.g., granulite.

Most of the rocks from Lunar Highlands collected during the second Apollo lunar landing are anorthosite. It also appears in some chondritic (stony) meteorites.

Anorthoclase is alkaline feldspar with composition between orthoclase (K-feldspar) and albite (Na- feldspar) – another example of solid solution.

NAMES: The three feldspar-related terms are rarely seen and to the unaided eye, are hard to differentiate. The three names are confusing in our memory. For clarification, they are: anorthite (mineral, or >90 % calcium-aluminosilicate, $CaAl_2Si_2O_8$),

Figure 3-12A: A tetrahedron of volcanic rock. LD = 13 cm; no cut; from San Bernardino County, California.

an*orthoclase* (mineral, $(Na, K)AlSi_3O_8$, solid solution between albite and *orthoclase*), and *anorth*osite (rock, >90% plagioclase). Other than using instrumental analyses, the specimens can be named with greater confidence in the context of field observations with reference to published geological maps.

3-12. Rocks Shaped in Tetrahedron/Parallelepiped

The specimen shown in **Figure 3-12A** is a tetrahedron made of volcanic rock. The base of each of the four triangular faces is about 12 to 13 cm wide. It is a mysterious wonder why erosion and weathering in the desert shaped it into a tetrahedron.

The rock is weakly inter-layered in red and grey. It has many irregularly shaped pores; some of the empty pores appear as black spots in the picture; and a few pores are filled with white caliche (carbonate). Vertical fractures also developed across the layering.

Figure 3-12B: Tetrahedron and parallelepiped. Side length of mirror = 6.5 cm; miscellaneous source locations.

The whole rock seems to have been partially transformed through silica replacement into a red fragmented, tetrahedron of jasper (?). The transformation also gnawed and dismembered the once continuous and coherent grey layers.

Two more tetrahedrons of quartz (light colored pair) are shown in **Figure 3-12B**, along with two parallelepipeds of quartzite (dark colored). Each is itself homogenous in mineral composition.

Figure 3-13A: Kyanite. LD = 23 cm from Arizona-California border area. One cut; courtesy of CTAL.

The parallelepiped block of quartzite has resulted from anisotropic stress field (horizontal compression coupled with vertical decompression or tension) as argued for Figure I1-9 (Lee, 2018). How the tetrahedron is formed, nevertheless, is not clear. My gut feeling for its occurrence has to do with: material homogeneity, isotropic (hydrostatic or lithostatic) stress field and for high stress/strain concentration. As a side note, tetrahedron is the most basic block used in finite-element numerical analysis for 3D modeling by engineers and scientists.

The tetrahedron in the front has been worn by erosion and weathering as well as stained yellowish brown in the desert. The white piece in the back is fresh looking. Disregard what may have caused the creation of tetrahedron or parallelepiped, the two are unusual in shape among the debris in the desert. The query for its occurrence is for curiosity only. Perhaps rocks of tetrahedron shape had inspired the construction of pyramids in different ancient civilizations.

3-13. Kyanite

Figure 3-13B: A polished slab of kyanite. LD = 15 cm.

Kyanite is a greenish blue, columnar aluminosilicate mineral. It is characterized by high degree of anisotropy in Mohs hardness – 4 to 5 along the length and 6 to 7 across. **Figure 3-13A** is a piece of kyanite from high-pressure metamorphic rocks in the Arizona-California border area. Frequently it is associated with staurolite (ferrous aluminosilicates with cross twin, but not visible here), quartz, and plagioclase. Here the brown is indicative of the presence of garnet.

Figure 3-13B depicts one polished slab of another kyanite specimen. It shows weakly NE-SW banding of the green kyanite (grey quartz; white plagioclase).

3-14. Columnar Rhyolite

I borrow a familiar term, columnar basalt, to make some sense out of this odd-looking rhyolite in **Figure 3-14** – travertine-like texture except its grey color, or trellis-like design without major grid pattern. Its layering in white versus greenish grey is subtly visible. More visible are short segments of cracks (grooves) and ridges that run across the layering and cover the entire exterior.

The white is quartz. The greenish grey is weathered product (clay?) of alkaline feldspar. Brownish streaks are also weathered products – originated from iron-bearing dark minerals. The short groves follow the crevices (cracks), which were generated as the rhyolite cooled and contracted. Uneven and severe weathering along the cracks disrupts the layering so much as to render the layering almost beyond recognition.

The top surface has a peculiar pattern as if the rock were a bundle of columns, like chopsticks, fastened together with their ends sticking out unevenly. One cut face at the base does not reveal equivalent columnar structure. Obviously weathering and erosion are at work in the desert to shape the exterior of this odd piece of rhyolite.

Figure 3-14: Travertine-like Rhyolite. LD = 8.5 cm; base cut; from San Bernardino County, California.

Unlike the columns in basalt that run from top to bottom across a layered basalt (see Figure I5-22a; Lee, 2018), the columns here are short and skinny; they are not well defined. Why? The rhyolite was spewed out in successive thin layers rather than a massive layer like the flood basalt famed for its column development due to cooling contraction. Each thin layer cooled and cracked before a new layer overlaid the old one, partly because the rhyolite magma is much more viscous than the basaltic magma. The more viscous the magma is, the more likely for it to hold more gas bubbles and to flow sluggishly. Those features facilitate faster rates of weathering and erosion too.

3-15. Mylonitic Gneiss

Figure 3-15A: Mylonite. LD = 26 cm; from Riverside County, California; base cut; courtesy of CTAL.

Mylonite is not defined for its mineral compositions. Instead, it is named for its texture that has resulted from granulation and ductile flow in fault zones. Ductile flow ramifies creeping at slow rate under solid state condition due to dislocation along grain boundaries and diffusion/ migration of inter-grain pores. The process tends to densify the rock by compressing grain size and increasing grain-boundary surface area. Unlike brittle fracturing along the fault zone near the ground surface, creeping happens under steady shear stress at elevated temperature at depths. Mylonite is formed by solid-state transformation, no melting, and hence it belongs to metamorphic rocks.

Figures 3-15A exhibits one stained or slightly weathered piece of mylonite. Its side face (about 5.5 cm thick) has subtle gneiss-like foliation. Both front and rear faces are striated at an oblique angle to the foliation. The striation and foliation qualify it to be called mylonitic gneiss. The striation is a relic of past slip surface but unlike slickenside (Figure 1-10G), it is hard to decipher the sense of relative movement; perhaps because the former was generated by fast brittle fracturing while the latter by slow ductile creeping.

The striation on the cut face shown in **Figure 3-15B** clearly justifies the naming of mylonitic gneiss. (The long white streak is artifact from edge trimming.) Before the cut, the two pieces together shaped like a rhomboid parallelepiped.

Figure 3-15B: Mylonitic gneiss. LD = 19 cm; base cut from Figure 3-5A.

This piece of mylonite does not clearly show texture of ductile flow. However, features of ductile flow can be clearly seen in two pieces of mylonitic marble (limestone) in the predecessor of this book (Lee, 2018, Figures I2-1 and -2). Both mylonitic gneiss and marble are respectively denser than the common gneiss and marble.

3-16. Fluorite

Fluorite (CaF_2) is widely used for production of hydrogen fluoride (an extraordinarily strong, corrosive acid) and commonly used as flux to reduce the melting point for steel production. Typically, it occurs as a vein mineral in igneous rocks, and it can also deposit with sedimentary rocks.

Figure 3-16A: Zoned fluorite. LD = 11 cm; cut but not polished; source unknown; courtesy of Ms. Andrea Morales.

Frequently fluorite appears in cubic or octahedral crystal forms. It serves the defining hardness of 4 in the Mohs scale. Because it is susceptible to scratch as an individual crystal and is also brittle as aggregate, it has rarely been set as precious gemstone despite its beauty for decorative ornament.

Depending on types and amounts of impurity in trace elements, fluorite can display various colors, covering the entire visible light spectrum. **Figure 3-16A** depicts a zone-colored fluorite: purple and green. The white zone is quartz or quartz veinlets interspersed between the fluorite zones. A packet of druse quartz occurs in one cavity of the middle quartz zone (middle right).

The appearance of druse quartz and the distribution patterns of quartz suggest silica-bearing fluid infiltrated into the cracks after the existing fluorite had been fractured earlier.

Because of its softness, multi-color zoning, and semi-transparency (translucence), fluorite in big chunks can be sculptured to have a beautiful art piece if its brittle fracturing can be effectively managed.

Figure 3-16B displays 10 pieces of fluorite crystals with white and green or pale green color. Each crystal is isometric, and each has octahedral crystal faces. None fluoresces under UV light despite the original naming of fluorite for fluorescence, or vice versus.

Figure 3-16B: Fluorite crystals. LD = 2 cm; unknown source location.

3-17. Lava

Figure 3-17A: Three distinctive lava types. LD = 28 cm; uncut; from San Bernardino County, California.

Lava is magma that extrudes from volcanic vents or associated fractures. In common usage, lava also refers to rocks that have solidified from the extruded magma.

Figure 3-17A depicts a piece of lava that has three distinctive parts with intervening white, thin quartz veins (chalcedony). Its lower member is vesicular with visible cavities (black spots). The middle member between the two white quartz veins is reddish and non-vesicular. It could have been partially altered to agate. The upper member looks like the lower member without visible vesicles. A fourth member (on the middle-right corner) is jagged. Unlike other members in texture, it is a later added-on quartz sliver as exposed by a few white spots.

OBSIDIAN: Some felsic lava (i.e., similar in chemical composition to granite or rhyolite) is very viscous for its high silica content. Upon exposure to atmosphere or cold rocks, it cools rapidly such that crystals will not have time to develop. Instead, it forms black obsidian – a non-crystalline volcanic glass (**Figure 3-17B,** base slab). Sometimes, radiating, white spherules appear as phenocrysts (cristobalite, a high temperature variety of quartz) amid the black glassy groundmass. It is nicknamed as snowflake obsidian. Impurity in trace metals

Figure 3-17B: Obsidian. LD = 25 cm; unknown source locations; gifted by Mr. Danny Sweeny.

may change its color. The reddish-brown piece here holds fragments from earlier eruptions. Vitrification in the base slab yields a few white quartz specks.

Obsidian is amorphous, homogeneous, and brittle. Upon impact, it produces conchoidal fracture. It has been used for experimental scalpel blade for its sharp fracture edge. Since ancient time, obsidian has been knapped into stone tools, such as arrowheads.

PUMICE: **Figure 3-17C** exhibits two pieces of foamy volcanic or pyroclastic rock – pumice. It is glassy and very vesicular with rough surface. Pumice is the only type of rock that can float in water. Another vesicular, glassy pyroclastic rock, scoria, will sink after floating in water for short time.

Like granite and rhyolite in chemical composition, pumice has high silica content. Hence, its parental magma or lava is very viscous. Beside silicates, the magma has volatile components (e.g., water, carbon dioxide), which stay dissolved in the magma under high pressure. Upon sudden volcanic eruption, both temperature and pressure drop abruptly. Like carbon dioxide bubbles out when a soda or beer can is opened, drastic pressure reduction causes the dissolved volatiles to exsolve from magma immediately to form gas bubbles but the gases cannot escape freely owing to inhibition by the hosting viscous magma. Furthermore, the magma is quenched swiftly to form glass, and the partition cavities (vesicles) instantly trap the gases. As the temperature declines, gas pressure decreases further to reduce the tendency for the gas to escape.

All those interactions are completed in short time after eruption such that those tiny gas bubbles do not coalesce into bigger ones. However, the vesicles dominate the volume of pumice to result in low density; but the vesicles do not interconnect, leading to impermeable pumice. Both the abundance of vesicles and the inability for water to migrate between pores allow pumice to float in water indefinitely. (Diatomite has high porosity and permeability; hence a piece of dry diatomite can float in water for short duration only.)

Figure 3-17C: Pumice. LD = 35 cm.

Because of its high silica content, pumice is typically light-colored, like other felsic rocks. But exception happens. The top piece in Figure 3-17C is pitch black, like black obsidian. The piece was bought from a gravel shop for building and construction.

The bottom piece is whitish grey but slightly tainted brownish in contact with desert soils. It is believed to have originated from the Obsidian Butte at the southeastern end of Salton Sea in Imperial County, California. Its parental Butte site, however, is almost devoid of any pumice now because of exploitation. I picked the specimen three decades ago near a sand dune several miles northeast of the Butte.

3-18. Hydrothermal Graphite

Graphite is one of the two common minerals of carbon; the other is diamond. Graphite is weakly linked by sheet layers. Each sheet is bonded together by carbon atoms spread out in hexagonal structure. The sheet, the so-called graphene, is 100 times stronger than the strongest steel per unit mass basis if one can isolate it. However, the weak link between sheets makes it one of the softest minerals with a Mohs hardness of one (as defined by talc). It serves as a good lubricant and, for writing, as lead pencils or charcoal paints.

Graphite can be recognized by four attributes: black metallic luster, extremely low hardness, low density (light weight for comparable rock size), and black smudge on hands upon touching. The last feature distinguishes graphite from anthracite (nicknamed smokeless coal) by touching.

It occurs as a high-grade metamorphic rock with purity in carbon greater than that of anthracite (highest-graded coal), but graphite is not combustible. It can also appear in non-minable, minor stringers or seams in schist or gneiss and sometimes in association with igneous rocks. **Figure 3-18** depicts two pieces of graphite, along with one piece of anthracite for comparison. The botryoidal knobs on the left piece are indicative of hydrothermal origin, as shown additionally by layering (not schistosity) on the right piece and fiber-like threads across the layers. The 'junk' on the right is part of its enclosing country rock.

Figure 3-18: Hydrothermal graphite, except that the top piece is anthracite. Left: LD = 4 cm; bought.

3-19. Suiseki Gneiss

The art of rock appreciation is now quite popular around the world whether the rock stands alone or in conjunction with bonsai. The suiseki stone can be placed in outdoor garden or indoor on desktop. Its beauty is appreciated in the eyes of beholders. As practiced traditionally by Japanese, only one cut to the stone is allowed for display stabilization; in other cultures, anything goes, including artificial carving and staining. Usually, a suiseki stone is set in custom-made display wood stand.

This book and its predecessor have assembled quite a few uncut stones suitable for suiseki. Here is one more, uncut, natural stone – a piece of gneiss (**Figure 3-19A**, and the book cover) – which is presumed to have come from a southern California desert.

Like similar high grade metamorphic rocks, this piece of gneiss is composed of alternating black and white bands, with the former consisting mostly of biotite and hornblende and the latter of quartz and feldspar; it is a mix of mafic and felsic minerals. The grooves and the windows (holes) align with the foliation or banding, suggesting the natural engraving of the stone is structurally dictated.

Figure 3-19A: Suiseki gneiss. LD = 15 cm; no cut; bought from a desert rockhound.

The piece lay flat naturally with its rear side facing the ground; hence water and wind could not have sculptured its sky-facing surface by brute force of particle abrasion. However, the edges or rims of grooves, holes, and windows are smoothly and delicately engraved. Why?

Mafic minerals are unstable at the ambient ground temperature and pressure. Their foliations fissured and the interfaces between different mineral grains loosened owing to differential thermal expansion/contraction during hot day and cold night. The resultant microscopic cracks sucked in condensed moisture through capillary action during cold nights. Sometimes the moisture froze, expanded, and enlarged the fissures. Through endless freeze-expansion-breakage-suction feedback, the processes were enhanced, but the rock was still degraded at slow rate around the margins of fissures. Denudation of mafic minerals leads to decay of felsic minerals too. The rock is eroded grain by grain to have the grooves cut and holes dug and is eventually tunneled and carved. Wind blows away the eroded dust and exposes new surface for further fine-tuning of natural carving. The perpetual interactions among rocks, air, and water lead to the appearance of this piece of suiseki gneiss. This artistic sculpture, however, is rare and it can be found only by chance encounter in the desert.

Figure 3-19B is an addendum to Figure 19A for suiseki although it is a piece of chalcedony. The piece abounds with smoothly worn holes that align to form troughs. No tunnel

Figure 3-19B: Suiseki chalcedony. LD = 12 cm; no cut; from San Bernardino County, California.

has developed from the holes. The ridges and troughs are sub-parallel to one another and spread over the entire rock surface.

Silica-bearing fluid had infiltrated into foliated host rocks such as gneiss and solidified to become chalcedony. The weaker host rock was then weathered and eroded to form the 'ridge-trough landscape'. A few visible spots of residual host rock remain in some deep holes. One white streak across the rock is not calcareous caliche; it is a seam of translucent chalcedony which appeared long after the emplacement of the primary brownish chalcedony.

Figure 3-20: Sphalerite. LD = 15 cm; base cut; bought.

3-20. Sphalerite

Sphalerite (zinc sulfide) dominates many zinc ore deposits. The piece in **Figure 3-20** is heavy for comparably sized rocks. It has shining black faces with vitreous metallic luster. Multi-reflections make photo-taking a challenge, even equipped with a circular polarizer filter. For example, the green is a photo-illusion; the rest of the color representations, although still skewed by shadowing effects, seem fair after filtering out blinding shining patches.

What led to the identification of sphalerite are: It has white streak, as supported also by milky white goo when it was saw-cut or during belt-grinding; and it is soft but heavy. On the dull cut face, it shows two sets of subtle cleavages crossed at right angle, reminiscent of cubic crystal structure.

3-21. Labradorite

Figure 3-21: Labradorite. LD = 12 cm; the right piece from building supply store;

Labradorite is an intermediate mineral in the albite-anorthite solid-solution of plagioclase. Slabs of labradorite are readily available at many building and supply stores. It is attractive for its bluish iridescence, known as schiller optical effect or labradorescence. The optical phenomenon comes from reflection off laminae, which have resulted from solid-to-solid exsolution between sodium and calcium plagioclase as the rock is slowly cooled.

Labradorite occurs usually with mafic igneous rocks. **Figure 3-21** depicts one dark piece of labradorite along with one corner of a commercial slab for comparison. The blue schiller optical iridescence may not be readily observable amid the dark minerals. To spot it, turn a specimen around under sun light. Once the blue is spotted, one must finely cut it and have the cut-face polished. Otherwise, the blue iridescence may not appear; for example, it is not observable in the unpolished faces of the commercial slab (unless it is sprayed with water).

Not all labradorite will display schiller phenomenon. Minerals with schiller reflection are not necessarily labradorite. For example, bytownite (another plagioclase with greater calcium content) can show off blue schiller reflection too.

3-22. Magnetite

Two pieces of magnetite are displayed in **Figure 3-22**. Both respond to magnet, show black streak against white ceramic plate, and have a feel of heavy compared to common rocks. Both also exhibit metallic luster on the polished faces but the left piece is more resistive to grinding while the right piece is easy to grind. Furthermore, the right piece yields brown goo during grinding, suggesting some cubic magnetite ($FeO \cdot Fe_2O_3$) has been oxidized to maghemite (an unusual cubic hematite instead of a common hexagonal hematite, Fe_2O_3). If so, the right piece could have been

Figure 3-22: magnetite. Left, LD = 9 cm. Sources forgotten.

transformed from peridotite or dunite (ultramafic rock with high content of olivine) during serpentinzation and the greenish white, fibrous patches represent another end product – asbestos.

Common magnetite is not a magnet; it will not attract an iron nail. But it can be turned into a permanent magnet under a strong, artificial, inducing magnetic field, which far exceeds the Earth's natural magnetic field strength. However, a lodestone, an unusual type of magnetite with impurity of titanium/manganese/ aluminum, will attract iron nails. A lodestone acquires its permanent magnetism through strong magnetic field generated by lightning near the ground surface. A properly shaped lodestone, suspended or pivoted, had been used as a navigation tool in ancient time, before the usage of compass with magnetic needle or modern navigation with GPS (Global Positioning System).

Magnetite is one of the major ore minerals for iron. It can occur in igneous, metamorphic, and sedimentary rocks (see Section 4-5: Banded Iron Stone). The fine particles of magnetite can be washed-up on the beach in small, black stripes or patches (see Section 5-7: Modern Analog), where one can scoop up magnetite sands with a magnet for kids to play around.

Also, magnetite can be deposited with sediments. As the fine magnetic particles settle through non-turbulent water columns, the particles will align with the ambient geomagnetic field. Thus, in conjunction with age dating of sediments, geologists can chronicle the variations of geomagnetic field through geologic time. (A sinking, big chunk of magnetite cannot do for the job because it is too big for the magnetic force to overcome the gravitational inertia for re-orientation.) By means of paleomagnetic studies, in addition to other scientific endeavors, the theory of plate tectonics, which tells the plate motion on Earth, has been well established since the 1970s.

Magnetite can be generated biologically in some bacteria and animals too. Well known is magnetoreceptor, in the upper beak of some species of birds, that aids navigation for the birds' seasonal migration. Post-deposional biogenic magnetite, especially the bacterial type, could potentially perturb the magnetic records accumulated through particle by particle settlement.

3-23. Granite Spiny Lizard

I have lived in Riverside, California since 1974. It is my family's hometown in America. My house is seated over the Southern California Batholith. The campus of the University of California at Riverside, where I had taught geophysics and hydrogeology for 35 years, sits at the foothill of the Box Springs Mountain, a granite hill. Before I came to Riverside, a big concrete logo 'C' was poured by students over the hill face just below its summit. That is a man-made landmark.

Figure 3-23: Granite Spiny Lizard over granitic rock. The lizard is about 25 cm long.

One day during the period of 'stay-at-home' mandate to minimize person-to-person spreading of coronavirus in 2020, my wife and I hiked two miles along a trail in the eastern backside of the hill to the granite summit near that logo C. Fittingly to the occasion, a picture of *Granite Spiny Lizard* was taken (**Figure 3-23**), about one mile south of the granite arch in Figure 3-1. Ignoring the flying predators, this black lizard was enjoying a sun bath by resting on pale granitic rocks.

Chapter 4: SOFT ROCK TALK

Soft rocks refer colloquially to sedimentary rocks that are formed at the ground surface or sea floor, as distinguished from igneous and metamorphic rocks which, except volcanic rocks, originate from the deep interior of Earth. As used elsewhere, soft rocks mean rocks that are indeed soft mechanically.

Sedimentary rocks are compacted, cemented, and consolidated sediments. Sediments occur in three modes: deposition of rock fragments derived from existing rocks through mechanical transport by wind, water, glacier, or debris flow; chemical precipitation through evaporation and solute saturation; and accumulation of biologic remains.

Clastic sediments (i.e., mechanically derived) range in grain sizes from clay, silt, sand (from 1/16 to 2 mm in diameter), to gravel [granule (greater than 2 mm), pebble, cobble, and boulder (greater than 256 mm)]. At a given locality, sediments are rarely uniform in grain size; usually sediments are a mixture with various grain sizes. Sorting is an index to gauge the uniformity in grain size distribution. Roundness of grain increases with transportation distances. Size, sorting, and roundness, in addition to layering, are the main attributes of sedimentary texture. In terms of dominant proportion of grain size distribution, the equivalent sedimentary rocks are shale (claystone, siltstone), sandstone, and conglomerate. 'Clasts' refer to grains or fragments in sediments. Breccia denotes sediments or rocks with large, angular, poorly sorted clasts, in contrast to conglomerate with greater roundness in clasts.

Beyond the textural classification, the naming of clastic sedimentary rocks is further refined by constituent compositions. A popular scheme is based on relative abundances of quartz, feldspar, and rock fragments. With the naked eye, we cannot visually identify those constituents for grain sizes smaller than sand, we will not venture to naming clastic rocks based on compositions.

Sandstones are usually porous. Those with open pore space are called arenite ('clean' sandstone); if more than 10% of pores are filled with mud or clay, it is 'dirty' sandstone (called greywacke which generally derives from undersea avalanches). Arkose derives from granite with feldspar dominating over quartz sands. Most exploitable groundwater is held in sandy layers (aquifers) that have high porosity and permeability. Mudstone has high porosity, but extremely low permeability prevents it from becoming a workable aquifer. Oil shale bears abundant oil and gas but requires hydraulic fracturing (fracking) to open flow paths for extraction.

Layering is the main characteristic for most sedimentary rocks, which may or may not bear fossils. Layer interfaces are usually smooth; and grains do not interlock one another. However, sediments and sedimentary rocks can appear chaotic with no orderly layer structure; for example, deposits of debris flows, landslides, and glaciers are poorly sorted mixtures of jumbled, angular rock fragments. This chapter deals with sedimentary rocks other than limestone which has been addressed in Chapter 2.

4-1. Layered Structure

Figure 4-1 is a typical section of layered sedimentary rocks, exposed in the coastal area of San Diego, southern California. Differential erosion in sandy and clayey interlayers creates the stair- or terrace-like landscape. A lot of cobbles or boulders scatter over the horizon or atop the ground surface. Those are remnants of erosion, not necessarily nodules or concretions that were released from the hosting formation after their exposure or cropping out.

If those remnants are buried by new sediments and become part of a new formation, they are alien clasts that pre-date

Figure 4-1: Layered sedimentary rocks, from San Diego County, California.

their younger, enclosing host sediments. They are not nodules – post-depositional products of replacement; nor are they concretions – contemporarily accreted or developed with deposition. Nodules and concretions may not be distinguishable to the unaided eye despite their difference in modes of occurrence. Hence the two are often exchangeable in common, amateur usage.

4-2. Twirl Structure

The picture in **Figure 4-2** was taken during a misty morning when my wife, our three-year-old grandson, and I toured along the coast in San Diego to watch seals. Viewing from the bottom to top, we first see beach sands (Formation Unit A).

Next to or atop of the beach sands sit two types of sedimentary rocks with distinctive structures. On the right (Unit BR), the horizontal sand-clay layering is very well developed; to the left (Unit BL), there is no layering to speak of although it is still made of the same gray sandy-clayey mixture.

Overlying Units BR and BL is the weakly layered sandy Unit C. In comparison to the well-developed layering in BR, Unit C may be deemed massive (i.e., no clear layering) and its cliff-like wall has been defaced unfortunately with graffiti (visible at enlarged picture scale), which will be removed naturally by erosion if no new graffiti incur.

And of course, there stands the brown bluff (Unit D). Layering in the bluff is barely visible at the bottom one third of the cliff; the rest could have been covered with and hence obscured by rock-fall debris, which piles up and scatters near the base of bluff. The brown hue suggests Unit D, formed at high oxidation state, is a recent continental deposit.

In contrast, the gray Units B and C are marine deposits, formed under oxygen-deficient conditioner or reducing environment. Both are parts of turbidite – deposits by turbidity currents

Figure 4-2: A swirl structure in sedimentary rocks, from San Diego County, southern California.

which are undersea turbulent currents originated at shallow water and loaded with suspended particles, grains, or fragments to become a dense body of fluidized mass flow. Upon reaching deep, calm water over flat sea floor, the turbidity currents slow down and lose their carrying capability. Large grains settle first to the ocean floor, medium grains follow next, and finally fine grains precipitate last to form a graded formation, i.e., grain sizes decrease from 'coarse' at the bottom to 'fine' at the top. Figure 4-2 is opposite to the expectation – an inverse gradation with fine-grained layer underlies coarse one. How do we get around the paradox?

Turbidity currents can recur and give the appearance that a coarse-grained layer lays directly atop a fine-grained layer if the sedimentary section is only partially exposed and viewed. In other words, Units B and C can be deposited by two different turbidity currents. The key to resolve the issue is to inspect the interface between Units B and C in the exposed outcrop. Is it an erosional surface? One criterion is to see if parts of the underlying Unit B have been scraped and incorporated into Unit C.

The interfaces between units B and C, and C and D are unconformities, which signify time gaps in the depositional sequences. Specifically, they are disconformities because the layering is parallel to the interfaces. (An unconformity is angular if layering is oblique to the interface.)

Next, let us consider the lateral transition between Units BL and BR. The two are disjointed in layer structure. Is there a fault bisecting the two? If yes, the faulting pre-dates the deposition of Unit C which appears to have blanketed horizontally over 'the presumed fault' without any disruption. On the other hand, can the boundary between BL and BR be an ancient erosional surface? If yes in this case, Unit BL was younger to Unit BR and occurred prior to the presence of Unit C. For sure, Unit BL is too soft to have wedged under C.

Figure 4-3A: Cobble bored by gastropods. LD = Long Dimension = 12 cm; no cut; from Los Angeles County, California.

The swirl or twirl in BL is the most intriguing feature here. How did it happen? The feature is preserved amid its laterally jumbled surrounding. Was it a local happenstance in submarine slumping when a part of the strata met resistance to its forward motion (rightward, landward) and curved back to form the swirl? Was the slumping triggered by earthquake or tsunami? Or simply, was it triggered by gravitational instability when sediments piled up, like a snow avalanche during heavy snowing?

Someone with a broader perspective about the geology around the area may have a ready answer. Meanwhile I invite you to speculate what has happened on this picture alone.

4-3. Boring in Rocks

If you walk along a rocky shore, you will have encountered cobbles like that pictured in **Figure 4-3A**. This semi-spherical calcareous clay ball is covered with many holes drilled by boring gastropods. These holes are each isolated, i.e., there is no network of tunnels to connect the holes together.

A gastropod does not have teeth or claws to chew or scrape the rock. How can it drill a rock, up to 4 cm deep? It secretes acid to dissolve or weaken the rock as it bores its way. How does a gastropod know acid is useful? And why is it capable of producing and using the acid to build its dwelling? Evolution is not preordained to have a goal, but organisms go along and somehow some adapt and flourish while others perish.

There are many small and big holes. Each hole tapers inward, seemingly to conform to the shape of a conical, spiral gastropod – apex (posterior) pointed inward and aperture (anterior, mouth) open outward to the sea water for food. How can a gastropod burrow with its apex as the inward leading prick? The apex is sealed or dead and no secretion of acid comes out of it to ease the path for burrowing. In short, can a gastropod drill backward? Why? How?

A baby gastropod starts with a tiny hole. As it grows bigger, it needs a larger dwelling. Does it come out to drill a larger hole? Or does it stay in? And somehow it can amazingly enlarge the room as it grows.

When I picked up this cobble at beach, I did not see any live or dead gastropods in the holes, only a couple broken shells. Why did all the 'colony of gastropods' disappear?

Figure 4-3B depicts another cobble with holes drilled by unknown sea creatures. It is sandy with fair amount of clay – a piece of greywacke (dirty sandstone). At least, one hole was inhabited by one bivalve clam. That inhabitant cast doubt about the gastropods as the drillers, as speculated for Figure 4-3A.

Figure 4-3B: Sandy cobble with sea clams. LD = 23 cm; from Los Angeles County, California.

4-4. Breccia

GLACIAL DEPOSITS: **Figure 4-4A** depicts a piece of breccia. Its grains are mostly angular with various shapes. It is poorly sorted: a mixture of visible grains with sizes varying over orders of magnitude and a silicified matrix with visibly indistinct grains.

Figure 4-4A: Glacial breccia. LD = 24 cm; no cut; from eastern San Bernardino County, California.

Its clasts (fragments or grains) have a diversified mineral composition, as reflected in different shades of colors and shapes. The breccia is well cemented in a siliceous matrix, as shown by many protuberances but tightly held grains or fragments around the periphery of the rock specimen.

This piece of breccia comes from a Precambrian glacial deposit (more than 541 million years old). Its angularity distinguishes itself from conglomerate which is composed of rounded clasts (see Figure I4-9 of Lee, 2018 for a picture of conglomerate). However, without the context of field observations, a hand specimen of glacial breccia could be confused sometimes with breccia from debris flows or landslides.

Figure 4-4B: Annealed breccia. LD = 12 cm; multi cuts; unknown source location; gifted from Mr. Jim Wolford.

RE-CEMENTED BRECCIA: Another piece of breccia with very distinctive and picturesque outlook is presented in **Figure 4-4B.** In short, it has been brecciated and then re-sealed by quartz veins. All sides are either saw-cut faces or hammer breakage faces.

The original rock would look like a Nevada wondering rock (trade name) with Liesegang banding (around Z), which, when polished, shows vivid inter-banding of red, brown, and white. The parent rocks were shattered into fragments and displaced from one another such that their pre-breakage configuration cannot be reconstructed within the view of this specimen now. The open cracks were filled by siliceous fluid while cracking was in progress because the fluid had engulfed fragments or particles of various sizes before the fluid precipitated as the white quartz vein.

As expected, the siliceous fluid infiltrated and matched the crack peripheries before its solidification or crystallization into white opaque quartz. The quartz vein is rimmed with a thin dark brown seam (about 1 mm wide). The very dark patch of the seam (V), however, was slightly broadened by a relief shadow during picture taking. In the rear side (**Figure 4-4C**), a good chunk of the quartz filling is banded or zoned. More widespread in the veins are mixtures of quartz and unknown alien mineral grains. No quartz shows recognizable crystal form except the druse quartz that partially fills several vugs (see D in the front face).

ZIGZAG MATCH: Most intriguing in this picturesque specimen is the zigzag boundary between two fragments of rock with distinctive Liesegang banding (near Z). Neither fragment could have been liquid at

the time of their perfect zigzag match. Then, how could two solid fragments fit to each other so precisely or intimately? If one of the two had to be a liquid when the matching happened, the pale one with less banding on the left of contact would be my choice. Could it be a batch of mud or volcanic ash? Did it get the Liesegang banding after its emplacement into a void? If so, why did the late banding stop at the contact, showing no visible infiltration or diffusion to the right fragment?

Similar 'solid-solid' contact also seems to have happened between two fragments at the bottom middle of Figure 4-4B (S). The left fragment is well banded, but the banding stops at the contact; there is hardly any banding in the whitish right piece.

So, two major development stages are implied after the breakage of the Liesegang-banded host rock. The first introduced a liquid that yielded the pale white fragments

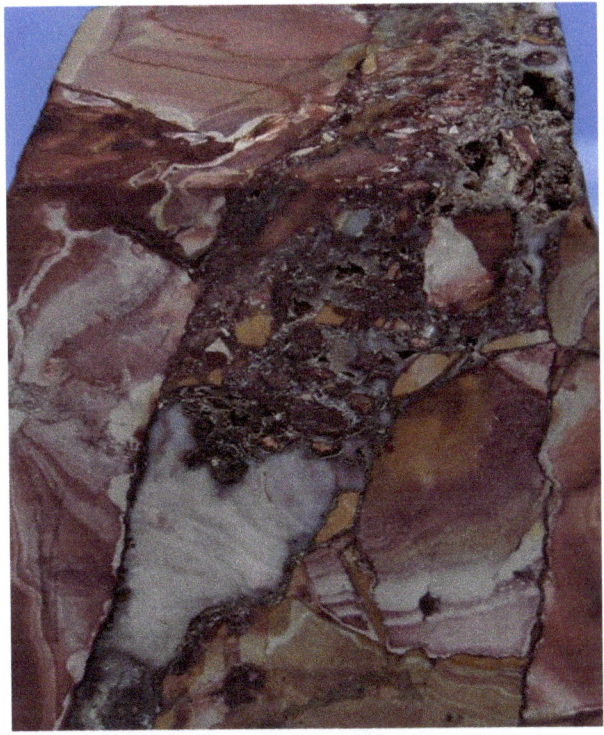

Figure 4-4C: Breccia; rear side of Figure 4-4B.

with sparse banding. The second stage induced invasion of siliceous fluid and eventually the deposition of vein quartz. The first is subtly clear but the second is unambiguously conclusive. Some loose ends still need to be tied, nevertheless.

Figure 4-5A: Banded ironstone. LD = 29 cm; no cut; from eastern San Bernardino County, California.

4-5. Banded Iron Stone

Banded iron formations or ironstones make up about 60 percent of known iron ore reserves in the world. **Figure 4-5A** depicts a piece of banded ironstone from an abandoned mining dump in eastern California. The black bands are rich in magnetite/hematite, and the pale-colored bands are sedimentary chert (amorphous silica) tinted with reddish iron oxides. The two alternates in banding or laminating on a sub-centimeter scale. This piece is dull, compared to a vibrant piece from Australia (**Figure 4-5B**), because it lacks significant presence of fully oxidized iron although it responds to neodymium magnet.

Figure 4-5B shows red and grey bands which are respectively hematite and magnetite; only the latter reacts with a tiny neodymium magnet disk. The light-colored stringers are secondary calcite, which filled the gaps opened when the banded ironstone was folded.

I would like to use both pieces as steppingstones to introduce an idea: How the availability of free oxygen, as implied by the banded ironstones, affect the origin of life in the early era of Earth. Besides stromatolites (see Section 5-8), no other rock has played such a global role.

OCCURRENCES: All banded ironstone formations occur in Pre-Cambrian sedimentary deposits (more than 541 million years ago). Most clustered globally between 1,800 and 2,400 million years before present – a long period when cyanobacteria had busily built a global stromatolite empire and simultaneously claimed credit for the great global oxygen generation that incubated the hydrocarbon-based lives on Earth.

Figure 4-5B: A polished slab of banded ironstone from Australia. LD = 12 cm. The tiny neodymium magnet interacts only with the grey magnetite band. Courtesy of Mr. Jim Wolford.

Ancient ocean water was acidic (our current ocean water is slightly alkaline) and there was little free oxygen (i.e., oxygen unbonded chemically with other elements) in the air and ocean; and the sea water carried a lot of dissolved or soluble ferrous iron. Then, the cyanobacteria came along in seawater to do photosynthesis and produce free oxygen. The iron was oxidized, and the resulting ferric oxides precipitated down to the seafloor to form the black (magnetite) or red (hematite) bands. When free oxygen became deficient or scarce, chert or mud formed predominantly. The alternating banding between iron oxides and chert corresponded to fluctuations of available free oxygen.

SNOWBALL: Another cluster of banded ironstones occurred around 750 million years ago when Earth was covered extensively by ice to become figuratively a global snowball. Under a global ice envelope with some broken windows, the ocean water was mostly shut off from the atmospheric oxygen, but it continued to receive ferrous iron that was spurted through hydrothermal vents in undersea rift valleys. When the global snowball began to thaw and the dissolved iron re-contacted with atmospheric oxygen, the accumulated ferrous iron in sea water resumed oxidization to result in precipitation of banded ironstone again. The banded ironstone depicted in Figure 4-5A was formed in association with the thawing of global snowball.

FREE OXYGEN: It took extra 200 million years to replenish the sea water with enough free oxygen for nourishing more marine invertebrates (no plant and nor land animal during that period). Then, suddenly in geological speaking of time, a Cambrian biological explosion detonated: many new organisms proliferated and began their evolutionary journeys. Trilobites dominated the Paleozoic Era for 290 million years. Dinosaurs followed and roamed Earth for the next 190 million years during the Mesozoic Era. The late comers, mammals, crawled out of their lairs (burrows, caves) after one gigantic asteroid struck Earth and wiped-out dinosaurs 66 million years ago. Thus, began the Cenozoic Era; we humans arrived at a later stage of this latest Era.

(As a footnote: Another theory stipulates that dinosaur were wiped out by mercury poisoning before the asteroid could have played the role of an exterminator. The mercury gas was released by super volcanos that made the vast Decan basalt plateau in India. The killing was witnessed, to name one example, by seashells of which the fossils have recorded high dosage of mercury consumption.)

IRON DEPOSITS: Five hundred million years after the Cambrian biological explosion, you and I come along. We exploit the banded ironstones, which took millions and millions of years in making, for our civilized usage in years, months, or days. By way of talking about ironstone, I have introduced a few keywords for the interested readers to surf on the internet for fascinating subjects like oxygenation of Earth, theory of global snowball, and Cambrian biological explosion.

Before we leave the subject, you might also be interested in the story of another asteroid impact that created a 1000-meter-high seawater column at the impact center about 1,800 million years ago, and then generated the banded ironstones over a long period of time in what is now Minnesota State.

Figure 4-5C depicts a piece of medium to coarse grained sandstone. It is banded with each band consisting of finer sub-layers. The top one-third of the section displays some layer truncation.

Changes in color and grain size reflected supply changes, which in turn had resulted from small-scale short-term climate changes that influenced sediment supply, transport, and deposition.

Figure 4-5C: Sandstone. LD = 20 cm; no cut; from southeastern California.

The layering patterns suggest the specimens in Figures 4-5A/B and 4-5C were both formed in proximity of their respective sources. The difference is that the very-fine grained sediments in the banded ironstone were 'rained' down through a sea water column while the layered sandy deposits were transported laterally by water before their settlement.

4-6. Diatomite

Diatomite is a rock composed mostly of fossilized diatoms, which are aquatic single-cell algae living in the sea or freshwater lakes. Diatoms have microscopic silica shells, rarely exceeding one mm in diameter. They grow through photosynthesis and hence thrive only in depths where sun light can reach. Radiolarians are another dominant silica bearing micro-organism, but radiolarians are animals living in the sea only.

Figure 4-6: Diatomite, LD = 17 cm; surface scraped; from Los Angeles County, California; gifted from Dr. Ting-Chang Huang.

Diatomite is fragile and powdery. Its dry density is less than one because of its high porosity. Dry diatomite can float in water for short duration only because its pores will soon be soaked with water for its high permeability. On the other hand, pumice – a felsic (or acidic) volcanic rock – can float like foam in water indefinitely for its high porosity, poor permeability, and, of course, low density. (Pumice's air pores are so poorly connected to one another as to have extremely low permeability and will not absorb water to sink itself. See Section 3-17 Lava.)

Pulverized diatomite is called diatomaceous earth (DE). The combination of powdery silica, white color as well as high porosity and permeability allow DE to be used in various applications for filler, filtration, drugs, pesticides, and arts supplies. For health-related usage, only fresh-water originated diatomite can be used because sea-derived diatomite often carries undesirable heavy metallic elements.

In the real world, diatomite is not pure. In addition to diatom fossils, it may hold up to 20% of clay and iron. **Figure 4-6** depicts one specimen from a late Miocene formation (ages between 5.3 to 25 million years) in Los Angeles County, California. According to Dr. Ting-Chang Huang's microscopic observations (e-mail communication, 2019), the diatomite also bears significant amount of radiolarian fossils and minor amount of calcareous nannofossils. The relative abundance of siliceous over calcareous fossils suggests these organisms used to live in a colder environment under which calcareous shell debris could be dissolved easier in seawater.

The piece is indeed soft and fragile despite its old age and having gone through potential diagenesis, compaction, and cementation. It can be cut easily with a hacksaw, leaving a bumpy, crumbling face. It could also chip off upon touching to yield rough, crumbly surface overall.

Amid the rough surface, there are quite a few small patches with smooth, slightly greenish surface (see one big patch at the top surface). These patches, being still fragile, might have resulted from the incipient chloritization of clay minerals.

SQUARE BLOCK: The most conspicuous feature in Figure 4-6 is a square block, which protrudes out of the diatomite layering and extends to the rear of the specimen as well. Recovered from an old residential area, the block could be relics of a passageway for water dripped from irrigation pipes. But why was groundwater confined to a narrow passage with a square cross-section?

The square block is bordered with a distinctively light-gray toned band. The band, like the ruin of a fortress wall, has uneven width and relief (in part due to photo distortion) and bears many grayish brown specks. The largest speck at the upper-right corner in the square is clayey and can be pried loose with a bamboo toothpick; but others are resistive. Interior to the band, there are hardly any brown specks.

Could the specks have been silicified to make the band (or wall) stand out? Could iron oxidization play a minor role in congregating the specks although they are scattered randomly in the band? I cannot answer with observation by the naked eye only. Even if an answer is available, a long way still lies ahead to explain why that block is squarely configured. Is it by chance inherited from the original distribution that somehow had more clay and iron oxide contents to begin with? Or alternatively, is it structurally controlled?

4-7. Sandstone Ridge

The specimen in **Figure 4-7A** was a loose sandstone piece near an outcrop of travertine in the Mojave Desert. Despite the presence of calcareous veinlets and a few small patches of caliche, the sandstone is not well cemented overall. Its grains can be rubbed off with free hand, as shown with a few fine sand grains on the wood stand.

Figure 4-7A: Sandstone ridge. LD = 16 cm; no cut; from San Bernardino County, California.

As positioned on the stand, the sandstone's bedding dips steeply. One bedding plane is exposed on the right. The stone is uniformly grey, but it is not greywacke. Besides veinlets and fractures, the sandstone is homogenous in composition and is very well sorted. The deposit was distal to its parental rock sources.

One peculiar phenomenon happens when its bottom is submerged about 0.5 cm deep in vinegar. Through capillary suction, vinegar rises and deposits powdery white crystals on the ridge top a few hours later. The stone would look prettier with a snow-like cover on the ridge if the powder would not turn into messy dust. Those vinegar crystals can be easily washed out with water; and cleansing of the interior can be done likewise by immersing the stone in clean water. Some residual vinegar crystals that rim two vertical cracks are still visible in the picture (one at the upper left corner and the other at the middle bottom).

Figure 4-7B: Shale and sandstone. Shale LD = 19 cm; base cuts; from Inyo County, California.

Displayed in **Figure 4-7B** are shale and sandstone from Inyo County, seating on a vein quartz plate from Kern County, California. Both shale and sandstone have one common feature: calcite veinlets, which can be scratched with a pocketknife. The veinlets stand about one mm above their respective surfaces of host rocks because the veinlets are more resistive to surficial degradation.

4-8. Evaporites

Evaporites include a wide variety of minerals that precipitate chemically out of water bodies, typically in the dry desert environment. Evaporites such as table salt (sodium chloride) are very water soluble. Nucleation of a particular mineral begins in standing water when the water is being evaporated and when the solubility of that compound is reached (i.e., water is saturated with dissolved solids). For multiple-component brines, different minerals precipitate at different stages of evaporation and so, zoning of evaporites occurs depth-wise and laterally. Overlapping in zoning also happens because different solutes can precipitate simultaneously from the residual brines as evaporation proceeds.

Frequently columns of evaporites can stand in brine pools; some rise above water and others stay submerged, pending on fluctuation of water level. A variety of natural shapes in evaporites can create fascinating scenery. I have visited evaporation ponds run by a solution mining company in the Mojave Desert. The salt columns and pedestals in the ponds are the desert's wonder, albeit

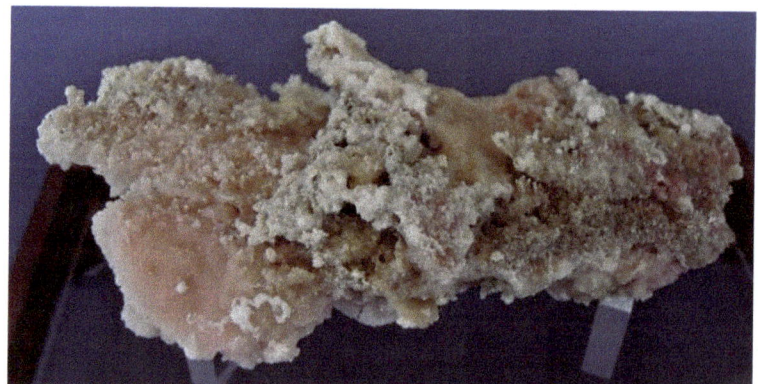

Figure 4-8A: Evaporite of sodium chloride. LD = 24 cm; no cut; from Inyo County, California.

artificial. Those wonders, however, cannot be preserved as specimens because they crumble to powder in dry air and can also be worn down by exposure to moisture in the air.

Figure 4-8A displays one specimen of salt from a shallow evaporation pond in the Owens Valley, Inyo County. It is not as beautiful as the ones from the Mojave Desert mentioned above and it is very fragile too.

The piece mostly consists of sodium chloride. The coloration could be due to the presence of some trace elements. More likely the grey is indicative of clay mixing. And the pink and yellow signal residues of salt-water algae – a cyanide yielding type. Be aware of potential hazards of consuming naturally colored salt, which is available in some specialty stores.

Nature always creates something wonderful. We try to explain its creation. **Figure 4-8B** illustrates such a piece in an evaporative environment in the desert. It is a piece of gypsum peppered with sand grains, most of which are quartz. Gypsum can crystalize in various forms. Common are transparent or translucent selenite and the nicknamed 'desert rose'. [See, for example, Figures I4-1 and I5-4a of Lee (2018)].

Figure 4-8B: Sand-peppered gypsum crystal. LD = 10 cm; no cut; source forgotten.

Three horizontal layers of gypsum crystal were laid first. Then, the top two layers were 'cut' or ended abruptly. A new gypsum layer grew and abutted the cut faces at sharp right angles (near 90 degrees). More layers were later erected, parallel to the central, dominant column. Those additions sit atop the horizontal layers at sharp angle too.

Figure 4-8C: Gypsum. LD =13 cm; no cut; from San Bernardino County, California.

I am short of words to say why the gypsum makes such a 90-degree turn during crystallization. There appears no obstacle on the growth path that forces crystallization to change orientation. It appears like the so-called 'gypsum dovetail twin; if so, the twins are stacked.

Here is another piece of beautiful gypsum (**Figure 4-8C**). The shining, fibrous gypsum is demarcated by grey clay layers. Each clay layer is depositional during a short-wet period, and it has been fragmented by dehydration cracking during later dry period. Gypsum as evaporite fills the cracks and grows atop the clay layers through evaporation of calcium-sulfate bearing solution, which has been scavenged (dissolved) from surrounding rocks, transported to a depositional center (basin or pond), and precipitated over a long period of time.

Figure 4-8D shows another piece of columnar gypsum, which is not as fibrous as the piece in Figure 4-8C.

Figure 4-8D: Gypsum. LD = 16 cm; gifted by Mr. Calvin Shipley.

4-9. Layered Black Chert

Chert is an aggregate of silica (silicon dioxide) in the form of cryptocrystalline quartz. It originates from sedimentary rocks, as diagenetic products of silica-producing organisms such as diatoms and radiolarians or as replacement products of pre-existing organic debris. It may accumulate in fresh water or seawater, either fossiliferous or fossil-free. Silicified woods are replacement chert but usually the name of chert is reserved for other types of replacement. Frequently cherts appear as dark colored nodules. And cherts can appear in layers. Darkness arises from impregnation with organic matter.

Chert in marl or chalk is named flint for its better quality for tool making in ancient civilization or ornamental making. Other cryptocrystalline silica minerals, as related to magmatic or hydrothermal activities, are named agate (colored, translucent, curved, and banded), onyx (plain layered), jasper (red, opaque, cavity filling, irregular shape), and chalcedony. The latter is a catch-all term for odd shapes other than nodular chert. Opal is hydrated silica mineraloid (a gel, not a true mineral) with or without opalescence.

How is chert recognized visually? It is compact, hard (Mohs hardness: 6 ~ 7), and brittle (conchoidal fracture); its color spans reddish brown, gray, green, and black. Unfortunately, those characteristics in hand specimen are too ambiguous to distinguish it from others. In the field, chert can be recognized by its mode of occurrence: sedimentary or otherwise. So, I usually name a hand specimen as chert by process of elimination, i.e., by ruling out other options.

Figure 4-9A: Layered chert. LD = 24 cm; two cuts; from Inyo County, California.

Figure 4-9A depicts one piece of layered chert, which was retrieved from alluvial deposits but was originally imbedded in limestone, as inferred from outcrop nearby.

Both sides were covered with clay (marl) in the field. Partial removal of clay by scraping and cleaning reveal the piece is full of micro-cracks. But the piece remained intact when it was saw-cut. The cut face suggests a part of the piece can be polished.

Figure 4-9B depicts one relic patch of chert which still sticks with a relic limestone piece.

4-10. Fluorescent Bark and Geode

Petrified or silicified wood is a popular item in rock gift shops, in part, because the specimen can be easily polished to become a memorable souvenir such as bookends. Most petrified woods, including those in Petrified Forest National Park, have been silicified from the woody part of fallen trees. Their barks are rarely preserved.

Figure 4-9B: Limestone with relic chert. LD = 16 cm; base cut.

SILICIFIED BARK: One exception is the specimen in **Figure 4-10A**. The bark is preserved but the woody part is missing. In the field, the piece was mostly encrusted with caliche (redeposited calcium carbonate near the ground surface). Partial removal of the caliche with vinegar reveals the piece is dotted with many oval chalcedony nodules. Those nodules immerse in a net of interconnected, brownish yellow or dark brown, bark-like strands. Both the nodules and strands also appear to align vertically, like along a tree trunk

Figure 4-10B is a bottom cross-section of the silicified bark in Figure 4-10A. It shows multi-layering or scaling in the brown bark and the bark is interspersed with grey lenticular chalcedony.

Figure 4-10A: Silicified bark. LD = 19 cm; from eastern Riverside County, California; one base cut; courtesy of Mr. Donald Alexander.

Figure 4-10B: A bottom cross section of Figure 4-10A. The bark is about 2.5 cm thick.

It is not clear why chalcedony occurs in dispersed, segregated, nodular forms, rather than forming a continuum as prevails in typical 'woody' petrified wood. Is it the scaly or flaking nature of bark that preferentially favors certain locations for replacement of bark to form the chalcedony nodules? Is it the greasy or oily resin that prevents the chalcedony from coalescing together? Or is it short of silica supply?

FLUORESCENCE: Most amazing about this silicified bark is its intense green and dim blue fluorescence (**Figure 4-10C**) under ultraviolet (UV) light at either long or short wavelength. Only the chalcedony fluoresces; and the whole piece will fluoresce more broadly if more caliche cover is removed. See Section 4-16 for one more fluorescent bark.

Pure chalcedony does not fluoresce. The 'activator elements' as impurity in chalcedony promote the fluorescence. When an orbiting electron in an activator is excited by absorbing UV irradiation energy, the electron was kicked from low to high orbital energy levels (i.e., from stable to unstable states). Then, that unstable electron falls right back to its stable ground state and emits the absorbed energy as visible light. The light color varies with the energy exchange: stronger

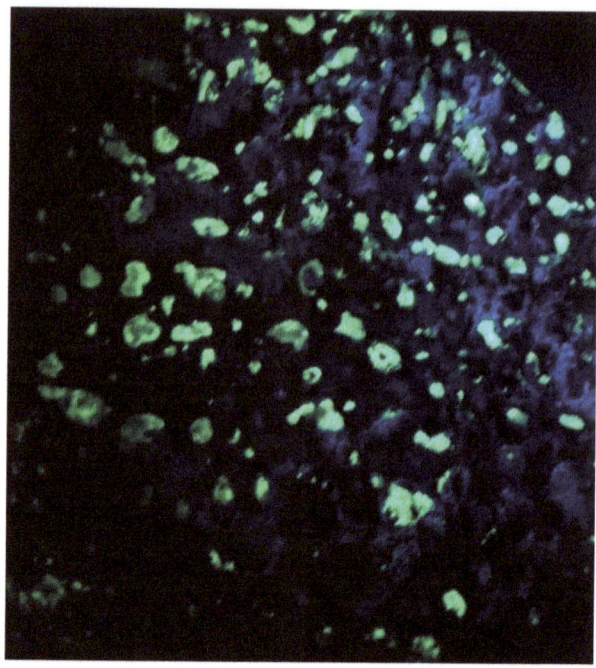

Figure 4-10C: Fluorescent chalcedony nodules (green) in the silicified bark; part of Figure 4-10A.

toward violet and weaker toward red spectra. The piece glows continuously if UV continues to shine on the activators.

Once the UV source is turned off, the fluorescence ceases at once. If the light emission lingers for a while after UV is off, the material is said to be phosphorescent.

The impure activators include some rare earth elements and a few heavy metallic elements such as tungsten, molybdenum, lead, titanium, chromium, and uranium. Which is the culprit for the fluorescence? I do not know without instrumental analyses.

URANIUM: Being cautious, I presume the fluorescence is due to radioactive uranium. The seriousness of the radiation, however, cannot be assessed without using a device (e.g., Geiger counter) to count the strength of particle emission or chemical analysis for uranium content. The sampling site of the petrified bark is not known for uranium exploitation. For safety measure, long term exposure to similar silicified bark should be avoided, especially in enclosed space, until the radioactivity as a cause of florescence is eliminated or uranium concentration is below the harming level.

FLUORESCENT GEODE: The bark specimen came from the Wiley's Well area in eastern Riverside County, California, where rockhounds have long explored for geodes. The chalcedony and quartz in open geodes from that area also shows fluorescence under UV bombardment as exemplified in **Figure 4-10D,** which was photographed from the same geode for Figure I1-18a of Lee (2018). For comparison, that picture is duplicated as **Figure 4-10E** with the understanding that the two photos are presented in slightly different scales and picture-taking perspective.

One could venture to claim that the relief in the floor under UV represents a 3D view of a transitory 'tub' before the newer chalcedony fills and flattens it as seen in daylight.

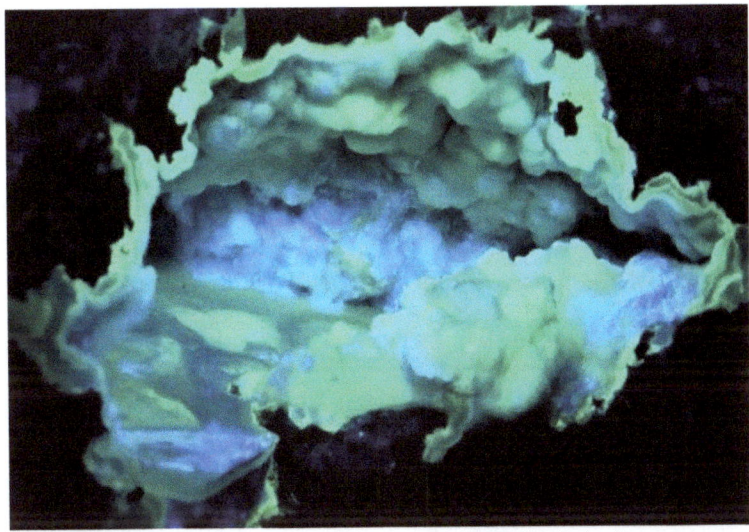

Figure 4-10D: Fluorescent geode under ultraviolet light for specimen in Figure 4-10E.

Figure 4-10E: Geode, about 10 cm across; one cut; from Riverside County. Reprinted from Lee (2018, Figure I1-18a).

Note that chalcedony and druse quartz inside the geode fluoresce but the brown encasing lava rind or crust does not. An uncut geode will not fluoresce unless the chalcedony protrudes through the rind. Noticeable are two distinctive fluorescent colors: blue and green. Is the color difference an optical illusion? Some narrow greenish-blue bands reflect the shadow at edge of amygdaloids (almond- or grape-like spherules). But why is it blue at the 'basin floor'? The basin is flat under white light but appears rugged under UV light. If the blue-green contrast is real, what is the cause?

To alleviate the concern whether the blue is an optical illusion, one pair of pictures for another geode is presented in **Figures 4-10F** and **10G.** As usual under the short-wavelength ultraviolet light, the greyish chalcedony turns green; the black hole (a former gas bubble) on the upper-right quarter becomes bluish grey; and again, the brown lava rind or crust disappears into darkness. However, cobweb-like threads emit faint blue or green light out of the darkness. Also, in the lower-left quarter, several pinkish-blue dots correspond to 'a chain of white chalcedony islands in the sea of lava' that encloses the core body of greyish chalcedony. The core chalcedony appears zoned in both daylight and UV light, but its zoning is quite different from that in Figure 4-10E. The cause for the blue stays mysterious but its presence in Figure 4-10G is not an optical illusion because all light is reflected from a smooth flat cut-face (except the hole), not from a rugged, broken face as in Figure 4-10E, which may have been compromised by some light-shadow effect.

Figure 4-10F: Geode, About 13 cm across; one cut; from eastern Riverside County, California.

IMAGINARY: Just for fun or fantasy, one monkey, hiding near the center of the fluorescent picture, is enjoying a piece of bread. In the lower-right quarter, one black duck with a stick in its mouth appears to wade leftward. Carrying the imagination further, that duck image transforms into a server who is presenting a big box toward a bearded receiver on the right. Well, imagination under UV is unlimited because of strong color contrast between fluorescent and non-fluorescent objects. Look over Figure 4-10D again and fantasize whatever one cannot picture under daylight. (Lava is dark under UV light.)

MORE ON FLUORESCENCE: Below the reach of sun light penetration in the ocean, various deep-sea creatures fluoresce in the dark, but those creatures are not radioactive. Certain molecular structures yield fluorescence (bio-fluorescence) for the creatures to see and to be seen. A biologic miracle, indeed!

Here the green fluorescence by quartz or chalcedony is attributed, out of precaution, to enrichment of radioactive elements, e.g., uranium. Its source of origin is unknown, but it has spread to a wide area. Uranium can be absorbed by organic matter such as bark. But why or how is uranium incorporated with silica to replace some bark to form chalcedony nodules?

Geodes are products of magmatic (or volcanic) processes and associated hydrothermal activities. But crystallization inside geodes differs from replacement in the bark. For example,

Figure 4-10G: Geode under short-wave ultraviolet light; same specimen as Figure 4-10F.

crystallization is associated with declining temperature and changing concentration while replacement can continue isothermally. What is the common factor for enriching uranium in quartz or chalcedony that is formed in such different modes of occurrence?

Some geodes from Dugway, Utah are known to have uranium and fluoresce. I have yet to find geode or petrified wood, elsewhere from southern California, which will fluoresce under UV. Fluorescence is thus a diagnostic source indicator for my geode collections from the Wiley's Well area. Again, what is the cause for the different UV responses? Likely, the key is: presence or absence of uranium in the source hydrothermal fluids. The same uranium-bearing source fluids supply the silica needed to precipitate chalcedony in geodes, and to replace the wood/bark as chalcedony. (As a foot note: I was shown three pieces of geodes from the Wiley's Well area in May 2021. The chalcedony does not fluoresce but the bands in the rinds appear pink or red under UV. The bands are made of unknown laminated mineral.)

The next level questions are: where do the fluids collect uranium, and how do the fluids incorporate the uranium with silica precipitation or replacement?

Figure 4-11A: Silicified tree root. LD = 23 cm; no cut; unknown source location; courtesy of OBMS.

4-11. Silicified Tree Root

Petrified/silicified wood is a common collector's item. **Figure 4-11A** is an unusual specimen of tree root. Unlike the silicified tree bark in Figure 4-10A, this tree-root fossil is absent of bark, nor fluorescence.

Before the piece was silicified, it had grown twisted; a big chunk of it was split and separated, leaving gashing scars near the top one-third of the specimen. Amazingly, silicification has well preserved its delicate grainy, woody texture.

Petrified wood comes in different shades of colors, especially on cut or polished faces: grayish, yellowish, brownish, and reddish. Rarely is it greenish as depicted in **Figure 4-11B**. It could have been transformed from biomass other than wooden part of a tree in a reducing bog environment.

Figure 4-11B: Greenish petrified wood. Width = 7 cm; unknown source; courtesy of Mr. Gregory Vidler.

4-12. Stromatolite Jasper

Stromatolite and jasper in this section heading are not compatible because stromatolite is biogenic while jasper usually connotes a silica product related to volcanic activities. Nevertheless, the heading conveys the sense: how the specimen may look like.

Figure 4-12A: Stromatolite Jasper, LD = 12 cm; top cut; from northern Arizona.

The cobble in **Figure 4-12A** is covered with a mesh of fine, alternating red and white layers, occasionally interspersed with discontinuous grey quartz veinlets, or with narrow, elongated quartz lens. It has uncommon sedimentary layering. The layering is swirled, twisted, and convoluted into some local knotty closures. My attempt to unravel the sedimentation sequence has failed. The red-white lamination leads to the suspicion that the cobble is a piece of stromatolite.

One saw cut reveals the specimen is red 'jasper'. It has been brushed naturally with broad, elongated, light greyish brown 'paint'. Each 'brush stroke' is distinct and together they are beautifully configured in the red background matrix. All are individually rimmed with a dark brown rind, which was the protective membrane or cell wall to the organism or colony of organisms. The combination of elongation, irregular shape, and brown rind in those brown blobs leads again to the suggestion that the blobs are biogenic, viewed as stromatolite – a multi-million years, if not billion, old fossil assemblage.

Figure 4-12B depicts another view at the other end of the cobble, about 7 cm apart, down from the preceding cut face. The broad-brush painting in Figure 4-12A has changed over a short distance into a fine, delicate painting. Again, the features support the contention that the specimen is stromatolite jasper.

Figure 4-12B: Another view of Figure 4-12A. The brown patches outside the cut face were defaced by a failed attempt to polish.

CYANOBACTERIA: Stromatolite is produced by cyanobacteria (used to be taken as green-blue algae). Through photosynthesis, cyanobacteria slowly enriched an oxygen-deficient young Earth (less than one billion years old, or more than 3.5 billion years ago) into an oxygen-sufficient Earth atmosphere over one billion years. The abundance of oxygen allows other organisms including us humans to sprout and evolve.

Oxygen, however, is a waste product and is toxic to cyanobacteria. Most cyanobacteria species died long ago at the peril of what they are good for – sustaining themselves by producing oxygen – and other consequential ecological competitions. To this date, only a few species of cyanobacteria survive to build stromatolites at some desolate places of environmental extremity, which is hostile to most of other organisms. Such a long surviving period for cyanobacteria is an amazing feat, considering many other species that see prosperous years but eventually meet their demises for various causes over the past 3.5 billion years. See more narrative on stromatolite in Section 5-8.

REDDENING: Why is the rock reddish? Obviously, the rock has ferric iron to stain itself reddish. For iron to turn or oxidize from greyish ferrous (Fe^{++}) to reddish ferric (Fe^{+++}) states needs oxygen, lot of more oxygen. Cyanobacteria cannot flourish well in oxygen-rich environments. It is hardly believable that those stromatolites were produced at the time of an oxygen-rich Earth when the presence of ferric iron was favorable. Likely, the coloration to red happened long after the stromatolites were buried and fossilized.

Figure 4-12C: Jasper with stromatolite lamination. LD = 12 cm; two cuts; from northern Arizona.

The sediments surrounding the stromatolites are fine grained and collectively the fine sediments are poorly permeable to groundwater flow. Thus, fine grains allow slower transformation but better preservation by silica-rich and ferric-ion carrying groundwater over eons to jasper. The transformation is so thorough that the jasper appears homogenous. The so-called jasper here could be alternatively named red chalcedony in line with the naming of petrified or silicified wood fossils. Compared to the sediments, the stromatolites are less altered by ferric ions and hence keep darker tone.

(Note: My stromatolite story could be tossed if the dark brown rinds are geochemical reaction rims rather than biological envelopes or skin. That would be another story down the road.)

LAMINATION: The intricacy of layering shown in Figure 4-12A & B is hard to untangle. In contrast, the layering in the cobble depicted in **Figure 4-12C** is easy to unravel; it is like an ordinary sedimentary rock. Both specimens came from the same general sampling area and appear to look alike in color features but differ in layering fabric.

Two saw-cut faces expose no surprise. It is brownish red overall, laced with short, pale-brown strings. Unlike the unexpected internal textures revealed in the first specimen (Figures 4-12A & B), the cut-face textures can be envisioned from the outside of this second specimen.

Again, jasper comes to my mind for its red and homogeneous attribute, although the red-white lamination stands in the way of so naming. The lamination points to the contention of stromatolite and hence returns to the incongruous section heading of stromatolite jasper.

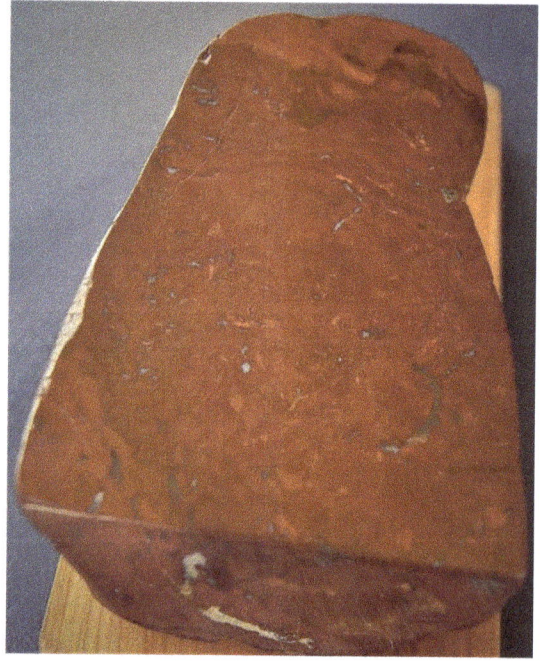

Figure 4-13A: Red chert/jasper. LD = 12 cm; two cuts; from central California.

4-13. Red Chert/Jasper

Figure 4-13A and **B** depict another set of red cobbles. All are massive without any visible layering. The stones are hard, and brittle as reflected by the presence of dents incurred during the transportation by stream water.

The grey or whitish speckles and patches on the cut face in Figure 4-13A are quartz or chalcedony. Otherwise, the piece is red and homogenous. This piece of red chalcedony is amorphous solid silica which had originated from sedimentary processes, post-depositional diagenesis or alteration of silica-embodied diatoms or radiolarians. To achieve red color, incorporation of ferric ions was a must activity in the past.

The dots of quartz appear like pore filling and the larger patches of quartz look like crystallization in cracks, as implied by irregular interface with the red host. Both are post-depositional, secondary filling, not contemporary with chert forming.

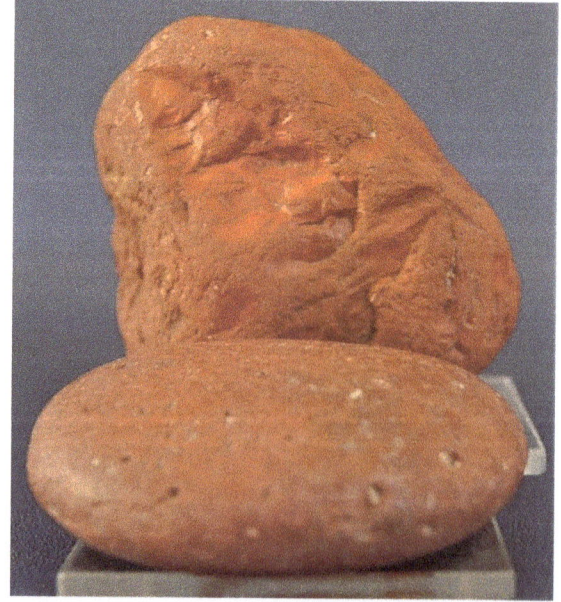

How does one tell the difference between red chert and jasper? Both are cryptocrystalline chalcedony. A definitive answer comes from seeing their occurrence in the field or outcrop. Chert is sedimentary while jasper is related to volcanic rocks. In the absence of field-observation, the visual differentiation for a solitary stone is an educated guess: Jasper is usually more varied in color and texture; and it shapes like coming from crevices and is small in stone

Figure 4-13B: Red chert/jasper. LD = 8.5 cm; no cut; from central California.

size. (The above-mentioned stromatolite jasper is an awkward exception.) Chert is typically more homogeneous in color and texture, and it could go far beyond handful in size.

Figure 4-13C: Red chert/jasper. LD = 12 cm; base cuts; from central California.

Figure 4-13C displays another set of chert/jasper. Naming it as jasper could be more profitable for the prospect of making it a potential cabochon or other jewelry deco. Each could be a beautiful red stone if it passes a crucial test: can it be well polished? Figure 4-13A demonstrates that all the stones presented in this section can be well polished.

4-14. Dehydrated Nodules

A nodule is a lump or clot of mass that differs from its hosting sedimentary rock in hardness, mineralogy, or chemical composition. It is a product of post-depositional, secondary replacement or selective cementation. If the host is disintegrated, the nodules can be released as solitary stones because of their greater resistance to weathering and erosion. Most nodules are calcareous or siliceous and sometimes ferrous (pyrite) or phosphorous. Usually, a nodule has simple internal structure.

Figure 4-14A: Sandstone nodule. LD = 9 cm; source unknown; gifted by Mr. Tony Gilham.

Figure 4-14A is an example of fine-grained sandstone nodule, formed by selective cementation. The cut face reveals this sandstone is monotonous clayey or silty, barely showing any layering. It is mysterious how the two spheroids are stuck together by either replacement or cementation. The cut face reveals subtle crack lines which radiate out from an interior point but do not visibly reach the periphery of the nodule. That pattern favors the contention that the cracking was started by interior dehydration.

SEPTARIUM: Can the internal dehydration cracking in a sandstone nodule be extended analogously to explain the occurrence of septarium (**Figure 4-14B**)? A septarium starts out as a marl or calcareous mud nodule. With respect to the sandstone nodule, the marl nodule holds expansive clay and hence more water for greater shrinkage in volume when it dehydrates and cracks later. Most cracking does not breach the periphery to allow efflux of water and, in exchange, for influx of carbonate-bearing fluid for calcite precipitation. The access routes are not clear in Figure I5-21a of Lee (2018), which was re-cut here for solving the puzzle: how the fluid fills the cracks. After a few trials, this slab comes closest to the desired cut for finding the fluid access routes.

How the calcite (the white filler) was emplaced is another puzzle. It cannot be a one-time fluid influx; it should have remained an open system for some time because solid cannot migrate into the cracks. Precipitation of calcite and replenishment of fluid must have run simultaneously. At end, there should have unfilled cavities inside the septarium because solid is less voluminous than the fluid from which it precipitates. The brown linings are aragonite. Inside the linings or cavities are tiny calcite crystals that have room to grow during crystallization.

Figure 4-14B: Septarium showing the dehydration cracks. LD = 13 cm.

4-15. Accentuated Layer Marking

Figure 4-15 depicts an odd-looking siltstone or mudstone. Looking at the alternating black-grey banding on its vertical front face (*V*), one may incline to say the banding is indicative of layering. Indeed, the banding reflects layering, but it is not primary, as formed when the sediments were deposited. Instead, the black bands stand for secondary, post-depositional

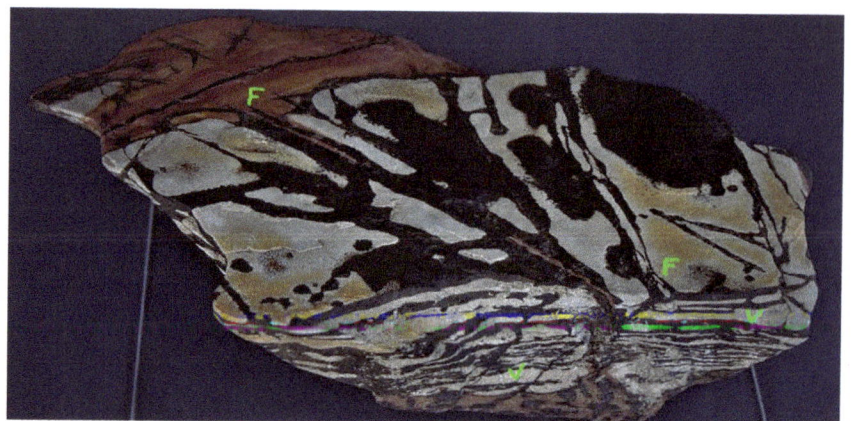

Figure 4-15: Siltstone/Mudstone. LD = 18 cm; unknown source.

infiltration (dispersion) by dark fluids or fluids that were oxidized later to black. The coloration accentuates the layer marking in an otherwise invisible mudstone layering.

BROWN DISPERSION: On the upper-left corner of the bedding plane (*F*), two distinctive fluid incursions (brown and black) onto a grey mudstone bedding plane are registered. The first is iron rich and it created dispersion lobes (tongues) with different shades of yellow to brown zoning – signaling variations in iron concentration or state of iron oxidation. The lobes are time marks for the advancing dispersion. And note the unstained grey tongue west of the upper *F* marking.

The iron stain spreads across the bedding to the rear and bottom faces and re-emerges at the base of the frontal vertical face (*V*). The two brown patches are linked via one disrupted brown, diagonal thread of veinlet on the bedding plane (*F*) and through a bloated segment of the brown veinlet on the front vertical face (across the bedding *V*).

This first phase of incursion happened during early stage of mud consolidation. The veinlets followed the micro fissures which developed owing to post-depositional dehydration of mud.

BLACK-FLUID INCURSION: Following the dehydration cracking, the black-fluid incursion happened. Dehydration enlarges slightly bedding spacing and causes occasional across-plane fissuring too. The in-plane dispersion (F) accounts for most of the odd patterns on the top face (which is actually a layer interface – bedding plane): strips ('tree branches') and blotches. One notorious feature is an imaginary animal figure hiding amid the branches. Some of those in-plane black imprints have fuzzy or hairy boundaries, suggesting post-emplacement diffusion from high to low concentrations. The equivalent black strips or veinlets in the brown part (F) of the mudstone have clear-cut outlines, suggesting the brown staining and filling have reduced the permeability to impede further diffusion from the newer black fluid.

The black fluid also migrated along the old fissures that were previously filled by the brown veinlets; the brown diagonal veinlet mentioned earlier is almost over-printed by the black, and the other two brown veinlets are barely visible through the black cover. Besides narrow strips, many black spots or patches pop out randomly in the brown area. Those features favor the conjecture that all black, including the layer-like ones, is post-depositional product.

LAYERED PATTERN: Why did the second fluid incursion make a layer-like pattern? In detail, the black bands do not always run the entire course of the rock width on the frontal vertical face (V). Dehydration induced differences in hydraulic properties between in-layer and across-layer, resulting in anisotropic dispersion. Unless fractured, the mud would impede the dispersion away from fissures. Thus, layer-like pattern arises.

Another but more convincing argument against the depositional black-and-grey layering is the presence of cross-cutting black veinlets, which happens post-layering because crosscutting cannot concur with horizontal, depositional layering.

What is the black material? It could be manganese dioxide, which forms interlayered dendrites in some limestone (see Figures 12-12a and 12b of Lee, 2018). Alternatively, the black fluid could be organic-rich or oxidation-induced. The molecules or particles of 'organic dyes' are likely bigger than the manganese equivalents and are less diffusive away from the fluid conduits of fissures.

Figure 4-16: Silicified pine bark. Height = 13 cm; one base cut; from Riverside County, California; gifted by Mr. Gregory Vidler.

4-16. Silicified Pine Bark

Figure 4-16 depicts another silicified pine bark, which comes from the same sampling site as in Figure 4-10A, but the specimen here is scarcely masked by caliche.

The chalcedony is exposed as white patches, which become green under ultraviolet light. On the inner side (underside), some chalcedony patches stretch up-and-down linearly and thus show greater contrast between UV green emission and no-emission black.

The bark suffers little wearing due to transport, suggesting that it was silicified in situ. Again, where did the woody trunk go? How does the chalcedony fluoresce? Does uranium-bearing volcanic ash play a role?

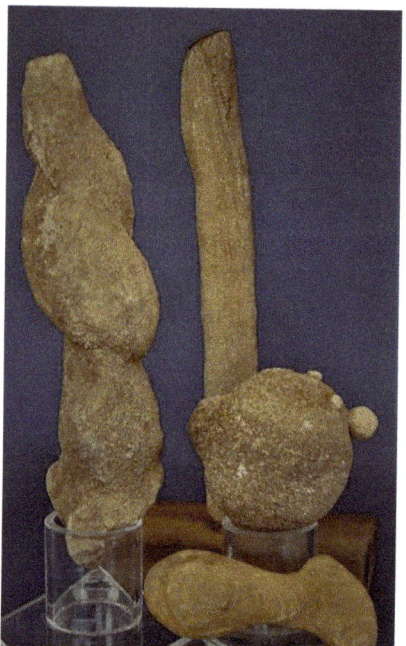

Figure 4-17A: Sandstone nodules and fragments. Left, LD = 15 cm.

4-17. Sandstone Nodules

Controversy can arise over the occurrences of some sandstone nodules: Are the 'nodules' post-depositional replacement products or erosional relics of the detached rock fragments as seen in Figure 4-1A?

Figure 4-17A depicts two nodules and two relics of sandstone fragments. The elongated nodule on the left is ropy or twisted, like the ropy, silicified (chalcedony) coprolites shown in Figures 5-1A & B. The spherical nodule is weakly layered and has three (or four?) sub-nodules or nipples, like the equivalents in the biogenic chalcedony nodules displayed in Section 1-1; its protrusion is like the silty sandstone nodule in Figure 4-14A too. Those sand sub-nodules do not doubly stack up. The column in the middle is a sandstone rod with visible traces of bedding while the bottom one is an erosional relic of a sandstone fragment.

Figure 4-17B: Five sandstone nodules. central piece, LD = 8 cm.

Although all chalcedony nodules cited in Section 1-1 are biogenic, it is difficult to envision how the sandstone nodules can form through biological processes.

All four pieces appear to have originated from loess, but different processes yield different nodules and relics. Nor can I reconcile the argument that erosion has carved out the spherical sub-nodules.

Another set of five sandstone nodules are presented in **Figure 4-17B**. The coarse-grained sandstone in all but the central piece is homogeneous with no visible layering. But layering appears in the central piece; and its stem or 'panhandle' elongates along the orientation of bedding planes. It is hard to imagine a nodule would develop across the bedding.

For comparison, a much larger nodule is shown in **Figure 4-17C** (from Figure I4-6a in Lee, 2018). It is a little calcareous and its grain sizes are smaller than those in Figure 4-17B. It has some lineation but no clear bedding.

Figure 4-17C: Sandstone nodule. The ball is 13 cm in diameter; bought.

Figure 4-17D: Loess fragments. LD = 17 cm; from Imperial County, California.

Figure 4-17D depicts two more isolated fragments of consolidated loess from sand dunes in southeastern California. The right piece is cross bedded but the mid-plane between the two lobes on the left piece follows the bedding. Obviously the two are erosional relics, not nodules. With these two in mind, I wonder if all pieces depicted in Figure 4-17B are nodules; some are erosional relics, especially for the central piece. An unsettled question is: how do the relics achieve the ball shape with long panhandles?

4-18. Eluvial Deposits

The rock with pisolitic (pea-like) texture in **Figure 4-18A** is bauxite (an ore of various aluminum-bearing minerals). For comparison, a piece of vesicular basalt is also presented. The vesicles in basalt have been filled with secondary minerals but the oval grains in bauxite are residues of weathering. The 'vesicles' in basalt are linearly aligned and the 'peas' in bauxite are similarly aligned too but the bauxite is not weathered from basalt. Instead, the parent to the bauxite could be other types of volcanic rocks: tephra or pyroclastics.

Figure 4-18A: Bauxite. LD = 10 cm; bought; bottom: vesicular basalt, gifted by Mr. Jim Wolford.

In tropical or subtropical areas where precipitation far exceeds evaporation rates, dissolvable constituents in some igneous rocks can be leached out by percolating subsurface water and the resulted residuals often have high concentration of hydroxyl aluminum minerals to form bauxite deposits – collectively called eluvial deposits which differ from the common fluvial or alluvial sediments deposited by river transport.

(As used in soil science, the leachate from the upper soil horizon *A* can be redeposited in the lower horizon *B* as illuvium and the residual above it is named eluvium. Geologists call eluvium for the residual products of *in situ* weathering and leaching, for example, eluvial diamond, gold, or cassiterite deposits. Eluviation means leaching.)

The black 'peas" in the brownish matrix are obsidian. Weathering causes the matrix to become brownish. Pea-like white spots are either fillings of secondary minerals (e.g., kaolinite) in cavities vacated by falloff of fragments or end products of weathering. Some dark obsidian has been lightened in color to brown by leaching; and a few grains are enclosed with white or brown reaction rims, again indicative of weathering in progress. Further weathering will lead to white and gray bauxite exemplified on the right edge.

Instead of viewing the rock as pyroclastic dominated by obsidian, the parental rock could be other type of aluminum-rich igneous rock that had been severely weathered to clay and leached to yield 'pea-like' texture.

Figure 4-18B is another piece of residual product of weathering – an eluvial deposit with one speculative twist that, after leaching, the eluvium has been transformed through opalization (hydration and solidification of silica from colloids).

Figure 4-18B: Opal. LD = 12 cm; some scraping; bought.

The rock is white, tinged with pink dots and stringers. The rough, yellowish crumbs are not superfluous add-on grains; rather, they are fragments disintegrated from parts of the main body. Some rough surfaces have been scraped or ground off artificially.

Overall, the rock gives a lightweight feel (low density) as compared to the common rocks of similar sizes. It exhibits conchoidal fractures and is resistive to scratch by knife. Its streak is white. The patchy fragmental attachments have resulted from dehydration cracking rather than superfluous additions or attachments of foreign grains. Those features point to the suggestion of opal although the stone is not opalescent, nor is it fluorescent under ultraviolet light. Hence it is regarded as a common opal, not precious opal.

It is not clear what the pre-alteration rock was. The protolith (parent rock) was transformed or altered through leaching by hydrothermal fluids to result in a light, homogeneous product. Whatever it was, the product is massive or chunky, unlike the 'pea-like' texture in Figure 4-18A. Somehow opalization occurred later, coupled with invasion of pink fluid along micro-fractures. (The invaders might hold mercury, arsenic, or manganese as guessed for their pink color.) After the opal was exhumed or exposed, dehydration happened to splinter the opal sporadically to yield those fragmental lumps.

4-19. Calcite in Mud Cracks

Figure 4-14B depicts a dehydrated nodule of which the internal cracks are filled with calcite to form what is a well-known septarium. Here **Figure 4-19** is a supplement to the septarium, showing another mudstone in which, the cracks are also filled with calcite seams (veins) and crystals.

The fractured, blocky mudstone came from a lake deposit in New Mexico. It is not a nodule. Unlike the tapered cracks in septarium, the cracks in this lake mudstone shape irregularly. Some cracks are big enough for calcite (some marked by red dot) to grow into visible rhombohedral crystal form (translucent, yellowish white), but most calcite grains in the veins or seams are too small to have visible crystal form (lower picture).

4-20. Groundwater Seepage

The picture in **Figure 4-20** was taken one day in March 2020 during the California's shelter-in-place decree to prevent spreading of novel coronavirus.

Present in the far background is a dim view of the San Jacinto Mountains, which trend northwest (left) to join the east-west trending Transverse Ranges. The Ranges rise owing to impingement by the Pacific tectonic plate against the North

Figure 4-19. Calcite (red dots) in Mud Cracks: Upper, LD = 13 cm. Lower picture is the back side of the upper one.

American plate. The Mojave Desert, where most of my rock collections come from, is separated by the Transverse Ranges from southern California, where I reside.

Note the hillslope of the frontal ranges is essentially barren in the semi-desert environment (or Mediterranean climate) in the Riverside area except for two parallel vegetation lineaments, which follow groundwater seepages along fracture zones. An oasis or water hole is a cherished site in the desert where groundwater upwells along a geologic fault that juxtaposes one water-permeable geologic block against an impermeable one.

Figure 4-20: Groundwater seepages. Picture was taken at a wildlife refuge in Riverside County, California.

Along the foothill base runs the main strand of the San Jacinto fault, which is the most active one in terms of the recurrences of major earthquakes (magnitude greater than 5) among the three prominent NW-SE trending strike-slip faults in southern California. The other two are the San Andreas and the Elsinore faults. (Strike slip means faulting along the strike or trend of a geologic fault.)

Most of the foreground where the blue heron stood belongs to the San Jacinto Basin. The basin, lying between two strands of the San Jacinto fault zone, is being pulled apart. It is widening, lengthening, and deepening. The resulting expansion and subsidence of the basin, however, is balanced in topography by natural filling of sediments eroded from the hills nearby.

I spent about one half of my professional career on the San Jacinto and adjacent groundwater basins: applying geophysics (mainly seismics and gravity) to unravel buried geological structures (e.g., water-filled underground basins or channels), defining subsurface basin configurations and their inter-connections; as well as analyzing hydrochemistry to characterize various subsurface water masses (types) for groundwater resources studies and environmental mitigation.

Chapter 5: FANTASY

Chapter 5: FANTASY

This FANTASY chapter includes all rocks that could have been grouped into one of the preceding four chapters. But here the narratives are speculative, imagined, or fantastic.

5-1. Coprolite

Coprolite is a piece of fossilized dung (animal's excrement or pooh), which often provokes 'yak' from a toddler who first sees it in the museum but soon after, he or she may dare to touch it out of curiosity. An inquisitive mind will ask how it was fossilized, especially for dung of land animals to be preserved and transformed.

Each of **Figures 5-1A** and **-1B** displays two specimens of coprolite. Every specimen is responsive to a neodymium magnet; it is highly silicified too; and its Mohs hardness is around 7. The body of each specimen is slightly twisted, ropy, knotty, spiral, and its surface cracks like a pinecone.

Figure 5-1A: Two pieces of coprolites. Long Dimension (LD) = 12 cm; no cut; courtesy of Ms. Kim Christensen.

The tips of two fossils were chipped and polished. Each reveals the knotty grains are white chalcedony and the rest is slightly coated with rusty yellowish, reddish, and brownish limonite, goethite, or hematite.

QUESTIONS: The replacement of dung by silica must have happened by way of water and the dung must have been submerged for a long time for the chalcedony to fully replace the dung. There are unanswerable questions. One: how was the texture of soft dung preserved under water during replacement?

Two: was the cracking inherited from the original dung? Or, was the cracking due to dehydration after replacement? Overall, the fossil configurations favor the choice of 'heritage'.

Figure 5-1B: Two pieces of coprolite. LD = 13 cm; no cut; courtesy of Ms. Kim Christenson.

All four specimens appear clean, free of sediment attachment. Does the cleanness result from effective ultrasonic fossil cleaning which shakes off undesirable dirts? Or, has the silica selectively replaced the dung but left the surrounding sediments alone?

Furthermore, it is difficult to decipher what animals have released those fossilized dungs. An educated guess can be made if the geologic setting at fossil recovery sites is known; but for these purchased coprolites, the info is not available. Because of their spiral morphology, these coprolites could be the excrements of Mesozoic marine ichthyosaurs, not the land-dwelling dinosaurs. Like sharks, the marine reptiles had spiral ridges in their intestines. This conjecture de-mystifies how silica replacement can happen without plentiful silica-bearing water on land. In brief, coprolites are replacement fossils, not the preserved, fossilized excrements or palaeofaeces, which can better reveal what the animal's diet is.

5-2. Snowman Rocks

Shortly after the predecessor of this book was published in late 2018, NASA released in 2019 the left imagery shown in **Figure 5-2** (Johns Hopkins University's Applied Physics Laboratory). It is a contact-binary space object in a post-Pluto belt which is about 4 billion miles from our Sun. I was amazed at its gross resemblance to a terrestrial bi-spherical geode from Riverside County, California (Figure I1-15a of Lee, 2018).

The snowman-like space object was nicknamed Ultima Thule for the big and small spheres, respectively, meaning figuratively beyond the known world. The imagery was taken with NASA's New Horizons spacecraft at 85,000 miles away. The object's orbital period around the Sun is 298 Earth years. It is a rocky planetoid with some impact craters on its surface. With a calculated density of 0.2 gram per cubic centimeter (one fifth of the density of water), it is porous. (Note: Ultima Thule has been officially renamed in late 2019 as Arrokoth, meaning 'sky' in Powhatan/Algonquin language.)

Ultima Thule symbolizes one stage in sweeping space dusts (particles) to form a planet or planetoid. The two started as independent spheres of dust; then they collided to forge a binary sphere by gravitational attraction at an impact speed so slow as to preserve most of their respective spherical shape.

Now, bringing us back to Earth, how did the two spherule geodes merge as one bi-spheroidal geode? It certainly does not result from collision of two geodes. Likely, two neighboring spheroidal gas chambers were formed in the lava flow and the barrier between them was breached when the geode-forming silica solution invaded the chambers.

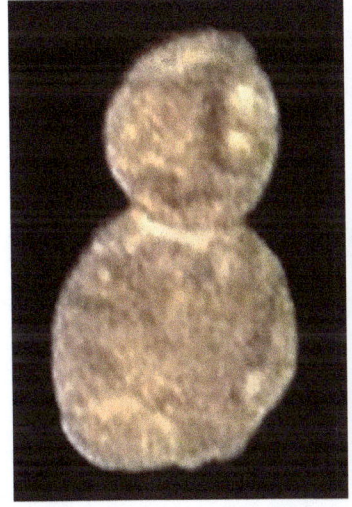

Figure 5-2: Ultima Thule (left, LD = 32 km) & Geode (LD = 8 cm).

It is not clear whether the bi-spheroidal geode is solid or only partially filled. But it can be found non-destructively by measuring its density in comparison with known solid geodes. By analogy to other geodes from the same suite, one may infer this bi-spheroidal geode is solid. That inference is a disappointment because good crystals can develop only when there is available empty space for unimpeded crystal growth. A sure assessment is to cut it open.

Figure 5-3A: Moqui and Chalcedony balls. Diameters range from 3.0 to 3.5 cm. Bought.

Like other geodes from the same sampling area (see Section 4-10), this bi-spheroidal geode will likely fluoresce under UV light.

5-3. Moqui Balls

RING: **Figure 5-3A** displays four Moqui balls, including the split-halves. Additionally, one chalcedony ball, which was presented in Figure 1-1C, is duplicated here for comparison of two distinct types of spherical concretion.

Moqui ball is a fine-grained sandstone concretion encrusted with hematite rind. The sandstone is light reddish brown and poorly cemented; its grains can be rubbed off with fingers. The weak interior, however, is well protected by the hard hematite rind from erosion in its natural setting.

The chalcedony ball, as argued in Section 1-1, is biogenic. It does not have a ring structure except a thin white opal veneer cover; its interior is homogenous. In contrast, the split Moqui ball reveals one dark core (or nucleus), surrounded by concentric and diffused shells (or rings in 2D view).

RINGLESS: **Figure 5-3B** depicts one large Moqui ball (6.5 cm across) along with two pairs of split-cut balls. Each split-face exposes a hematite rind too, but its interior has different decor: One set (upper row) holds

Figure 5-3B: Moqui balls. Mr. Tony Gilham gifted the large ball. Others are split cuts from Figure 5-3A.

many, scattered dark specks and two short rind-like arcs that are embedded within a reddish brown but incomplete diffusion ring or band; the other set is pale red with short, light, subtle gray arc patches. Based on those split-cuts, such non-circular internal texture is probably more prevalent among the Moqui balls than the ringed texture depicted in Figure 5-3A.

Note that the large ball in Figure 5-3B is asymmetric with respect to its equator; the northern (upper) hemisphere is smaller than the southern one by 0.5 cm or 8% in diameter.

OCCURENCES: How do the Moqui balls form? Moqui balls come from the Navajo Sandstone formation in southern Utah and northern Arizona where several national parks and monuments reside. Moqui in Hopi Indian language means 'dear departed ones'; that is, the memento left in the night by the returning deceased ancestors to signal their offspring that the ancestors are happy in after life.

The Navajo Sandstone originates from eolian deposits (loess), vast sand dunes covering thousands of square miles, which appeared about 190 million years ago during the Jurassic Period when dinosaurs roamed on Earth. The spectacular reddish landscape of the Navajo Sandstone is due to coating by hematite on fine-grained, white quartz sand or interstitial filling of hematite between sand grains. The hematite was previously derived from weathering and oxidizing of iron-bearing rocks in the surrounding hills and was incorporated with sand to form dunes.

About 160 million years had elapsed since the dunes were formed. Then, the Colorado Plateau was uplifted about 20 to 25 million years ago during tectonic movement and the Navajo Sandstone was deformed. Associated with the uplifting, hydrocarbon from nearby organic-rich formations migrated and the groundwater chemistry changed owing to infusion of the mobilized hydrocarbon. The iron in part of the red Navajo Sandstone was leached by the carbon-bearing, reducing groundwater. The iron-depleted sandstone

Figure 5-3C: Patches of Moqui balls. Photo by Professor Marjori Chan. See text for more credits.

turned from red to pale milky white, adding to the fascinating, contrasting, picturesque landscape. Meanwhile the leaching water was loaded with dissolved ferrous iron. When the iron-bearing groundwater met oxidizing groundwater (hydrocarbon-free), the iron precipitated as hematite (ferric oxide) or goethite (hydrated ferric oxide), which congregated around sand grains; and the resulted concretions would appear in various shapes: balls, disks, tubes, or irregular aggregates (**Figure 5-3C**).

TWO MORE EPISODES: About 2 to 5 million years ago, the modern Colorado River started to cut its course in the plateau. The event reconfigured the drainage systems and groundwater flow patterns, and accordingly created another episode of Moqui-ball forming. The last or the third episode of Moqui-ball making occurred, according to radioactive age dating, as late as 300,000 years ago.

Among the explanations for various forms, the most interesting are stories about the origin of the spherical Moqui concretions. The general consent is that hematite nucleated around sand grains to form small balls, and the balls grow bigger by accreting more hematite (remember the cut sections of the balls indicate that hematite appears as rind only). The concretions may appear as solitary iron balls or merge as aggregates of small balls. Some argue that a Moqui ball began as ferrous carbonate (siderite $FeCO_3$) for the availability of hydrocarbon, and later, microbial activity turned ferrous into ferric oxides [hematite Fe_2O_3 or goethite $FeO(OH)$].

Protected by erosion-resistive hematite rinds in the dry desert, some concretions were later dislodged from the soft hosting sandstone formation by wind and occasional rainwater erosion. Eventually the dislodged concretions were transported to and swept into spectacular patches on low, flat, sloping ground (Figure 5-3C). The globular ones are the classical Moqui balls, which are objects of my story.

(Note: The preceding six paragraphs begun with the subheading *OCCURENCES* are based on online Life Science, and Wikipedia, 2019; and the photo in Figure 5-3C was downloaded from an article in Life Science by Becky Oskin who credited it to the original photo by Professor Marjori Chan, University of Utah. I have not yet seen any Moqui balls in the field. Following is my armchair dream: stories for two short questions. How does the rind come about and why are Moqui balls limited in size? *Skip the rest of this lengthy, speculative section if you wish.*)

QUESTION 1 (RIND): Why does the hematite form a hard, dark rind but leave behind a soft, unconsolidated, pale reddish interior with occasional ring or shell imprints?

By an exaggerated and distorted analogy to the Earth's major internal structures and for the convenience of using familiar terms as well for imagination, the cut-faces in Figure 5-3A reveals that a Moqui ball has inner core, outer core, mantle, and crust. The Earth's divisions originate from gravitational differentiation, i.e., layer (shell) settling due to density differentials with heavier compounds (minerals) sinking inward or downward in exchange for lighter ones floating upward. This differentiation occurred when the infant Earth had been melted because of intense accretion impact and radioactivity heating (of which the rate far exceeded the heat dissipation rate into space) shortly after its birth about 4.6 billion years ago by accretion/ aggregation of cold space particles, like the space dust collection by Ultima Thule (Figure 5-2).

The inner core of a Moqui ball originates from nucleation of hematite around sand grains. Then, the hematite diffuses from the darker inner core to form a pale *solid* outer core (unlike the Earth's *liquid* outer core) and a light-colored mantle. Like Earth, the Moqui mantle has a transition zone, discernible by subtle tone disparity, which divides itself into the upper and lower mantle. The dark Moqui's crust or rind is unusually thick if scaled analogously with the Earth's size. The rind fortifies a sand ball to form and preserve what we see and call the Moqui ball.

DOUBTS: The conventional interpretation implies that the ball grows bigger and bigger by padding more and more hematite onto an initially tiny globular nucleus blob. Such padding will result in an iron ball of homogeneous composition, like the homogeneity in the chalcedony ball shown in Figure 5-3A. This expectation, however, is inconsistent with the fact that some Moqui balls are stratified by diffusion of hematite. Also, it is dubious to suggest that the transition zone has resulted from diffusion because there is no obvious source reservoir (zone) to diffuse from. At best, the zone is the relic of a former rind which had diffused outward and inward to leave behind a diluted trace of hematite band. Despite the ambiguities, unequivocal evidence for diffusion is the presence of a short, red swath inward of the rind. Strangely or coincidently that inward diffusion from the rind appears to have stopped at the 'mantle transition zone' (Figure 5-3A, cut faces). Confused? Yes! But we need to face the question: how to make a rounded rind by diffusion or accumulation of hematite. Diffusion cannot spread from a dark core through a pale mantle to a darker crust (rind), or vice versa.

Awkwardly, the simplistic model narrated above cannot be easily generalized to explain the texture of the split faces in Figure 5-3B. The basic premise is that the making of Moqui balls was started by nucleation but there is neither visible core of nucleation nor diffusion zoning in the interior sandstone. The crux of the story should be how a spherical sandstone ball, or a proto ball comes into being before a 'hematite rind' wraps it up to deliver the desired Moqui ball. In other words, how was a sandstone proto ball formed before the hematite encrustation to form the rind?

SOIL NODULES: A plausible analogy is to look at iron-manganese (Fe-Mn) nodules in some types of soils. Tiny nodules occur in soils through redox reactions (reduction and oxidation) in conjunction with microbial activities through cycles of wet and dry seasons that subject soils to alternate between water <u>saturated</u> and <u>unsaturated</u> states. (See the meaning of *underlines* later.) Consequently, the nodules accrete or recede in concentric spherical shells or other irregular shapes. But those nodules stay typically on sub-centimeter sizes. Unlike the exclusive composition of quartz sand and hematite for Moqui concretions, the soil nodules may embrace rock fragments and organic matter in addition to Fe-Mn oxides and quartz. (Note: Soil scientists' nodules are equivalent to geologists' concretions, which mean they grow together with the host sediments. But geologists reserve 'nodules' generally for post-depositional replacement products. Let us treat the two terms interchangeable in practice.)

NUCLEATION: Laboratory experiments show nucleation occurs in two modes: homogeneous or heterogeneous. Homogenous nucleation requires a long time to initiate within an unstable, supersaturated (oversaturated) solution. Heterogeneous nucleation takes a shorter time to start at the interface with other solid media or at the introduction of a seeding solid into the supersaturated solution. Once started, accretion or crystallization accelerates exponentially with time until the fluid becomes unsaturated.

In natural condition for Moqui balls, nucleation happens in pores of sandstone. Those pores are too small to be seen with the naked eye. The nucleation is not of the homogeneous mode; nor is it a case for the classical heterogeneous nucleation in laboratory experiments. The quartz sands are readily available for iron in the pores to nucleate around but the flowing pore water is not supersaturated with iron. So, how did nucleation begin in the iron-unsaturated water? It is incredibly challenging, therefore, to simulate and see nucleation in groundwater which is flowing through porous media. So, let me make some conjectures about the encrustation for Moqui balls.

REDUCTION-OXIDATION: Redistribution of iron in sandstone involves three major steps: dissolution from solid ferric to aqueous ferrous states, transport of iron solutes, and re-deposition of the ferrous back to ferric states. In short, it needs redox for making concretions: reduction achieves dissolution and subsequent oxidation elsewhere reverses the process to cause deposition.

As the water is being evaporated or dissipated, the solution will become supersaturated, and the dissolved iron will nucleate around sand grains to form concretions. Each concretion grows radially and circumferentially, like an expanding 3D-spider web, into a ball as depicted in Figure 5-3A. However, most balls develop without visible nucleation points (cores), or shell structures as shown in Figure 5-3B. If the concretions begin as siderite (iron carbonate), oxidization will have to follow later to transform siderite into hematite or goethite with the aid of microbial actions. A prerequisite: somehow the oxidizing microbial must be introduced into the groundwater at shallow depths. An immediate question for this siderite-bypass scenario: what has happened to the released carbon dioxide? Are there any carbonate minerals in the hosting sandstone around the concretions?

In lieu of routing via siderite precipitation and microbial oxidization, an alternative is to have the reducing groundwater met oxidizing groundwater. Thereby the oxidized product (the insoluble hematite or goethite) settles through nucleation and ball growth to form Moqui balls.

RIND and PROTO BALL: Some aspects of both theories have been presented in the literature. However, how a rind comes into being is still intriguing. Do the rinds reflect sudden surges in iron-bearing groundwater? Let me venture to an alternative suggestion that the birth of rinds has resulted from variations in hematite precipitation rate induced by change in groundwater flow rates.

Now, image the probabilistic occurrences of proto balls, which are lightly laden with hematite, immersed in groundwater. Each proto ball is much less permeable than the sandstone around it because of the infilling of its pores by iron precipitates. The flowing groundwater will diverge slightly from the upstream face of a proto ball, skim over its upper and lower hemispheres, and converge toward its downstream face. This local perturbation to the general flow field (pattern) results in slowdown of the flowing groundwater in front of the proto-ball's surface (upstream face) owing to viscous drag along the 'fluid-solid' interface. The slowdown favors the solutes to adhere to the interface and hence to grow a rind.

An impermeable and thickening rind will hydraulically isolate its interior from the ambient groundwater. Diffusion from a well-developed core and rind yields the interior zoning as depicted in Figure 5-3A. However, there is no zoning (Figure 5-3B) for proto balls which are absent of visible nucleation cores except some traces of inward diffusion from the rinds.

Is there any supporting evidence for perturbation to the groundwater flow field? The big asymmetric Moqui ball in Figure 5-3B may provide a clue: Its equatorial plane aligns with the plane that splits the upper and lower perturbed flow field. The slight disparity in size between the upper and lower hemispheres of the big Moqui ball is due to gravity-induced asymmetry between the flow over and the flow under a proto ball.

QUESTION 2 (SIZE LIMIT): Next, why does a Moqui ball stop growing beyond a certain size? An obvious answer: the supply is exhausted. But all balls are similarly sized to well within one order of magnitude (Figure 5-3C). Like size-limitations for animals or plants, what is the common size-limiting factor for the growth of Moqui balls? As mentioned above, the slowdown of groundwater around a proto ball caused a rind to form. At a little distance away from the ball surface, the slowdown is compensated by speedup because the total mass flow should be conserved. [The regional velocity (the Darcy's) for groundwater is slow, likely on the order of a few meters per year or less.] If the speed ratio of local to regional flow exceeds an unknown but threshold value, no deposition of the suspended particles will occur there. Only the solution within the loci of the threshold value can unload its solute to the proto balls. A rind of finite thickness is thus formed, and the ball size is limited. Because of small-scale heterogeneity in sandstone, slight changes in size of proto balls will lead to variations in the perturbed flow patterns and hence threshold values. And the unknown but varied threshold values account for a size-diversified assemblage of Moqui balls.

Rind-making is a onetime deal because a Moqui ball does not have multiple hematite rind-like shells.

SATURATE/UNSATURATE FLOW: The above conjecture for Moqui ball forming is anchored on continuous, steady, <u>saturated</u> groundwater flow. While I am on the subject, let me throw another monkey wrench, <u>unsaturated</u> groundwater flow, into the potential causes for forming Moqui balls. Groundwater may or may not <u>saturate</u> the porous space in sandstone. Note here the underlined <u>saturation</u> refers to the state of pore filling; while, elsewhere, the underline-free saturation (or supersaturation) refers to the extent of solute dissolved in water. Unfortunately, this is a bad practice for using the same word in different contexts in the same topics. Because there is no alternative term for common usage in different situations, I underline the word <u>saturated</u> or <u>unsaturated</u> for usage in groundwater flow.

Hydraulic conductivity in a homogenous, <u>saturated</u> medium (sandstone) does not change as the flow proceeds (assuming no deposition on or dissolution from sandstone). However, if water infiltrates into an <u>unsaturated</u> region, the hydraulic conductivity will start with extremely low value and increase to a steady <u>saturated</u> value. So, the infiltration would begin at low rate and rise to a normal, <u>saturated</u> groundwater flow rate when the hydraulic conductivity has evolved from <u>unsaturated</u> to <u>saturated</u> values.

So, when groundwater encroaches from <u>saturated</u> into <u>unsaturated</u> regimes, the <u>unsaturated</u> region would act like a temporary groundwater barrier (because of low hydraulic conductivity) and the flow rate at the leading front is impeded. The slowdown provides a favorable condition for groundwater to dump its load of solutes or suspended particles during random, multiple-point nucleation or during build-up of an impermeable cortex-like hematite envelope over a proto ball of sandstone.

UNANSWERED: I have tried to give a simplistic view, but it turns out anything but simplistic: how the sandy proto-balls and hematite rinds come about and why the Moqui balls have similar sizes. There are three major geologic episodes in the making of Moqui balls. Does each follow the same script? There are perturbations or exceptions that cannot be individually addressed. There are countless paths for the advancing <u>saturated</u> and <u>unsaturated</u> groundwater flows that mingle to further complicate the role of flowing groundwater in shaping the balls. I suspect from the comfort of armchair that Moqui balls were formed during short period of time along with the advancing fronts of groundwater flow rather than over long period of time in the steady <u>saturated</u> flow regime. And there are many shape variants awaiting explanation. In brief, let me paraphrase a Zen copout: No answer is the answer to the intrigue of genesis for Moqui balls.

Figure 5-4A: Nucleation in limestone. LD = 11.5 cm; multi-cut; from San Bernardino County, California.

See Section 5-9 for remarks on the Martian 'Blueberries' or concretions.

5-4. Nucleation in Carbonate

As exemplified by Moqui balls in section 5-3, solitary nodules or concretions are usually found in alluvium because they are more resistant to weathering and erosion than their parental host rocks. **Figure 5-4A** is a cross-sectional view of hydrothermal carbonate deposits with nodular clumps. The specimen came from a discarded exploratory mining site. It is ambiguous whether we can call those circular or elliptical nebular clusters as 'concretions' because they interlock one another; that is, the host rock and concretions are indistinguishable. Hence, there will be no residual solitary globular objects as the end products of weathering and erosion. However, we do see products of nucleation and each cluster will be called a 'concretion' for short of a better term.

NUCLEATION AROUND QUARTZ: Two patches of white quartz in the lower half stand out as the seeding nuclei for the brown calcite to emanate into elliptically zoned clumps (or dubious concretions). The two clusters are bordered with many smaller clumps with concentric zoning: some have distinct white or black nuclei, and a few are absent of discernible nuclei. Such absence does not imply those individual concretions start without seeding nuclei because my saw-cut of the rock may have missed the nuclei in their central cores.

Figure 5-4B: Nucleation in limestone, rear view of Figure 5-4A.

Note that the quarter around and west of '*F*' marking has been brecciated and re-cemented. The light gray spotted patch of mineral east of *F* is calcite, not quartz. That calcite did not serve as a nucleation seeding;

instead, it filled a crack only. Inconspicuous nucleation also happened during the re-cementing of breccia in the vicinity of the brecciated *F* quarter.

CONCRETION GROWTH: All concretions developed simultaneously because they interfere with one another to yield truncated interfaces. An exception happened in the quarter marked by *F*. The misalignment of zoning patterns among sub-blocks within the *F* quarter (block) shows that the block had been cracked and then rehabilitated by infiltrating fluids, which later yielded small concretions. Also, the rehabilitation was marked by growth of arc-like curvy zoning, which demarcates the *F* quarter from the rest of the rock. The remaining cracks in the region were filled eventually with distinct, small grayish patches of calcite.

Figure 5-4C: Pre-cut front face of Figure 5-4A.

Obviously, the concretion started with incipient quartz nucleation. As the quartz grew lengthwise, it was suspended in semi-mobile hydrothermal fluids which were rich in calcium carbonate. But it did not yield any recognizable crystal form, apparently because silica precipitated out of the solution rapidly and soon after, each cluster of quartz was enclosed by thinly zoned brownish calcite. Owing to exhaustion of silica in the solution, many concretions could nucleate only with tiny bits of quartz.

To have a glimpse of the 3-D perspective of nucleation, the rear side of Figure 5-4A is pictured in **Figure 5-4B**. There is no correlation of surficial features between the front and rear faces. Hence each concretion extends less than the thickness of the slab, 5 cm.

However, one can see unmistakably elliptical (ellipsoidal) nucleation along the elongated patches of quartz: one surrounded by brown-zoned calcite on the polished rear face (*Q*) and the other enclosed by red calcite zoning on the unpolished top surface (*T*). Near the top middle (*R*), one eye-catching red 'concretion' encircles another brown 'concretion' which in turn embraces a tiny bit of quartz as nucleus. In addition, there present several small, circular concretions with visible nuclei. The variations reflect changing fluid composition as the concretions were forming. Segregation of colors is indicative of differences in chemical affinity, like birds of same feather flock together.

ABSENCE OF ZONING: Several blobs of quartz appear on the lower-left half of the rear face (*S*, Figure 5-4B). Each blob appears to be offshoots squirted into its surrounding brown calcite, like firework shooting.

Figure 5-4D: Rectangular nucleation in limestone. LD = 8 cm; from the same sampling site for Figure 5-4A.

Unlike other part of the specimen, there is no visible zoning or concretion there.

The nucleation sequence for the rear face (Figure 5-4B) repeats what is seen in the front face: starting with quartz and ending with brown or red calcite zoning. However, the sector marked with *S* appears to have resulted from competition between quartz and calcite during the late stage of development. There is no clear sign which one started first and the nucleation zoning (shell) is absent.

ODD ZONING: **Figure 5-4C** is the natural cover of Figure 5-4A before the specimen was cut. Three elliptical (ellipsoidal) concretions predominate over its lower half. The relief in zoning reflects difference in resistance to weathering and erosion. Unlike the elliptical nucleation shown in the two preceding figures, the nucleation here does not appear to have wrapped around a slender strip of quartz. The quartz nucleus may be hidden, revealed only if the surface is scraped.

However, the features in the upper right resemble nucleation features elsewhere. To its left, the quarter marked by *F'* corresponds to the *F* quarter of Figure 5-4A. It is dominated, of course, by small, inconspicuous post-fracturing concretions.

The complexity of nucleation is further muddled by the rectangular zoning features (or four-side concave outlines) in **Figure 5-4D**. Again, we see no nucleation seeding for this specimen. As in Figure 5-4C, the nucleation seeding could be hidden beneath the surface. But why did it develop into rectangular mesh in lieu of elliptical form?

FILLING BY QUARTZ: Sometimes I wonder why the crack-filling carbonate (or limestone vein) does not have any void or cavity. Do all carbonates derive from a hydrothermal fluid that fills the entire fracture before it solidifies? In such a closed system, how remarkable the solid phase occupies the same space of the liquid phase without leaving an unfilled void which is to be filled later with an 'alien' material. In an open system, the precipitation of carbonate is being

Figure 5-4E: Nodules in limestone. LD = 12 cm. multi-cut, unknown source; gifted by Mr. Tony Gilham.

replenished with continuous flow of hydrothermal fluid. Again, the supply (input of the replenishing hydrothermal fluid) and demand (the precipitation of carbonate out of the fluid) is so balanced as to leave no void in the carbonate (limestone) vein.

A partial answer is provided in **Figure 5-4E**. Here we see three solid phases: Conspicuous, brown concretions (phase A) embed in light grey carbonate (phase B). Inside some clusters of concretions are white quartz (phase C). All phase-A concretions have visible nuclei of unknown mineral. One of the two-merged concretions (A) resembles coincidently the outlooks of twin geode or Ultima Thule in Figure 5-2 (simply curious happenstance, no implication). Phase-B 'host carbonate' in turns also carries concretions with tiny brown nuclei. The relation between phase-A and -B is not clear. Could phase-A precipitate (or condense) out of the host phase B? Or instead, phase-B fills the gap amid phase-A concretions. The chemical compositions of the two phases are certainly different.

Figure 5-5A: Liesegang banding in silicified volcanic ash. LD = 15 cm; slab; from Nevada.

Phase-C quartz grows inside the cavities of phase-A concretions. Unlike the situations in Figure 5-4A and 5-4B, the quartz does not serve as a nucleation seeding for the specimen in Figure 5-4E. Instead, the quartz here is a secondary mineral, crystallized from silica-bearing fluid which invaded the cavities after phase-A and -B had been formed. The cavities have resulted from dehydration cracking of phase-A concretions rather than fracturing.

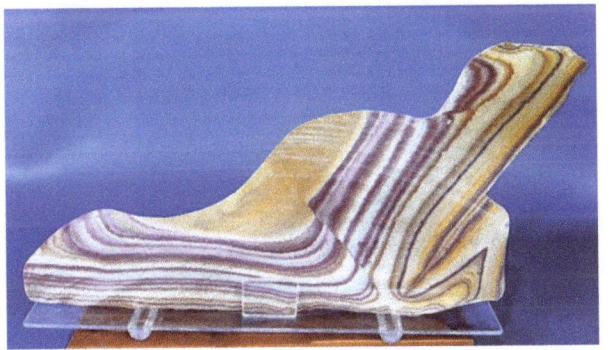

Figure 5-5B: Liesegang banding in silicified volcanic ash. LD = 30 cm; slab; from Nevada.

5-5. Liesegang Banding

Occasionally we see spillover from lawn sprinklers onto concrete or asphalt pavement and the relics of water migration tracks after the spillover is dried. The residual marking is Liesegang banding in action. Liesegang, a German chemist, discovered analogous color banding in his laboratory two centuries ago. We have also seen similar banding or ringing in rocks. Those natural beauties differ from laboratory observations in the causative chemical and physical processes, but his name is honored.

Figures 5-5A and 5-5B exemplify Liesegang banding in two pieces of lithified volcanic ash of rhyolitic composition, which is equivalent to granite in chemical and mineralogical compositions but differs in texture (fine versus coarse grained) and occurrence (volcanic versus plutonic). Both pieces are known in trade as Nevada wonder rocks or stones.

The original rocks were pale white. Its banding was created by advective (advancing) water which dissolved and scavenged ferrous iron (Fe^{++}, with two positive charges) along its flow paths in porous ash; and on the way as the water was being dissipated, the dissolved iron was oxidized to ferric iron (Fe^{+++}), and then deposited as the reddish iron oxides. The resulted pattern exemplifies advective, solute transport in porous media.

Each band signals one event in water advance. Repetition of banding marks multiple recurrences of groundwater flow of which the rates reflect weather or climate changes. The ordering of banding, however, does not necessarily chronicle the sequences of different flow events because some later events may override earlier ones, depending on supply/dissipation rates and durations as well as changes in hydraulic properties as the volcanic ash is being transformed by silicification and deposition of brownish/reddish ferric oxides.

Figure 5-5C: Liesegang rings in siltstone. LD = 14 cm; no cut.

Once each band was formed, Fick's diffusion proceeded slowly. Such diffusion follows the concentration gradient from high to low concentration areas, resulting in the observed fading of color from dark to light zoning within individual band. Fick's diffusion re-distributes solute (ferric iron) much less effectively than the advective dispersion.

After the completion of Liesegang banding, a tiny fault with an offset of 0.5 cm occurred in the mid-section of Figure 5-5B. But the fracturing in the lower-right corner was contemporary with banding because it perturbed the banding around it. Two dark blobs in the mid-section of Figure 5-5A along a fracture were also contemporary with banding.

The influence of fracture on Liesegang banding is self-explanatory in **Figure 5-5C**. Three major water advancing events were registered; two of them made a sharp bend around the southeast-trending mini-fracture in this piece of siltstone. Curiously, why did the inner band turn before reaching the mini fracture?

Figure 5-5D: Liesegang in sandstone cup coasters. Diameter = 10.5 cm.

Figure 5-5D is a collection of sandstone cup coasters with Liesegang banding, which are readily available in rock gift shops. Such 'landscape-like' diffusion patterns are common in porous sandstone in arid areas. A cup coaster made of porous sandstone can be irreversibly stained by spillover of any liquid. Diffusion and dispersion can often turn a rock, especially limestone, into a beautiful landscape slab if it is finely cut and polished, as exemplified in Figure I2-12a and -12b of Lee (2018).

Another example of Liesegang banding in sandstone is pictured in **Figure 5-5E**. The banding appears on a natural split-face – a two-dimensional view on a bedding plane with shining specks of mica. It reflects dispersion of fluid with episodic changes in composition. The staining fluid advances inward in such varying rates that the shape of the banding mimics the periphery of the cobble. The permeability of the sandstone (and accordingly the flow rate), is likely anisotropic, being greater along the water flow direction than across the flow when the sand was deposited, even though the sandstone is visibly homogeneous in composition and texture.

Figure 5-5E: Liesegang in sandstone. LD = 16 cm; Courtesy of Mr. Vincent Wing.

5-6. Concretions of the Unknown

The cobble depicted in **Figure 5-6A** seems to have dark brown nodules immersed in a mesh of frail, brownish yellow strands, or strips. The slice atop the main piece in the display shows that the dark nodules have been stretched into elongated form and aligned with the broken yellow strands. The notion of nodule designation, however, is a little dubious.

Figure 5-6A: Concretions of the Unknown. Top piece, LD = 14 cm; one cut; from Arizona.

Another cut face in **Figure 5-6B** reveals convincingly the presence of nodules. However, those globular knobs are growth concretions, not replacement nodules because most of them have visual cores with tiny nucleation seeds. And each concretion is also enclosed with a thin, dark brown rind. The yellow strands in Figure 5-6A appear, here, to have infiltrated the gaps between concretions to form a matrix. Alternatively, does the rind represent a reaction rim? The 'Siamese' concretion at the lower-right corner of Figure 5-6B is equivalent in geometry to the one marked by 'A' in Figure 5-4E. This similarity assures its status as a concretion. In this cut face, all concretions appear again to have been stretched and aligned with the top-bottom oriented yellow strands.

However, it is still challenging to decipher whether the brown concretions have immersed in the brownish yellow matrix; or on the contrary, the latter have infiltrated the interstices among the former. This a matter of time sequence in occurrences. The specimen was collected by chance two decades ago from an unmemorable

Figure 5-6B: Concretions, mid-section of Figure 5-6A; triple cuts; a slab.

hill slope in northern Arizona. It could have precipitated originally as carbonate from hydrothermal fluids. Over the ages it had been silicified to reach a quartz-like Mohs hardness. It was also tainted with iron and manganese to have various hues of brown. The light strands and dark concretions are different minerals and hence different origins. In short, its parental rock had been stressed and metamorphosed before it was detached and tumbled to become a well-rounded cobble. The mineral constituents of the cobble are, unfortunately, beyond my observation with the naked eye. I cannot relate this piece to any existing rock name. Enjoy the beauty of this piece of uncommon, yet-to-be named rock.

5-7. Modern Analog

RING FEATURES: **Figure 5-7ABC** exhibits three pictures from the tidal zone along a San Diego beach in California. I would like to make an analogous comparison for the genesis of Moqui balls (Section 5-3) and concretions with the caveats of the following limitations: The pictures are truly two dimensional rather than the three dimensional concretions or Moqui balls; they are created by surface water of which the flow is million times faster than groundwater flow; the features here are created in seconds while the concretions are made in years or longer; the markings are preserved only for a couple of tidal wave splashing, not millions of years; and the processes here are advective (particles carried by water movement), absolutely not diffusive (particles moving along concentration gradient).

The dark nebular clusters in the upper picture manifest distribution of magnetite/biotite particles. Dark patches are common on the beach, but I do not know why some particles are assembled in circular or ring patterns. The marking fades northeast with the retreating tidal water; a dark patch can be completely obliterated in the next few water whipsaws; and new ones can re-emerge elsewhere.

In the middle picture, the sea clam shell retards sand erosion under the valve covers but around it, the retreating water has scoured a furrow. Also note the difference in relief at the upstream and downstream ends.

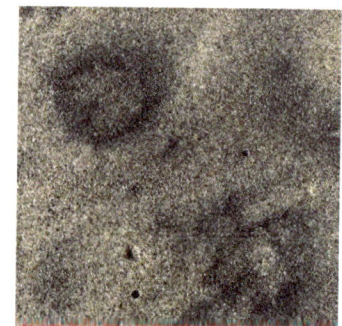

Figure 5-7ABC: Analog to concretions. The clam shell is one cm wide, and the circles are about quarter coin sized. from San Diego.

Most intriguing is the scouring of ring-like moat or rind, around a dark 'central core' in the lower picture. Could it be conjectured that black particle fill the moat, and then evolve to the configuration shown in the upper picture? But groundwater does not move solid particles; it carries dissolved or tiny suspended constituents to form Moqui balls. Nucleation of carbonate concretions is another story (see Section 5-4).

Note that the feature in the middle picture is common at the beach. The other two types of features are quite localized, and an observer must search for those circles in the tidal zones. They are very transitory, built-up, and wiped out quickly in a few pulsations of advancing and retreating tidal water.

Are those modern features applicable to the features in Moqui balls: the rind, shape, and size?

Figure 5-7D: Channel piracy. The picture is about 1.5 meters wide; Riverside, California.

RIVER PIRACY: Now let us turn to a picture of channel piracy in landscape development (**Figure 5-7D**) on the clayey berm of an evaporation pond. The picture depicts a small northeast-dipping drainage system. The water collects at the upper basin and drains along a channel northward to a braided delta at the northern edge of the picture.

To the west of the main channel lies a short arc of channel (in the middle of the picture). That channel was beheaded and abandoned because greater erosion or deepening along the main channel deprives its supplies of water. This meter-scale drainage system is an analog model for the piracy of river channels in a large-scale regional evolution of landforms or drainage systems.

5-8. Stromatolite

Now we extend the narrative about concretions in Section 5-6 with one more specimen (**Figure 5-8A**). Both cobble specimens came from the same general area of sampling and share similarity: light grey concretions (marked by B and C) embedded in reddish brown matrix (R) with many, scattered, small spherules. But the two specimens also show differences: The piece in Figures 5-6A & B has widespread, light brownish yellow strips or strands, giving an overall brighter outlook; while here, the equivalent yellow patches are speckle and less plentiful, yielding a dull outlook even if polished.

Figure 5-8A: Oncolite/stromatolite. LD = 27.5 cm (27.5x11.5x11.0 cm); one cut; from Arizona.

The cut face shows gross layering by grey, elliptical concretions, some of which merge to form strands with lengthwise, irregular bulge and constriction. The lineage is often disrupted or offset. Some strands are branched or split in the middle with fillings, which look like the background matrix. A few concretions are also marred by light greyish, shining, sericite-like sediments as exemplified near the 'B' mark. (Their presence can also be felt with finger touching on the polished surface.) Those features point to a scene of colonization by some organisms with entrapment of sediments between colony mats. A designation of stromatolite comes to mind again, but the layering does not resemble a stromatolite's telltale signature textures. Hence an alternative naming, oncolite or thrombolite, is suggested too.

FEATURES: All three names refer to sedimentary structures built by cyanobacteria ('cyano' means blue in Greek) with added entrapment of sediments and precipitation of carbonate in their colonial mats. Stromatolites (stratified rocks) are characterized by internal lamination despite their external appearances as mounds, columns, or sheets, etc. Thrombolites have clotted mass bodies without lamination while oncolites possess spherical or ellipsoidal concretions.

Here the three terms are used interchangeably for ambiguity due to contextual absence of field observation although oncolite is my choice despite the elongated morphology in the picture. The provenance (parent) to these cobble specimens is believed to have been constructed by cyanobacteria during Paleozoic, or earlier, during Proterozoic eras, that is, respectively, hundreds of million years or a couple of billion years ago.

Figure 5-8B: Bottom view of Figure 5-8A. LD = 28 cm; base cut.

The grey polygons exemplified by C marking are not stromatolite per se. They are free of contamination by 'sericite', and line up like a broken twine laid in parallel with the concretion strands. And being free of any rinds, those polygons are trapped sediments (clay) in the colonial mats or biofilms, which were built mostly upward in shallow sea as the bacteria grew upward to absorb solar energy for photosynthesis. But it is still challenging to decipher which way was pointing upward in this cut face.

By photosynthesis, cyanobacteria consume carbon dioxide to build their carbohydrate bodies and accordingly, the carbon dioxide concentration in sea water declines. The reduction in carbon dioxide and the accompanying decline in acidity prompt calcium carbonate to precipitate out of sea water as calcite or aragonite. The minerals congregate around the colonies as bright, light, brownish yellow specks and fill crevices between the bio mats and hence appear in various shapes.

Some specks scatter in the background matrix too. Overall, the matrix is brownish red (R). In addition, the matrix bears innumerable tiny spherules, each about one mm in diameter. These spherules in 3D view are akin to oolites, which appear in some limestone. Or, just image those spherules like a picture of clustered fish eggs. But here, the spherules appear in at least two distinct types, unlike the monotonous oolites or fish eggs.

The dark spherules are incipient concretions produced by cyanobacteria and the light ones are their carbonate byproducts. Both immerse in a submatrix of much finer, reddish particles. The overall redness reached likely long after the colonies had fossilized.

Figure 5-8C: Three-dimensional view of oncolite/stromatolite. LD = 13 cm; two cuts.

An uncut surface of Figure 5-8A, or its underside, is shown in **Figure 5-8B**. It displays some erosional depressions on the cobble. As it stands as an erosional relic, the mound should not be construed as an evidence for stromatolite. The view justifies the need to cut the rock for better visualization and insight.

Figure 5-8C depicts a three-dimensional view of the stromatolite. The piece is part of the missing half of the specimen in Figure 5-8B. It displays all the features mentioned earlier. But what else does it reveal?

The longest linear length of the strands that straddle the two orthogonal cut faces is 11 cm. The 3D view shows the strand is not column-wise; instead, it spreads out in expansive sheet form, like the spread of seaweeds. Also noted is the thin, dark brown rind around each concretion. Those rinds are sticky biofilms that not only wrap the colonies as protective sheaths but also trap and glue suspended particles to fortify the rinds and darken the rinds as well by attracting more ferric oxide.

SUBTLE FEATURES: **Figure 5-8D** is a slab face. Here if we could view the concretions or strands as fossils of individual creatures, their interiors would appear to have been stuffed with material like the reddish background matrix and those creatures with guts would perch higher on the evolutionary tree branches rather than the rightly placed rooting spot for the colonies of single-cell, nucleus-free cyanobacteria. Obviously, some colonies are breached or fragmented during fossilization.

Figure 5-8D: A slab of oncolite/stromatolite. LD = 27.5 cm.

The band that links discrete polygons of 'trapped sediments' (C in Figures 5-8A, and -8D) appears to run left-to-right across the entire slab width. Acting like a leaky barrier, this 'trap band' seems to have demarcated two distinct patterns of stromatolite colonies: one having solitary concretions and the other with merged or aggregated concretions. Those added observations, again, point to biogenic narrative for the specimen instead of abiotic origin as reasoned in Section 5-6.

A close-up picture of one section in Figure 5-8D (centered near the left C) is presented in **Figure 5-8E**. It amplifies some views displayed in Figures 5-8A and 5-8D. The bright, pinky white specks are calcite – a byproduct of photosynthesis by cyanobacteria. The reddish

Figure 5-8E: An enlarged section, around the left C in Figure 5-8D.

background matrix (R) is composed of debris broken from former stromatolites and calcite; some small elliptical concretions are abundant despite defects or breakage; calcite acts like interstitial fillers, as inferred from their short and irregular shape.

Each grey, elliptical concretion (B) encloses a tiny part of matrix material as its reddish 'internal gut'. Does it? In my view, the organism grew as a colony around the matrix debris rather than one individual that encompassed the matrix-like material in its body frame. Then, why did each concretion grow elliptically as in 2D view? It should be more varied in shape if the colony thrived by wrapping around the debris. The concretion marked by B' is dotted with tiny spots of white 'sericite'.

The strand of gray clay polygons (C) in this enlarged picture (Figure 5-8E) does not have any dark rinds, as noted earlier. Observables are two strands or filaments west of the large 'C' polygon. Let the imagination run high, are those sub-strands flagella-like used by protozoan as a swimming gear? How about the single clay strand to the right of 'C'? The answer is negative because it is composed of disrupted clay strand with varying width and it does not carry compatible implications in the context of cyanobacteria, which belong to flagella-free bacteria (used to be a member of prokaryote), not the eukaryotic animal. Additionally, those clay strands are also bordered sporadically with thin red line segments. It is not clear whether those red lineaments are biogenic or abiotic chemical reaction rims.

Furthermore, it is noted that some concretions in Figure 5-8E overprinted some white specks. Or alternatively but more likely, the fluid carrying white specks infiltrated the gaps around the concretions. There are no reaction rims between the reddish concretions and the white specks. Hence, the contacts are physical rather than chemical. Also, each of those concretions appears to have grown radially from a central nucleus. In short, the nature of contact and growth pattern points to biologic origin for the concretions – i.e., the contention of stromatolites.

CYANOBACTERIA: Recall the stromatolite jasper in Section 4-12. The stromatolite specimen there and the specimen here do not look alike externally or internally. We face the choices: one specimen is wrongly named stromatolite; both are not stromatolites; or both are stromatolites in different forms. The third one is my preferred choice or predisposition. Irrespective of the designation, let us pay some tributes to cyanobacteria, the creators of stromatolites/oncolites/thrombolites and by implication, the forerunners to innumerable if not all organisms on the Planet Earth.

In recent years, the studies of cyanobacteria and stromatolites have turned hot for some paleontologists and astrobiologists. They would like to project our earthlings' perspectives about early lives onto other planets or moons in our solar system and beyond. Hopefully, some clues can be discovered from stromatolites for finding extraterrestrial creatures and eventually, unraveling the origin of life. One challenge: the stromatolites are structures, not the builders.

Cyanobacterium, under the well-accepted biological classification scheme, is a phylum ranking name for bacteria; under the phylum, there are many classes, orders, families, genera, and species. Cyanobacteria are ubiquitously present on every corner of the Earth's marine and terrestrial environment (oceans, lakes; dry land, wet land; tropics, arctic; desert, forest; and indoor, outdoor around us) if moisture exists with sun light exposure. Those bacteria thrive on photosynthesis that uses solar energy to split water molecules and then combine them with carbon dioxide to yield carbohydrates, and to produce and release oxygen as byproduct. Cyanobacteria contribute about 20 to 30% of annual global production rate of photosynthesized oxygen. Some cyanobacteria can digest sulfur and nitrogen compounds too and can be used for toxic waste treatment.

To humans, cyanobacteria can be beneficial, toxic, or neutral. For example, algal blooms can wreak havoc to marine ecosystems. As a group, cyanobacteria have outlived any other organisms, as recorded in stromatolites, spanning from at least 3.5 billion years ago to the present.

RECORDS: Fossil records suggest the construction of stromatolites started about one billion years after the birth of Earth when the Earth's atmosphere was still abundant with methane, carbon dioxide, nitrogen, and water vapor, like the present atmosphere surrounding most of our sister planets in the solar system. The primordial ocean waters differed very much from modern ones in chemistry, temperature, circulation patterns, and of course, the inhabitants (if any). Somehow, somewhere, a spark of life transpired in the ocean. That very-first spark organism, against all probabilistic odds, survived to reproduce by split duplication (asexual cell division) and to propagate. It took hundreds of million years for that primitive organism to evolve to cyanobacteria and leave trace evidence of life in stromatolites, the oldest age of which is about 3.5 billion years. The primitive predecessors to cyanobacteria had lived there before 3.5 billion years ago because cyanobacteria could not hop up suddenly and be so sophisticated as to construct the stromatolites that have stood for more than 3.5 billion years – a feat insurmountable to any human's brag about architecture. Any existential evidence for the primitive predecessors is waiting to be discovered if it is still hidden somewhere.

As mentioned previously, cyanobacteria thrive through photosynthesis by using solar energy to split water molecules and combine the resulted protons (hydrogen) with carbon dioxide to form carbohydrates. Meanwhile, the sticky mats attract carbonates precipitated out of sea water and other suspended sediment particles. Together all are calcified later with the bio mats to form the basic framework of stromatolites. As the bacteria migrate upward to seek more sunlight, layers upon layers of stromatolites are laid and interspersed in various forms: laminated, columnar, mound, dome, or globular. The specimens for Figures 4-12, 5-6, and 5-8 are silicified and hardened versions of former fossilized carbonaceous stromatolites.

ROLE OF OXYGEN: Oxygen is generated during photosynthesis. Over billions of years, cyanobacteria had slowly converted the atmosphere from reducing to oxidizing states (conditions) and changed sea water chemistry. Consequently, new oxygen-dependent organisms appeared in sea water. Again, we have no clue about how those new and more advanced creatures came from and we still do not clearly know the linkage between new arrivals and cyanobacteria.

Disasters followed the success of cyanobacteria. 'Created' when free oxygen became available, the growing numbers of burrowing creatures foraged or minced the mats of cyanobacteria, eroding or consuming the stromatolite framework. Furthermore, the increasing oxygen contents in sea water became intolerably toxic for their survival. The once prosperous stromatolite builders therefore suffered drastic population decline and the construction of stromatolites in shallow coastal water was hence disrupted. Meanwhile, Earth turned rusty as grey ferrous iron was oxidized into reddish ferric iron by the available stockpile of free oxygen. (Mars owes its reddish nickname, the Red Planet, to the presence of hematite on its surface.) Those interactions were not one-way processes; intermittent back-and-forth actions and reactions kept going for a long time at local and global scales, as testified by the presence of laminated or banded iron formations during Precambrian era (before 451 million years ago, see Section 4-5 on banded ironstone). Volcanic activities, global glaciations, and tectonic plate motions added to the complexity of interplay by various performers.

Cyanobacteria survive through challenges arisen from their own evolutionary success. Construction of stromatolites reached a peak at 1.25 billion years ago; then activities declined, as the biodiversity intensified, by 20% when the Cambrian biological explosion happened at 451 million years ago. Thence after, the construction was suspended and resumed on and off. Greater activities in stromatolite construction restarted at the end of Ordovician Period (about 400 million years ago) and during the transition from Permian to Triassic Period (the end of Paleozoic and the beginning of Mesozoic Era, 252 million years ago) when an overwhelming majority of genera on Earth became extinct. Then, after each great genus extinction, global biota reshuffled, and new inhabitants populated Earth again; and stromatolite making was suppressed to leave no trace of fossil records during the prosperous period of new and more advanced inhabitants.

MODERN STROMATOLITE: Now, surprise discoveries in recent years! Modern active construction of stromatolites thrives in some desolate, highly saline waters in western Australia, Chile, Brazil, and Mexico where grazing creatures cannot survive. More surprises! Freshwater microbialites (stromatolites + oncolites) also appear in Canada, Mexico, and Turkey. Stromatolite was also found to sprout in an abandoned mining pond in Canada – an incidental man-made niche environment. What an amazing grit for cyanobacteria! As a group, cyanobacteria have persisted and prevailed for more than 3.5 billion years in good and bad times and when the opportunity comes, the bacteria will build stromatolites to last 'forever'. Cyanobacteria are indeed the fittest for survival!

5-9. Martian Blueberries

In 2004, NASA's Opportunity Rover (a spacecraft) touched down on Mars. Soon after the landing, a field of nodules or concretions was discovered near the landing site (actually, confirming earlier findings by

Figure 5-9A: False color picture of Martian Blueberries. Frame dimension: 3 cm across; from NASA/JPL-Caltech/USGS.

one orbital spacecraft). In excitement of the discovery, those pebbly rocks were nicknamed blueberries. The discovery inspired interest anew in studying the analogous Moqui balls (see Section 5-3) for better understanding of the origin of Martian concretions.

Figure 5-9A is a false color picture of the Martian Blueberries. It was downloaded from an internet article by Dr. Meghan Bartels (Dec 5, 2018; Space and Astronomy, Space.com). 'False color picture' means the picture was taken or processed in spectra outside the normal visual range of light. The practice is used to highlight certain features that are not readily visible under white light, but it can distort an object's normal color too. For example, green foliage becomes red in an infrared picture; the ultraviolet picture in Figure 4-10D is another false color picture that shows roughness in green of a smooth white floor inside a geode in Figure 4-10E.

Figure 5-9B: Martian Blueberries on sand and in formation. Picture dimension 3 cm across; from NASA/JPL-Caltech/Cornell/USGS.

The Blueberries stand out or partially imbed in the Martian sandy sulfate evaporite. A berry is less than 0.5 cm across, which is much smaller than a typical Moqui ball in Figure 5-3A (3 cm in diameter), but it is on the same order in size as the sub-centimeter nodules in terrestrial soils.

The Moqui ball is a concretion of sandstone encrusted with hematite rind while the terrestrial soil nodules are irregular iron-manganese spherules (Section 5-3). What are Martian Blueberries? Setting the color aside, if those berries were found on Earth, undoubtedly, they would be alluded to well-rounded pebbles in a fluvial deposit of sand, excepting that a couple have been split on site 'fairly recently'.

Unlike Moqui ball, two split faces show the berry has no hard rind and there is no interior layering either (a tiny core nucleus could be present though). The absence of rind and layering favors the conjecture that they are concretions congregated in situ by seeping groundwater. It has also been suggested that the berries started as calcite and the calcite was replaced later by hematite, resulting in hematite berries. If this is the case, the replacement must have occurred with the aid of water.

There is hardly any resemblance in how the Moqui balls and the Blueberries are formed. The equivalency of berries to terrestrial soil nodules is in doubt too because soil nodules are accumulated through cyclic water saturation/desaturation and microbial activities. Nonetheless, the presence of berries shows that water had once existed on Mars surface no matter the berries were formed in situ or transported from somewhere else.

As revealed by **Figure 5-9B**, the blueberries do not necessarily congregate over the evaporite sand through seeping subsurface water; they can occur inside layered formation and the formation is sedimentary too, either aeolian or alluvial. The concretions inside the formation must have grown with the aid of water that brings hematite to infiltrate and strengthen the 'proto-berries'. The resulted berries become more resistive to erosion/weathering and hence can keep their individual, solitary spherules. A split berry cannot be transported without impairing the sharp edges of split faces. We see 'intact' split berries over the sand and inside the formation. Also, the splitting is half-half or symmetric. So, can dehydration ignite the splitting of some berries – an implosion? If so, why is the split face so flat?

If the semi-spherical berries had resulted from splitting, where are the missing halves? One may argue the fallen but missing half from the cliff (right, Figure 5-9B) was washed away out of the picture area because the cliff is a relic of fluvial erosion. There is no track showing the missing halves were dragged out in Figure 5-9A and the left of Figure 5-9B. Could the traces if ever existed have been covered by renewed deposition of sand? Why do the ball-type berries stay in place, no trace of rolling? One may conjure question and question. Would he or she offer some answers?

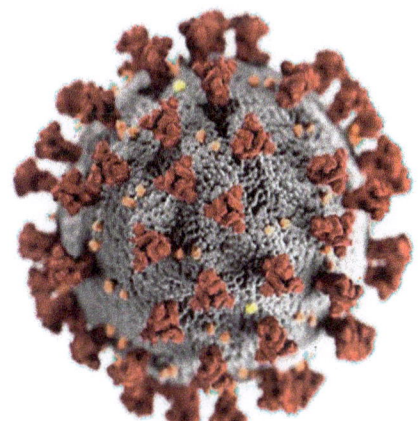

Figure 5-10: Novel coronavirus (SARS-CoV-2). Amplified ~ one million times; downloaded through Wikipedia from the US Centers for Disease Control and Prevention.

5-10. Beyond Stromatolite

Life begets life until death. All living beings have predecessors. Then, what is the zeroth or first organism that assembled lifeless organic compounds and survived to evolve and diversify the phylogenetic tree of organisms? It defies our dignity to contemplate whether you and

I may be offspring of bacteria and viruses. In time of 'stay-at- home' mandate against the spread of novel coronavirus (SARS-CoV-2) during 2020-21, let me entertain myself for a break during this period of life doldrums. Are we haunted by our dear ancestors now?

BACTERIA vs. VIRUSES: Cyanobacteria are reputed to be the builders of stromatolites of which the oldest have stood on Earth for more than 3.5 billion years. Based on fossil records, cyanobacteria are believed to be one of the first terrestrial organisms. The construction of stromatolites, however, has gone through boom-and-bust episodes in sync with the recurrences of biological calamity (genera extinction) and prosperity (genera renaissance) as Earth evolves. Nevertheless, cyanobacteria persevere in good and bad times. Today, cyanobacteria still strive to yield yearly 20 to 30 percent of synthesized oxygen globally through photosynthesis and, in extreme environmental niches which are hostile to common organisms, to build stromatolites.

A bacterium is unicellular; its cell membrane does not enclose a nucleus but other vital organelles function as an organism. It lives and produces, passes its gene by cell division, and it can benefit or infect other organisms while practices self-defense. Some bacteria are good at congregating with other individuals to form bacterial colonies that build, for example, stromatolites. A bacterium can tackle many tasks and is so sophisticated that it could not have popped instantly out of the primordial ocean when Earth was one billon years 'young'. What should have happened are presence of simpler and smaller predecessors. A virus could answer the call because a virus is 100 times smaller (about 10 nanometers in size) than a bacterium. But viruses have not yet been recognized in any fossil records.

Another obstacle: a virus replicates itself only when it infects cellular organisms. When a virus is not infecting, it stays idle as a particle called virion. Protected by a protein coat (capsid), a virion has genetic contents (DNA, RNA, etc.). A fancy virus like coronavirus has an extra lipid envelope. It does not have a cellular membrane or nucleus. Regarded as a particle, a virus is neither alive like an organism reproducing oneself through cell division, nor is a virus lifeless like a mineral grain. It stays on 'the margin of life'. Setting aside xenophobia against virus, to me, a virus is one of nature's artistic wonders (**Figure 5-10**) if it were visible to the naked eye and not infectious.

WAR GAME: A virus infects an organism by attaching itself to the organism's cell membrane, using its protein spikes to poke into the cell, and enslaving the infected cell to replicate itself. The virus multiplies rapidly to burst and kill the host cell, and then release the newly minted viruses to spread and infect more and more cells. When an organism detects an infection and if the organism cannot repair the damage, it may sacrifice the infected cell by committing suicide to protect the healthy cells because a virus cannot force the dead cell to labor again and the virus in the dead cell stops reproducing. Consequently, the dead cells become a defense barrier like a Maginot Line meant to be breached by the Nazis, but the virus will not starve to death because virus has no life; and the infected organism becomes a virus carrier. (Scars on some virus-infected plants testify the tactic of suicide protection.) However, some viruses can be fairly alerted to prevent such suicide from happening, thus begins a torturous ordeal to the ill-fated organism.

Beside passive suicidal defense, an infected organism will fight the intruders through its auto-immune system by yielding antibodies to engulf and yank out the virus' spikes. Vaccination stimulates and boosts the immune systems of animals or humans by injecting low-dosage or non-disease-inducing virus residues. An antibody is effective against a definitive strain of virus only and virus attacks selectively on a specific type of cells. Because of their simple structures, viruses are very nimble and can mutate often to new strains when an opportunity appears. Antibodies need to be updated to cope with new invaders, for example, taking annual vaccine (flu shot) ahead of the predicted variants (strains) of viruses. Some antibodies exist permanently with the infected organisms and thus insure life-time immunity to future attacks by the same strain of virus. However, immunity is not necessarily guaranteed for life.

Dead skin cells erect an effective barrier to virus invasion. However, virus in droplets or aerosol can find its way into our body through mouth, eyes, or nostrils, as well as blood transfusion or body fluid exchange. We wear protective masks to shield ourselves from becoming virus transmitters or receivers; we wash hands with soap to nix virus spikes from their basal lipid envelope which as a fatty acid is soluble in organic solvents but unfortunately or fortunately our body fluids are not organic solvents.

Although dead skin cells can act as a virus barrier, bacteria can inhabit in dead cells to cause infections. Good hygiene can keep infectious bacteria away but excessive cleaning to dismantle the dead-cell habitat is not a practical choice. So, we take antibiotics to fight infecting bacteria, not viruses. Unfortunately, prolonged use of antibiotics will enhance bacterial resistance and diminish the antibiotics' effectiveness (so-called drug resistance). We fall into a catch-22 trap. How can one escape from the quandary? Deploy viruses which are harmless to us but can infect and kill infectious bacteria. Bacterium-killing viruses, bacteriophages, have been used in therapy (in lieu of antibiotics), food processing industry, groundwater tracing, and waste treatment.

EVOLUTION: It has been estimated that in the oceans, the mass of bacteriophages is almost equal to the combined mass of bacteria and archaea (two of the three domains in phylogenetic classification of organisms, the third being eukaryote to which animals and plants belong). The bacteriophages are said to have killed *daily* 20 percent of prokaryotes (bacteria and archaea). This killing rate is unbelievably high; however, the killing is matched equally with incredibly high replication rate of prokaryotes. Such killing and replication revitalize the invisible ecosystem: some survive and evolve through gene exchange, modification (mutation), and recombination. Biodiversity is accordingly strengthened, and phylogenetic branching is triggered and advanced. And through eons of fighting for survival, somehow, we become what we are.

Virus cannot stand alone; it has no life but paradoxically it can thrive in host organism. It might have a cellular origin but because of its parasitic living, some organelles deteriorate to vestiges and eventually disappear for lack of usage – a Darwinian regressive evolution. It might have started from fragments of broken cell and gone their own way but still depended on a host for replication. It might have co-evolved with the first bacterial cell but somehow attached to the cell as a dependent. There are many other 'might-have' hypotheses, but none is beyond critics. And there are multiple stochastic happenstances for the origin of organisms and viruses.

Where is the fossil trace to document a slowly evolving transition between organisms? Does a new species mark a new beginning by quantum jump from an old one? Where should a species demarcation line be drawn on the drifting sands of evolution? Can a living thing be created out of abiotic organic compounds nowadays? If yes, it will be devoured instantly by the established organisms and there will never have any observable evidence. Could the first spark of life, in the absence of other organisms, have a greater chance to survive and propagate?

EXTRATERRESTRIAL: Let us broaden our options to look for an extraterrestrial incidence as the ignitor of terrestrial life. Our imagination is notably inspired by the Murchison meteorite. It was an observed meteor fall in Australia in 1969. It is pre-solar (7 billion years old); it is a carbonaceous chondrite (stony meteorite); and most crucially, it is rich in organic compounds, especially amino acids which are essential ingredients for organisms.

As the hypotheses go: when the solar system formed 4.6 billion years ago, the conditions at Mars were more inducing to chance conception of organisms than our Earth's. Knocked off by meteor impact, an organism-carrying piece of Mars landed on Earth about 4 billion years ago after hurling through the space for a few million years. Although its odyssey is beyond belief, the primal Martian seed sprouted and began life in a young Earth which was still too hostile for the organisms to germinate on their own but not hash enough for existing organisms to evolve.

EXTREMOPHILES: Unable to find yet any evidence of life on Mars by space crafts despite evidence for the presence of water and fluvial landscape during the unknown past (see Section 5-9: Martian Blueberries), some scientists revisit potential life incubators on Earth – deep-sea hydrothermal vents. Here, the hydro-environment (pressure, temperature, and chemistry) is extremely hostile to modern organisms, but it could better recapitulate the scene of a long-gone environ on the one-billion-year-young Earth. If any new microbe could come forth by chance in such uninhabitable hydrothermal vents, it would have the good luck of evading from being consumed. The low probability of initiation and high probability of escaping death coupled with low odds of being detected yields a slim probability for discovering new creation of organisms from abiotic compounds. The probability is not nil, however, because hydrothermal vents are distributed globally.

Nevertheless, the discoveries of modern stromatolites built by cyanobacteria in extreme environmental niches (isolated, anoxic, high salinity waters) are encouraging to all of us who care how we came from. But those cyanobacteria are descendants of existing bacteria. Extremophiles born without ties to any existing organism may hold the clues to the origin of life – we hope. In addition, we wish someday a brand-new organism, but not virus-like, can be created out of abiotic compounds in the laboratory for deducing the onset of life.

5-11. Tektite

I do not own any meteorite despite trying my luck in playas (dry lakes in the desert) to find one. The rock closest to it is tektite (**Figure 5-11,** tallest piece) but tektite is not meteorite.

Tektite used to be thought as an ejecta that was kicked into an orbit around Earth by volcanic eruption or meteor impact on Moon. The ejecta then fell as tektite from its drifting orbit onto Earth by gravity. Its chemical and isotope compositions, however, do not match well with those of the Moon rocks.

Now, most scientists believe tektite is an ejecta from meteor impact on Earth. The rock at impact site was melted by the intense impact heating and flung into the air by high impact momentum. Once airborne, the melt was twisted aerodynamically and cooled rapidly to form glass of various shapes (teardrop, dumbbell, spherule, etc.) before scattering back to the ground as solitary individuals. Based on its chemical and isotopic compositions, tektite is inferred to have been transformed from the terrestrial rocks at the impact site, not the impacting meteor.

Figure 5-11: Dumbbell tektite (bought, LD = 10 cm), brown hematite, black obsidian, and dark basalt.

Seemingly like the volcanic obsidian, tektite is glassy, usually black, or greenish black. It is brittle with shining conchoidal fractures. However, tektite has different suites of chemical and isotopic compositions, and especially, its low water content. But we cannot tell the two apart with the naked eye except by shape recognition or places of occurrences.

For comparison, Figure 5-11 shows, in addition, one small fleck of black, shining, glassy, conchoidal obsidian, which responds slightly to a neodymium magnet, in contrast to the nil response by the tektite. Also shown is one black piece of naturally polished basalt, which is attracted to a magnet but is short of glassy conchoidal fractures.

The brown piece is included here for its distinct conchoidal fracture, which is a little subdued because of its long exposure in the desert. It is not a meteorite; instead, it is nicknamed 'meteo*false*' or meteo*wrong*'. The specimen is hematite, as inferred for its brown color, brownish red streak, conchoidal fracture, hardness (around 6), dense feel (high density), and strong response to a neodymium magnet. Its front face was cut and polished, as copied from Figure I5-13b of Lee (2018).

Chapter 6: MISCELLANY

Chapter 6: MISCELLANY

This chapter adds stories for new specimens to supplement earlier narratives.

6-1. Leopard Jasper

The cutface on the top of **Figure 6-1AB** bears numerous circular concretions and it resists acid etching and knife scratching. Such slab might be traded by someone as a leopard jasper. However, the protuberances on the bottom piece, the uncut rear face, indicate the piece was originally a limestone rich in biogenic concretions but it has been highly silicified post-depositionally.

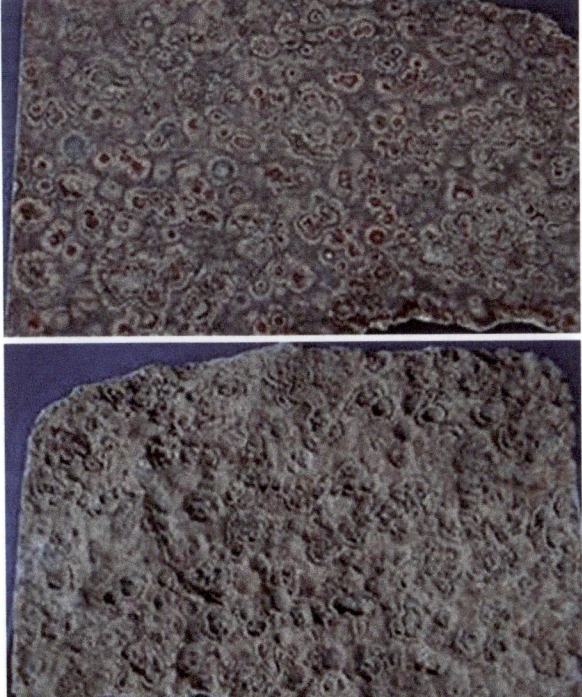

Figure 6-1AB: Jasper or silicified limestone. Each image is about 10 cm across; bought.

Figure 6-2: Porphyritic diabase. Slab; LD = long dimension = 12 cm; bought.

6-2. Porphyritic Diabase

Figure 6-2 depicts one slab of porphyritic diabase, which usually occurs in feeder dikes to volcanos. Its groundmass (matrix) is marked with characteristic dark green color. (Note: some people may regard diabase as an altered basalt, instead of a dike rock.) Feldspars crystalized out of sluggishly moving diabase magma. The green in the naturally exposed front face (bottom), however, has been weathered to brown. Unlike the phenocrysts in a silica-deficient magma as shown in Figure 1-3G for the occurrence of 'starburst jasper', here, the phenocrysts (white feldspars) do not align for infering flow direction; nor is there any cluster of feldspars. By the way, diabase may be alternatively called dolerite in the U.S.

6-3. Spiral Gastropods

I have visualized that the holes in the dome-shaped cobble in Figure 4-3A were dug by gastropods. That viewpoint needs to be re-examined in light of fossil gastropods in **Figure 6-3**. The cone-shaped gastropods sprial right-handedly in the sense of clockwise advancing screw. All are so silicified as to resist knife-scratching, except the surficial brown sediments which effervesces in 5% vinegar solution but the pitch black interior

Figure 6-3: Fossils of spiral gastropods. LD = 14 cm; courtesy of OBMS.

as exposed on the sides does not. The fossils stay flat on the bedding and orientate randomly. None appears to have dug into the sediments. In view of such fossil positioning, the taper-in holes in Figure 4-3A could have been drilled by other creatures.

6-4. Opalized Wood

The first impression upon touching the piece of rock in **Figure 6-4** was the feel of light weight (low density) relative to common rocks of comparable size. It is yellowish white, gritless with vitreous, greasy luster; and it is not scratchable with a pocket knife. The broken face on the front is weakly conchoidal and is not serrated. It is a chunk of opalized wood. Like the opal in Figure 4-18 but unlike the spherical one in Figure 1-12A, it is a common opal without opalescence and it does not fluoresce under UV light either. Nevertheless, the complete opalization is uncommon among petrified wood.

The front and rear faces mark the interfaces of annual tree rings and their interfaces also trend up-and-down on the left and right faces of the specimen. Representing the wooden fiber grain are faint, brownish yellow streaks that appear on the front and rear faces. The curvy pattern of the stripes on the bench at the lower-left corner reflects optical distortion caused by the union of the horizontal and the slanting breakage faces of tree rings.

Variations in stripe width or thickness suggest the growth of the parental tree, when alive, had varied yearly by more than a factor of two. However, I cannot decipher whether the specimen on display is upright or upside down.

6-5. Marbles

A pyramid of limestone is presented in **Figure 6-5A**. Its top part, however, was chopped naturally to end with a frustrum of pyramid. Section 3-12 listed some tetrahedrons of igneous rocks. But, here, the pyramid is a piece of limestone which has been infiltrated by silicious fluids to form a set of silica veins. The hardy veins protrude slightly above the otherwise plain limestone faces as ridges which circumscribe the pyramid. It is not understood why some rock pyramids pop out sporadically in the desert.

Next, a piece of broken marble is pictured in **Figure 6-5B**. It was a fresh, loose piece in the desert, but the environmental elements had yet to re-shape it significantly. The red atop the white marble is goethite or laterite.

Figure 6-4: Opalized wood. LD = 12 cm; bought.

Figure 6-5A: A frustum of pyramid limestone. LD = 14 cm; from San Bernardino County, California.

Figure 6-5B: A desktop suiseki marble. LD = 13 cm; from San Bernardino County, California.

In the mid-background, the marble is spattered with slender, black "pine-like trees" sprouting out of wavy dark brown siliceous seams. The strong color contrast is appealing for making this piece a small desktop picturesque suiseki.

6-6. Dendrite-like Texture

My eyes were fixated on the dendrite-like diffusion texture in **Figure 6-6** when I first saw it. Unlike the dendrites which branch off as they grow (e.g., Figure I2-12a and b, Lee, 2018), here, the 'tree trunks' swell as they grow in Zone B before tapering off. Some 'trees' branch off and fade out when they extend into the upper Zone C.

Figure 6-6: 'Dendritic-like trees' in fine-grain sandstone. LD = 6.3 cm; multiple cuts; gifted by Mr. Tony Gilham.

The 'trees' pop out of Zone A. The upper-right triangle of Zone A appears like rhyolite with undulating, slim, segregated gray quartz seams (less than 1 mm thick) while its counter lower-left triangle is almost free of such seams.

Zone C appears to be composed of tiny but visible grains. However, the grainy texture fades and vanishes into the upper, reddish, cloudy Zone D.

Gaze at the front face of the rock to get an illusion. Illusive is a sunset scenery. Foreground is covered with river sand. On the far bank of the flowing water stand a row of trees; the row turns into brown silhouette against a sun-setting reddish cloudy sky.

Wake up from the illusion. Look at the rock under a reflecting microscope. The rock is indeed granular and Zone C in particular bears innumerable, rounded grains immersed in a matrix of even finer particles. It is a piece of siltstone or very-fine-grained sandstone. It is well compacted and cemented but still scratchable with a pocket knife. The piece can be nicely polished because of its finely cemented grain texture. The brown and red hue is due to infiltration by ferrous fluids and their subsequent oxidation to ferric oxides.

The two cutfaces indicate the 'trees or bushes' emerge (diffuse) from a common base between Zones A and B, remain solitary as they grow upward, broaden at midway, then taper off. A few pierce into Zone C, then branch and fade away. The midway swell is likely to follow the tightly-held interlayer spacing; the branching in Zone C is allowed by relatively large pores and greater permeability as implied by the existence of visible grains.

Figure 6-7A: Amazonite showing partially crystal faces and fragmentation between cleavages. Height = 10 cm; no cut; courtesy of Mr. Gregory Vidler.

6-7. Greenish Blue Amazonite

Amazonite is a pretty bluish green to green variety of microcline, which in turn is a low-temperature variety of orthoclase. Amazonite and microcline occur typically in pegmatite dikes as offshoots of granite at the last stage of magma evolution. Its greenish is due to impurity of lead-bearing minerals and water molecules, not to copper component.

Figure 6-7A depicts a prismatic amazonite. Its four visible crystal faces are shining and vitreous. It has two sets of nearly orthogonal cleavages. One set prominantly runs through the crystal while the less conspicuous set appears as short segments between the dominant set. The development of cleavages generates numerous fragmental rectangles, which abound especially behind the visible crystal faces. It is not clear whether the cleavage-related fragmentation has destroyed an otherwise 'perfect' prismatic crystal, or prevented the crystal from being fully established.

Compare this picture with the amazonite in Figure 3-4B for color contrast and cleavage development.

A fragmented piece of amazonite is presented in **Figure 6-7B**. Fragmentation along the two well-developed sets of cleavages have rendered the crystal faces beyond recognition. Those fragments also attract deposition of caliche which masks the specimen's identity. The removal of caliche reveals this bluish green piece of amazonite is interpersed with white feldspar and gray, translucent quartz, plus some weathered brown, black mafic minerals. Some residual caliche stays as scattered, yellow patches.

Figure 6-7B: Fragmented amazonite with interspersed quartz and feldspar: LD = 9 cm; no cut; courtesy of Mr. Gregory Vidler.

6-8. Petrified Bark

Frequently our viewpoints on or interpretations of some phenomena have to be revised or updated as new data become available. Here is one example on silicification of tree bark.

In Sections 4-10 and 4-16, I described two pieces of silicified

Figure 6-8A: Petrified bark. LD = 9 cm; from Riverside County, California; no cut; gifted by Mr. Gregory Vidler.

Figure 6-8B: Petrified wood. Rear side of Figure 6-8A.

bark and wondered why the silicification of wooden part was not observed. The presence of petrified wood is now found in one small specimen (**Figures 6-8A**). Although the characteristic scales of bark are still visible, the rear side of the specimen (**Figure 6-8B**) clearly shows the petrified wood grains.

Figure 6-8C: Chalcedony geode in petrified wood. LD = 4 cm; from Riverside County, California; no cut; gifted by Mr. Gregory Vidler.

PETRIFIED WOOD: The yellow patches in Figure 6-8B are residues after partial removal of caliche. The greyish, milky white nodules of chalcedony, like the chalcedony in previous bark pictures, fluoresce in bluish green under ultraviolet light. The rest, including white patches (caliche), do not fluoresce. The three shards of chalcedony near the top of Figure 6-8A seem to have been squeezed out of the wooden grains.

The "extrusion" of chalcedony is compatible with the centrally located chalcedony in another piece of petrified wood (**Figure 6-8C**). It is like a geode in petrified wood with botryoidal chalcedony around its center void. In lieu of the grainy wooden texture on the periphery, there lie several strands of grey, elongated, buldging, bulbous nodules. The interior of those nodules is likely chalcedony, as suggested by exposures in the next two figures; but their grey covers prevent the chalcedony from fluorescing under UV light.

NODULES: The specimen in **Figure 6-8D** retains some bark scales but its woody grains are not apparent. Unusual protrusions emerge, nevertheless: At the lower middle, one grey semi-ellipsoidal nodule anchors on the surface; another semi-ellipsoidal nodule appears at the upper left edge. The latter's cover is broken, exposing bluish white chalcedony.

Most conspicuous is a circular chalcedony which occupies almost one half of the displayed surface. It has two major components: one geode and one curtain-like veil. The white veil, a thin sheet of chalcedony about one mm thick, has two windows. The smaller window near the top is barely visible but the larger one reveals bluish white botryoidal chalcedony inside the half-empty geode.

Figure 6-8D: Petrified bark and concealed chalcedony nodules. LD = 9 cm; one base cut; from Riverside County; gifted by Mr. Gregory Vidler.

The circular chalcedony is rimmed peculiarly by relics of a broken wall, which appears to be made of the same material as the rinds of grey nodules. If the wall was indeed part of a former nodule's rind, this geode inside the petrified wood would have a diameter of about 5 cm. It is a miracle that the veil remains almost intact after the geode's rind was wrecked. One may wonder how the veil or cover of the geoid has developed.

The rear side of Figure 6-8D is depicted in **Figure 6-8E**. It shows little woody texture and only feeble signature scales of bark. Instead, the entire surface is almost fully covered with nodules, some of which are broken naturally and thus expose milky white chalcedony in the interior. Note that, atop the specimen, the artificially exposed milky white chalcedony has a dark core of chalcedony. All exposed chalcedony fluoresces in green under UV light. The chalcedony is polishable while its rind is not.

A few questions await answers. Why does silicification of bark proceed by way of nodule making? Why does chalcedony fluoresce but the rest does not? Why are some, if not most of, chalcedony nodules enclosed with brownish grey rinds?

AN ALTERNATIVE: A conspiracy theorist suggests an alternative to the bark silicification. The host is volcanic ash, not wood. The ash turns into bentonite clay. Bentonite is light colored, soft, plastic, and moldable.

Figure 6-8E: Nodules saturated bark. Rear side of Figure 6-8D.

It expands when wet and contracts when dry. Through countless cycles of expansion and contraction, the clay cracks, forming nodular, scale-like clumps and elongated fissures that allow silica to infiltrate and solidify as chalcedony. A woody-like texture appears from the alternating layouts of the clay host and interpersed chalcedony. The two claims could be resolved by field observations or instrumental analyses.

Figure 6-9A: White geode with daisy-like concretions. LD = 7.8 cm; unknown source location; courtesy of Mr. Calvin Shipley.

6-9. White Geode with Daisy-like Texture

Geode is a nodule with cavity into which crystals grow. Generally, it has a rind of chalcedony for example, and sometimes the rind is in turn enclosed with a crust that is made of the material cemented or altered from its host rock. The rind and crust are very hardy such that the geode will preserve as a solitary nodule from weathering and erosion of the host rock. Without the protectve rind, a vug or crevice, which may also bear visible crystals, will fate the same way as the host rock, disintegrating into fragments upon weathering and erosion. See also banded agate geodes in Figures 1-4 and 1-9 and Section 4-10.

WHITE GEODES: **Figures 6-9A and 6-9B** depict two uncommon white geodes. The cavity in the former has single chamber while the latter has double chambers which are not visiblely connected with an empty passage way. Both geodes are rimmed by white chalcedony and each chamber is partially filled with well-developed, clear white druse quartz crystals, some of which may reach 5 mm in size. Worth noting are the cleanness and whiteness of the crystals and chalcedony. Why? Have the impurities of trace elements been absorbed by and thus filtered out by the host rock such that the fluid entering the cavity is like a pure silica solution? Note also the absence of crust. Was the crust removed from the geode or the geode not encrusted?

Figure 6-9B: White geode and its exterior. LD = 8.5 cm; courtesy of Mr. Calvin Shipley.

Grossly like cauliflower, the exterior of the two geodes is made of chalcedony with crisscrossing fissures. As indicated by the pictures, each geode is covered almost half-and-half by dark and light chalcedony, respectively. Could the color contrast reflect different burial depths before the specimens were unearthed?

DAISY TEXTURE: The most suprising surficial feature is the presence of daisy- or chrysanthemum-like disk features. One near-perfect 'daisy' is shown in Figure 6-9A; its whiteness stands out against the dark background. The rays of this white daisy extend radially about 5 mm and the rays are bundled to form four petal-like segments. Each petal is stacked with many arc contours, like the growth lines in clam shells. Many similar but fragmented daisies also scatter over the rest of the exterior.

How do those daisy aggregates originate? Why is the host crust missing? A simple answer: each daisy starts by nucleation, grows radially, and stacks up growth rings. Can the chalcedony do it? Not impossible but not likely. Can a chalcedony daisy be the replacement product of a former carbonate daisy? That is possible for the following reasons: 1) A host crust of carbonate can be removed relatively easier, naturally or artificially, as compared to the removal of a silicate crust. 2) Purification of the silica-bearing fluid to yield white geodes through absorption-filtering of trace metallic elements by a carbonate or clay host is more effective than by a silicate host. And 3) the standout of daisy color, white against dark background, implies that the daisies have been replaced by a different source of silica bearing fluid. (Note the 'daisies" in Figure 1-3G are phenocrysts.)

Another question to contemplate is: how can the nucleation for daisies begin on the exterior of a geode? One way out is: first, have the carbonate nucleation and daisy-making; second, excavate the carbonate by dissolution to form cavities; and third, infiltrate the purified silica-bearing solutions into cavities to make white quartz geodes and chalcedony rinds. Meanwhile, the carbonate daisies are replaced by chalcedony;

but unfortunately, most daisies are fragmented by subsequent fissuring in rinds. Some coarse fissures appear to have emanated from a few common depression sinks. Are those fissures due to dehydration cracking of spherical rinds?

The tender and clean exterior of the two geodes, in comparison to the rugged lumps that I used to see in volcanic geodes, seem to favor the contention that the two geodes have originated from solution cavities in carbonate or calcareous clay host.

Furthermore, the absence of crust as well as the purity of clear, white quartz crystals and chalcedony suggests favorably the potential hosting role played by carbonate.

Will anyone raise the ante that the daisies are silicified fossils, instead of starting from inorganic chemical nucleation speculated above? If yes, will you still entertain the storied sequences of events or modify the story?

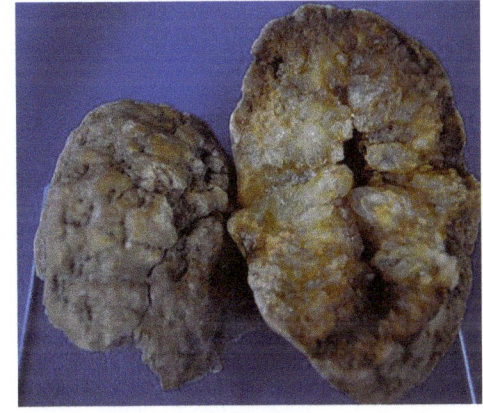

Figure 6-9C: Keokuk geode. LD = 9 cm. Gifted by Mr. Danny Sweeney.

KEOKUK GEODE:

Excluding the daisies, the two geodes look like the *white quartz* variety of Keokuk geodes from the tri-state area of Iowa, Missouri, and Illinois. Keokuk geodes, originated from dolomitic or argillaceous (clayey) formations, bear crystals of various minerals tinted with different shades of hues. I have searched on the internet but failed to find any geode with an exterior daisy-like texture.

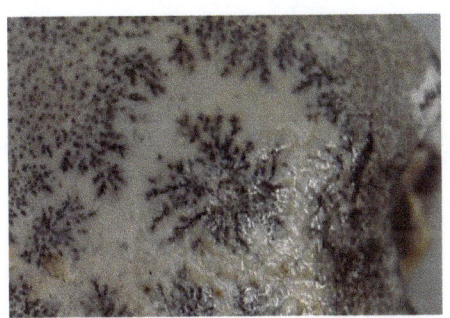

Figure 6-9D: Dendrite-like daisy on cast of a clam shell. The 'daisy', 6 mm across, appears near the bivalve hinge on the right edge of the photo.

After making the preceeding remarks, I incidently spotted two pieces of Keokuk geodes in a friend's yard. Later he retrieved two crush-open pieces from his collection, one of which is displayed in **Figure 6-9C**. But it comes from Indiana, not the tri-state area. The outlooks of the three pieces are similar except that the one in Figure 6-9C does not have any daisy concretion; however, the three do share similar exterior features of depression sinks. Also, the quartz crystals here are stained yellowish brown and are much bigger, not white and drusy.

DAISY ON CAST OF CLAM SHELL: The contention that those white geodes originate from infilling of silica in solution cavities in argillaceous-carbonate formation is underpinned by the appearance of dendrite-like daisy on one cast or external mold of clam shell (**Figure 6-9D**). The dendrite occurs near the bivalve hinge in one of my eight specimens of natural sandstone casts of clam shells. Those fine-sand casts imprint the cavities that have resulted from dissolution of carbonate shells. Other specimens are probably too grainy or too coarse for the dendrite to develop.

6-10. A Stone Wok

Sometimes we know the cause and effect and we are deterministic. But more frequently we are ignorant and attribute some phenomena to probabilistic happenstances and walk away from curiosity: for example, the occurrences of target-ring texture in granite (Figure 3-5B) and the square block in diatomite (Figure 4-6). Here we have another mistery – a 'stone wok (frying pan)' in **Figure 6-10**.

Figure 6-10: A stone wok. LD =13 cm; no cut; from San Bernardino County, California.

The wok is made of rhyolite, of which the subtly defined flow plane seems to be subparallel to the top surface of the specimen. The wok is supported by three massive legs but it is too small to have been a practical artifact. The question is: how nature excavates the stone wok. How does nature place the 'soup' repeatedly as to leave a permanent ring mark and to stain the rest of the wok floor except the part above that residual 'soup marking'? The stain does not seep to the bottom but it does smoothen the wok floor; and the infiltration seems to have altered the wok to be capable of yielding conchoidal fracture.

6-11. A Cluster of Hidden Agates

The rock shown in **Figure 6-11A** is not as picturesque as the geodes or agates in Sections 1-4 and 1-9 but its sharp, angular, protrusive, fragmental white aggregates invite a close look at the intricacy of crystal growth and configuration. It consists of three major components: a massive agate base, a thin double-banded agate, and a top, exterior layer filled with white aggregates, each of which is a multi-banded agate.

Figure 6-11A: Hidden geodes. LD = 12 cm; one cut with edge trim; from San Bernardino County, California.

Figure 6-11B: Agate underlying Figure 6-12A

AGATE BASE: The base (rear side) is a brownish red agate, varying from one to four cm thick without visible banding (**Figure 6-11B**). It is porphyritic-like with white flecks of 'phenocrysts', upto 2 mm in size. The cutface is crisscrossed by quartz veins and in addition, dotted with quartz specks. The grains in 'groundmass (matrix)' are not discernible but the groundmass responds magnetically to neodymium magnet – suggesting it might have been transformed from volcanic rock such as andesite which bears microscopic magnetites. Several reddish, grainless, patches of alteration, stand out against the lighter background. One one-centimeter sized agate appears near the lower-right convex edge. These visible quartz appearances are secondary fillings.

BANDED AGATE: Overlying the massive base are two thin laminae of quartz or chalcedony; each lamina in different hue is about one mm thick (Figure 6-11A). The two constitute as a curvy, thinly banded agate.

ANGULAR GRAINS AND DARK GAPS: Crystals grow from the curvy agate layer into a lava fracture. Probably, a big nodular geode has never been formed to emcompass all the crystals on display. Such geode would carry druse quartz. The crystals here as a group are distinctive: first, unknown tiny, black aggregates around the periphery of the specimen, especially along the lower margin (Figure 6-11A); second, one solitary, greyish translucent quartz blob (about 1 cm in diameter) at the lower left corner, just inward from the black mineral aggregates; and third, the protrusive crystals in white, angular habit forms. Those angular crystals do not look like quartz, nor plagioclase even though they exhibit orthoclase-like vitreous luster.

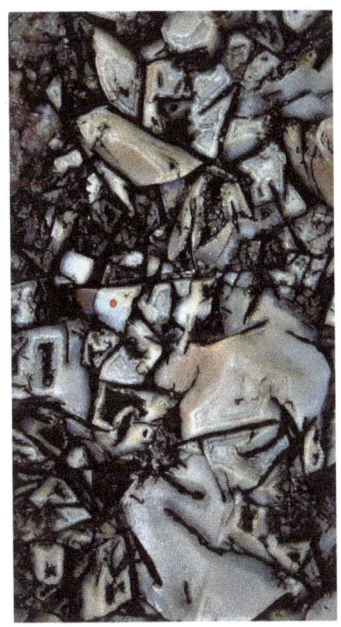

Figure 6-11C: Aggregates of geodes. Partially enlarged from Figure 6-11A, showing banding of some crystals.

The top layer also bears unusual dark fractures, which are short (less than 2 cm) and straight. And some fractures border on the edges of angular crystals but most stop short of breaching the entire grains.

Figure 6-11D: Another enlarged view.

ZONING: **Figure 6-11C** is an enlarged portion of Figure 6-11A (red dot for reference point). Each crystal has zoning that mimics its own periphery. Hence, each is an agate with subtle banding. As a whole, this outer layer is a cluster of agates, not an assembly of crystals with angular habit.

This viewpoint is further strengthened in a greatly enlarged picture (**Figure 6-11D).**

Surprisingly, the zoning in many instances bends around the tips of 'fractures' or stay parallel with the short, straight 'fractures'; and none of the 'fractures' cuts across the zoning (Figure 6-11C).

Such patterns preclude the convention that 'fracturing' occurs after crystal zoning. So, the fracture-like features in Figure 6-11A are not fractures. Most of them, if not all, are just dark gaps between aggregates as seen in Figure 6-11D. Are the gaps filled with unknown dark matter? The uniformity in darkness and the presence of a few white specks shimmering in the dark suggests the darkness is not due to optical shadowing.

The rectangularly zoned piece at the middle left edge is indeed a geode. And each of the white, angular aggregates is also a silica agate geode, not brecciated from a big piece.

Some mind boggling questions: Why does each geode grow angularly with straight edges, like brittle glass shattering? How do many small banded aggregates form and assemble? An anonymous geologist suggests that those small agates are relic casts, formed by the infiltrating silica fluid which mimics a former but now erased calcite wall of a fracture.

Figure 6-11E: A slab of geode. LD = 15 cm; unknown source location; courtesy of Mr. Colin Child.

A SLAB OF GEODE: **Figure 6-11E** depicts one slab of a geode, as a supplement to the cluster of agates in Figure 6-11A. The slab appears to have many subnodules as individual agates, especially in view of the area enclosed by the greyish white, saw-tooth-like contour.

Each subnodule has geode-like shades of zoning. Those are cross-sectional views of a cluster of columns or botryoids. Unlike the angular geodes in Figure 6-11A, they are not, separate, independent nodules demarcated by fracture-like dark gaps.

6-12. Multi-Celled Geodes

Sometimes we wonder at the mighty carbonate stalactites and stalagmites when we enter huge limestone caverns or do sight-seeing in Karst terrain. Occasionally we see silica stalactites and stalagmites at much smaller scales in hand specimens or museum exhibits.

Figure 6-12A and -12B show two opposing cutfaces of one stalactitic and stalagmitic agate geode, not the carbonate equivalents.

Figure 6-12A: Multi-celled geode. LD = 37 cm; bought; from Suwannee River Basin, Florida; red mark for orientation reference in Figure 6-12B.

SILICIFIED HOST ROCK: The host to the geode is porous silicified limestone of which lineaments are visible on the top and side faces of Figure 6-12B. The hardy lineaments and abundant cavities and vesicles might erroneously lead to the suspicion that the host may be rhyolite – a volcanic rock.

The features on the two cutfaces do not match well and the two parts of the interior do not look alike either because the geodes are highly asymmetric and an intervening slice between the two halves of the specimen was ground off during saw cutting.

Figure 6-12B: Multi-celled geode. Red marking refers to orientation for the counter face in Figure 6-12A.

MULTI-CELLED GEODES: This specimen hosts a big chamber which has been partitioned into smaller cells. Each cell is walled by seams of banded chalcedony or agate to become a hollow geode. Two neighboring cells do not share the same wall; each has its own wall, separating from its adjacent wall with a gap partially filled with silicified limestone, visibly like the host rock.

The cell geodes vary in color (white, grey, blue, brown, black), shape (botryoidal, spherule), and column (stalactitic, stalagmitic, or stalacto-stalagmitic); the specimen as a whole is an ensemble of cell geodes. Those geodes have one common attribute: spatial room for crystal growth. But there appears no visible crystal inside the hollows, not even a trace of drusy quartz of which the presence is common in silica geodes.

Absence of crystals means the geodes have not resulted from a cooling, silica-bearing hydrothermal fluids. Instead, it implies replacing existing minerals, particle by particle, with silica. Chalcedony, a cryptocrystalline form of solid silica, mimics the shape of the replaced at steady temperature. The replaced is carbonate in the buried fossil corals and the imitating chalcedony is the pseudomorph of corals. The replacement, however,

Figure 6-12C: An enlarged clip from Figure 6-12A. The lower-right cell is 7 cm across.

is an imperfect replica of coral because of disturbances during post-depositional diagenesis of sediments; some details are preserved while others are impaired.

STORIES: My story happened some tens of million years ago at where is now the Suwannee River basin in Florida. It began with coral reefs in the sea. The falloff debris of coral became sediments along with others. The carbonaceous sediments were buried deeper and deeper, and post-deposional changes occurred physically and chemically – the so-called diagenesis of sediments. In particular, the dissolution and silicification (replacement) of carbonate by passing subsurface waters altered the limestone formation. Dissolution created cavities for silica to form agate linens that underpin the cavity walls from collapsing; silicification of limestone encrusts cavities to form weathering-and-erosion resistive nodular geode. And this geode specimen is comparmentalized into more than ten cell geodes.

After tectonic uplifting of the silicified formation, some of those nodular geodes are exposed by erosion, released to river deposits (alluvium), or unearthed by man's digging.

Inside the cavities but outward from the agate linens are the spectacular subnodules (hereafter called nodules for short) that cluster to form botryoids, stack to form knotty string-like stalactites or stalagmites, and pave the cavity floor or wall in grid patterns. How do those nodules appear in different colors and complexity in geometric arrangement?

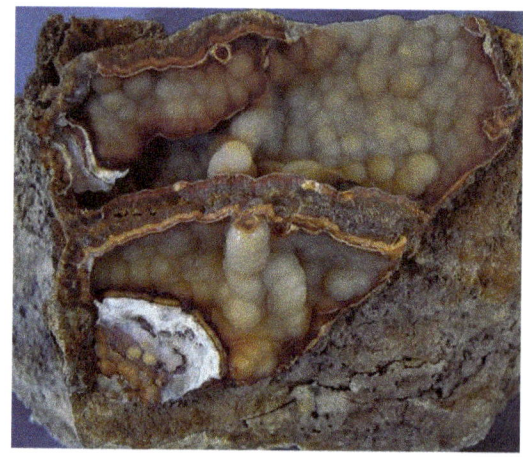

Figure 6-12D: Botryoidal geode. DL = 11 cm; atop and behind Figure 6-12B.

COLOR VARIATIONS: Coloration of geodes reflects trace element contents of the originating silica solutions. Over the space of specimen size (< 1 m), are the trace elements expected to vary so much in type or concentration as to cause color variations? Are those cell geodes formed simultaneously or sequentially?

One clue to color diversification comes from the white silica deposits in a cell located on the middle right of Figure 6-12A. That cell among some others is open to fluid infiltration from outside into the chamber to cover and alter partially the existing black botryoids. Contrarily to some open cells, two holes masked by black patches at the top of Figure 6-12B are free of any silica deposits; that is, the two cavities have been shut off from silica fluids since the cavities were excavated by dissolution. Furthermore, the leftmost cell in Figure 6-12B has agate walls but no nodule. The co-existence of open and closed cells leads to the following conjecture.

Replacement of carbonate by silica as nodules begins after erecting agate walls to form individual cells; all nodules start with the same color for the same influx of fluid. Inflow to cells will decline as the deposits accumulate. Eventually some cells, one by one, are shut off through self-sealing but the remainders continue to have inflow. A fluid evolving in quantity and composition instills different covers to the existing nodules.

Figure 6-12E: Additional stalagmitic & stalactitic geode. Stalagmite = 5 cm.

Thus, the outermost skins of nodules preserve the color from change when a cell is closed to the incoming fluid. Any supporting evidences? The chipping at some nodules in **Figure 6-12C** (which is located at the middle of Figure 6-12A) reveals colored rings that chronicle a sequence of color changes during the development of those cell geodes.

Figure 6-12D depicts one cell geode atop and outside the chamber in Figure 6-12B. Sub-cells followed the creation of the dividing agates. Those yellowish and brownish botryoids look pristine. The white patches mark new deposits or alterations in this open exterior cell.

Figure 6-12F: Stalactite and stalagmite. The cell is 7 cm across, from the lower right corner of Figure 6-12A.

One greyish white stalagmite in another external cell geode, outside the main chamber for the cell geodes, is on display in **Figure 6-12E**. Also shown are the lineaments on the exterior of the specimen. The picture is viewed from the right side of Figure 6-12B.

Figure 6-12F is an enlarged view of one picture clipping from Figure 6-12A. It shows all cell geodes are comprised of nodules. The color of nodules is registered when a cell is closed to influx of an evolving silica fluid. In other words, the color signals the last fluid incursion and coating.

DEPOSITION: I have explicitly said the nodules are replacement products of corals and also implicitly attributed the clustering, stacking, and paving of nodules to replacement of carbonate in corals by silica as agate and chalcedony. This statement is a convenient sidestep from explaining how deposition can yield the diversified patterns of nodule grouping. But there are features that cannot be claimed to be replicas of coral fossils; those have resulted from dripping deposition.

One example of dripping deposition is shown in in Figure 6-12F, which holds different dripstones: stalactite, stalagmite, and stalacto-stalagmite. And **Figure 6-12G** (an enlarged clip picture of 6-12A) depicts another

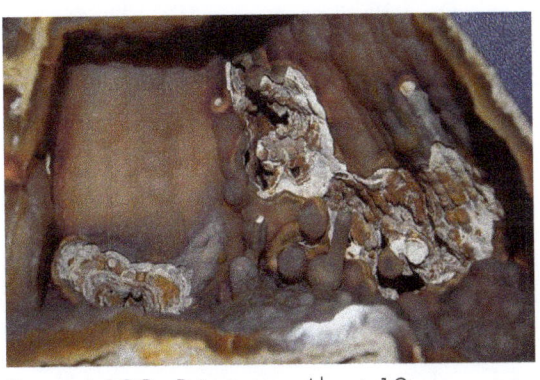

Figure 6-12G: Dripstones. About 12 cm across; from the right cell of Figure 6-12A.

set of dripstones. Note a pair of long-neck bottle-like dripstones at the lower middle of the picture and between them, one pair of spherules. Those four nodules appear to have popped out from a nodule-floor at one corner of the biggest cell in this specimen. As mentioned previously, some nodules in this cell have been altered by influx of water to yield curvy, white and brown zoning. Those alterations happen near the ground surface after the original encrustation of the geode has been punctured by weathering and erosion.

CHALLENGE: The upward necking of the two nodules contrasts with the downward tapering of small nodules inside the cell (hidden from the view) at the west edge of Figure 6-12C. But there is no pointed tip on nodules at their respective counter-ceiling, or -floor.

In the small world of this specimen, vapor pressure or moisture content varies slightly from cell to cell. Hence, the fluid viscosity and the rate of silica precipitation adjusts concurrently; and both adjustments differ from cell to cell too. The seepages into the cells could go slowly upward or downward, depending on local hydrogeologic conditions. Those minute variations, however, can lead to the presence or absence of tapering nodules.

Therefore, it is still challenging to unambiguously differentiate the floor and ceiling nodules and set stalactites apart from stalagmites. Perhaps such distinction is not a literally proper concept here, in the original sense of dripping deposition in limestone caves, but figuratively it is instruction-applicable. In short, this specimen of multi-celled geodes has resulted from replacement of carbonate by silica in the early stage of evolution and later, from modifications by deposition of silica to have a diversified set of celled geodes. Upon exposure near the ground surface, a new phase of alterations (as marked by white precipitates) by water builds up.

SILICA STALACTITE/STALAGMITE: **Figure 6-12H** shows a fiery agate. Inside the cavity, it comes complete with ceiling and floor botryoids, stalactites, stalagmites, and columns of stalacto-stalagmites. The agate forms through deposition of silica, not by way of replacing carbonate as is the scenario for the specimen described previously in Figures 6-12A through -12G.

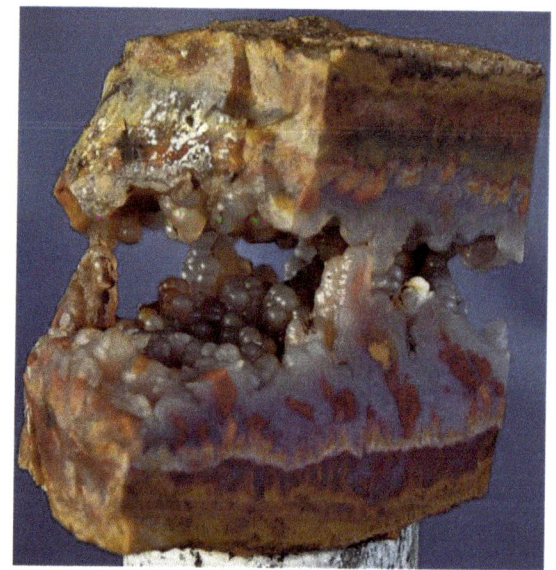

Figure 6-12H: Stalactitic and stalagmitic silica geode. LD = 7 cm; unknown source location; courtesy of Mr. Colin Child.

The encasing crust is a colorfully banded agate and the agate is symmetric with respect to the horizontal median plane. The 'red flames' spew downward and upward from the ceiling and floor, respectively, then sway to the west with the 'cloud' (greyish white chalcedony).

The relief or protrusion of botryoids on the ceiling is less than its equivalent on the floor. That is: the ceiling is flat relative to the rugged floor. This observation leads to the suggestion that the specimen sits upright on the granitic display stand as it would in the field.

Another argument for the upright posture of this picture is the contact geometry exposed at the mid-section, where two upper, bifurcated protuberances skirt around one lower, upward protuberance to form a stalacto-stalagmite. Note the presence of one pinhole at their juncture.

Lastly, what is the main difference in modes of occurrence between silica and carbonate stalactite/stalagmite? Upon seeping into a limestone cave, the partial pressure of carbon dioxide in the bicarbonate fluid drops instantaneously to the cave-atmospheric carbon dioxide pressure and accordingly, the calcium bicarbonate in the fluid precipitates to calcium carbonate as stalactite; and the excess dripping fluid falls to the ground to form stalagmite. There is no equivalent 'punch influencer' for silica deposition. Instead, the moisture content or vapor pressure in the air pocket affects the fluid viscosity and the evaporation rate of fluid, and consequently, the rates of fluid flow and precipitation. In short, silica precipitates through slow evaporation of water. Both dripping and oozing silica solution from crevices can result in botryoids, but there is no tapering or pointed tips on the silica nodules because of the sluggish silica conversion from liquid to solid phases – chalcedony.

6-13. Coral and Chalcedony

Figure 6-13 assembles three pieces of chalcedony and one piece of coral from different source locations. The stump on the right is a calcareous coral. Its top surface shows a well-preserved concentric ring structure with dividing, radial septa between the rings. The rings at bottom tend to be more elliptical. Its center hole opens to one tiny, top-to-bottom, see-through shaft.

Figure 6-13: Coral and chalcedony. LD = 7 cm (center); various source locations; all but the base gifted by Mr. Tony Gilham.

The coral serves as an analog for inferring (not proving) that the circular, cylindrical columns in the left piece of chalcedony has originated from fossilization of coral by chalcedony replacement. Each column looks like the the column in the geode on the left of Figure 6-12C; the similarity reenforces the idea that the geodes in the Figure 6-12A to -12H series started with coral fossilization.

Like the coral, every column at the left piece has ring structure with a center point and a bottom counter point but the two points do not have a see-through tube connection. Noteworthy are a few solitary tube-like tentacles that rim along and stem from the inner face of a brown stained, chalcedony wall or crust on the north edge – another biogenic sign. Similar tubing appears also at the bottom.

The milky white, translucent chalcedony has an outsized cavity, in which bumpy botryoids are poorly developed. Its cavity edge is dotted surficially with white opal specks amid scattered grey spots.

The base plate to the three pieces mentioned above is a slab cut from one 30-cm nodule, which looks like an agate or geode externally but the cut face says otherwise. Its silicification to chalcedony is incomplete but it does have dark brown agate veins and weak zoning.

GLOSSARY & INDEX

Note: The terms in red are new additions to the GLOSSARY in the predecessor of this book. The numerals are section identification for indexing. Prefix 'I' refers to section number in volume I.

Actinolite—A hydrous amphibole group mineral, green with needle-like radiation. I5-16, I5-19; 3-11.

Agate – A translucent variety of chalcedony nodule, usually curved with alternating color bands. It occurs typically in the cavities of other rocks. I5-12, I5-14, I5-21; 1-14, 1-19, 6-9, 6-11, 6-12.

Amazonite – A variety of bluish green or green microcline or orthoclase with well-developed cleavages. Its green is due to lead impurity. 3-4, 6-7.

Amethyst – A purple, translucent to transparent variety of quartz crystal. I1-15; 1-19.

Amorphous – Material or mineral without crystalline structure is said to be amorphous.

Amphibole – A group of dark rock-forming minerals which are hydrous ferromagnesium silicates, including hornblende, nephrite (soft jade). Amphibolite is a rock made of amphibole. 3-11B.

Andesite – A reddish brown, fine grained volcanic rock, of which the feldspar is primarily of andesine composition (sodium-calcium silicate). The name originates from the Andes Mountains in South America. 3-6, 3-17, 6-11.

Anhedral – As opposite to euhedral, an anhedral mineral means its crystal faces are not well developed.

Anorthite – Calcium feldspar, calcium-end member of plagioclase. See also anorthoclase, anorthosite. 3-11.

Aplite – Fine-grained granite (finer than pegmatite) occurs in dikes that cut across other rocks. I3-5, I5-6.

Aragonite – An orthorhombic crystal of calcium carbonate (with three orthogonal crystal axes at different lengths). It is identical with calcite in chemical composition. It often occurs in hot-springs deposits. 2-3, 2-7, 2-11.

Banded ironstone – It is a major iron ore deposit – a sedimentary rock with alternatively banded or layered iron oxides (hematite, magnetite) and chert. The former is reddish while the latter is greyish. 4-5.

Barite – It is a crystal of barium sulfate ($BaSO_4$) with high density. I4-8.

Bauxite – An ore of various aluminum-bearing minerals, with spherules and low density. 4-18.

Basalt – Dark, fine-grained, extrusive (volcanic) igneous rock, bearing calcic plagioclase and dark green clinopyroxene but little or no quartz. I5-7, I5-22; 1-6E, 3-14.

Bedding – It is synonymous with 'layering' in sedimentary rocks. 4-1, 4-2, 4-5, 4-9.

Bicarbonate – A chemical compound with bicarbonic anion HCO_3, e.g., calcium bicarbonate $Ca(HCO_3)_2$, or sodium bicarbonate $NaHCO_3$.

Biogenic refers to something produced or brought about by organisms. 1-1, 2-10.

Brecciation – Making breccia, i.e., forming angular fragments of rock. I5-11; 1-11, 4-4.

Brittle – Hard but liable to break or shatter easily at small deformation (less than 3 to 5%). It is used in contrast to 'ductile' material property.

Calcite – A common rock-forming mineral, calcium carbonate. It is a principal constituent in limestone, marble, stalagmite, and stalactite. It can be a minor constituent in other rocks. It also can be a cementing agent for sediments. Ch I2, I2-13, I2-14, I2-15, I5-1; Ch 2, 2-12, 2-13.

Cast – Natural replica or mold of shells. It also refers to filling of a sedimentary depression or small rock fragments in sedimentary rock. 6-9.

Cap rock – As loosely used here, it means a residual rock layer that overlies another layer, like a cap. I2-7.

Carbonate – As a mineral, it designates a compound with anion CO3, e.g., calcite, dolomite. As a rock, it means deposit of organic or inorganic debris from solution. Ch I2; Ch 2.

Carbonatite is an igneous rock with high content of carbonate. It occurs in continental rifting zones. Ch 2.

Cataclastic – 'Cata' connotes a rock formed during catastrophe and 'clastic' means mechanical origin. Clastic sediments are assembled through transport by water, wind etc. But a cataclastic quartz (as coined here) is formed in situ by extensive cracking, not assembled through transport processes.

Cataclastic rock – A rock composed of angular fragments that are formed by tectonic fracturing. As used here, it also refers to vein quartz shattered by cooling contraction or pressure reduction through removal of overburden. I1-1, I1-2, I1-13, I1-14.

Chalcedony – A cryptocrystalline variety of silica (intertwined quartz and moganite). It is translucent with wax-like luster, sometimes fibrous microscopically. It occurs as an aqueous or hydrothermal deposit. Chalcedony is a catch-all term, including multi-colored or curve-banded agate, onyx (parallel banded), jasper (reddish), and sedimentary chert, plus other varieties. I1-17, I2-15, I4-7, I5-5, I5-14, I5-23; 1-1, 1-2, 1-7, 1-10, 2-14, 3-19, 4-10, 4-16, 5-11, 6-8, 6-10, 6-12.

Chert – A hard, dense, dull to semi-vitreous sedimentary rock, consisting of fibrous silica (chalcedony). Its color varies from dark grey to brown. It has splintery or conchoidal fractures It is also named as flint if occurred in limestone. I5-2, I5-5, I5-23; 1-3, 4-9, 4-13.

Chlorite – A group of greenish platy minerals consisting of hydrous aluminosilicate with iron and magnesium, e.g., chlorite schist.

Clastic sediment – Sediment transported to the depositional site by mechanical means, e.g., water, wind. Ch 4.

Clay – Any rock fragment that is less than 1/256 mm in diameter. It may also mean clay minerals with platy crystalline structure, aka clay mineral.

Cleavage – The breakage of a mineral along its crystallographic plane, for example, rhombohedral cleavage of calcite. I2-13; 2-9, 2-12, 3-4, 6-7.

Conchoidal fracture – A shell-like fracture which commonly appears in obsidian, quartz, and flint. I5-14; 6-4.

Concretion – A lump of material or mineral congregation that is physically distinguishable from its host rock. It is often misused as being synonymous to nodule. Concretion connotes continuous growth externally by adding more source material. In this sense, deep-sea manganese nodule should be call manganese concretion. See also nodules. I2-3, I2-11; 2-10, 4-10, 4-12, 4-16, 4-17, 4-18, 5-3, 5-6, 5-7, 6-9.

Conglomerate – A coarse-grained, clastic sedimentary rock. Typically, it has large, grained granule, pebble, coble, or boulder embedded in fine grained matrix of sand, silt, or clay. Its grain sizes are greater than sandstone. Its unconsolidated equivalent is gravel. I4-9

Continental shelf – It is part of the continental margin that lies between coastline and continental slope (which deepens toward much deeper ocean floor). The continental shelf has a slope of 0.1 degree and at water depth of less than 200 m.

Copper minerals – 3-10.

Coprolite – It is a piece of fossilized dung – a replacement product (e.g., silica), not the fossilized excrement or palaeofaece. Dinosaur coprolites are better priced by amateur collectors, but some spiral ones came from marine ichthyosaurs, not land-dwelling dinosaurs. I5-9b; 5-1.

Coral – 6-12, 6-13.

Core – As used here, the core has three different meanings: 1) It is the innermost part of Earth at depth greater than 2,900 km, consisting of a liquid outer core and solid inner core. 2) It means drill core which is cylindrical sample collected from a drill hole. 3) It is a piece of rock that serves as a nucleation seeding for external chemical deposition from solution.

Correlation – As used in stratigraphy, the determination of contemporaries of geologic formations or units.

Crag – is a steep, rugged, protruding rock body. 3-1.

Cross bedding – An internal pattern of bedding within a formation, the newer sediments are deposited at an incline angle to an earlier depositional surface, in response to change of direction of current or wind. I4-5; 1-3, 4-5.

Crust – The outermost layer of the solid Earth. Its thickness ranges from a few kilometers under the ocean floor to a few tens of kilometers under the continent. Its lower boundary, called Moho, is the discontinuity in the depth-varying speed of seismic waves. It also has the ordinary meaning of crust – a hardened, enclosing shell or rind. 6-9.

Cryptocrystalline – It is used to describe crystals that are too small to be seen with ordinary microscope, but its crystalline structures are still identifiable with electronic microscope or by x-ray.

Crystal – A solid with repetitive, regular arrangement of atoms to show natural, external faces of definitive form. 'Glass crystal' is not crystal by this definition for lacking a crystalline structure.

Cyanobacteria – Bacteria that are capable of photosynthesis. They used to be viewed as blue-green algae, but not anymore. Cyanobacteria are the earliest recognizable organisms that built stromatolites – the oldest fossils. 4-15, 5-8.

Dendrite – A surficial, branching deposition at the layer interfaces. I2-12; 6-5.

Diapirism – The process by which the overlying rocks or formations have been ruptured or pierced by the underlying, low density layers such as salt bed that rises to form a salt dome. The piercing can also be mobilized by pressure change or heating to force the unconsolidated sediments to squeeze upward. Seismic vibration can induce liquefaction and piercing. I4-3.

Diatomite – a sedimentary rock composed of diatom which is single-cell algae. 4-6.

Differential erosion – A phenomenon resulted from difference in resistance to erosion.

Diffusion – Migration of elements or ions from areas of high to low concentrations. The diffusion can also be carried out by fluid transport in the mode of advective diffusion or dispersion.

Dike – As used for igneous rocks, a tabular igneous intrusion that cuts and fills across surrounding or host rocks. I3-19; 3-5.

Dispersion – Transport of solute by moving water in porous media, like advective diffusion.

Diorite – A plutonic rock with a composition intermediate between acidic (i.e., high silica content, like granite) and basic (gabbro, with high magnesium and calcium content). It is characterized by mixing of dark and light-colored minerals. I5-6.

Dolomite – A carbonate mineral with equal number of calcium and magnesium atom in its molecule. Unlike calcite, it does not effervesce in weak acid test. The name is also applicable to rock. To distinguish the two, the rock is often referred as dolostone.

Drag fold – A set of minor folds on the order of a few centimeters to meters, formed in the softer rocks between two rock bodies that move relatively to each other. It can be indicative of the direction of relative rock displacement. I5-13.

Dripstone – Carbonate rock formed through dripping of water or evaporation in a cave, e.g., stalactite and stalagmite. The usage is extended here to mean rock formed by water drops on ground surface through evaporation. See tufa. I2-10; 2-14.

Druse – A small cavity in which small, protruding crystals may grow, e.g., druse quartz. 3-16, 5-4E

Ductile – As compared to brittle, it can sustain 5 to 10% deformation before the rock is fractured. It is a property that allows solid-state flow. I2-2; 1-10.

Dune – An abbreviation of sand dune, which consists of loose sand piled or heaped up by wind along beaches or in the desert. I4-5; 4-17, 5-3.

Enclave – An inclusion.

Eukaryote is a cellular organism with distinct nucleus, which holds genetic material such as DNA. It includes all organisms other than eubacteria and archaebacteria.

Evaporite – minerals or rocks that form through evaporation. 4-8.

Exfoliation – The process by which thin shells of rocks are peeled off, like the peeling of onion skin.

Exhumation – The exposure of buried features or rocks by erosional removal of overlying rocks.

Exsolution – is the process whereby an initially homogeneous solid is split, as the temperature and pressure changes, into two or more distinct crystalline products without addition or deletion of material. 3-4A, 3-17, 3-21.

False color – is the color produced outside the normal visual spectra, for example, using infrared or ultraviolet light camera. For visual enhancement, it can also be digitally manipulated as such. 4-10, 5-9.

Fault – A rock fracture that has visible, relative displacement across it, on the order of a few centimeters to hundreds of kilometers. I5-3; 4-19, 5-5.

Felsic – is a light-colored igneous rock, usually consisting of quartz and sodium- or potassium-rich feldspar such as plutonic granite or volcanic rhyolite.

Figure I – The 'I' refers to figure number in the predecessor of this book.

Flash flood – A sudden flood caused by heavy rain of short duration. Its huge flow volume or rate can overflow channels, which are normally dry or with low flow rate.

Flint – It is synonymous with chert but a more restrictive usage for dark, brown variety in association with limestone. 4-9.

Fluorescence is the light emitted or reflected under ultraviolet light source. If the object continues to fluoresce for a short time after the UV source is switched off, it is phosphorescent. Some organisms can fluoresce without the UV stimulation, they are biofluorescent. 1-12, 2-13, 3-21, 4-10, 4-16, 6-8.

Fossils – Any records that are left by extinct organisms. Fossils are remains of body parts that have been calcified, silicified, or pyritized. Fossils also include the preserved activity products such as dungs, animal tracks as well as their biogenic mats and reefs. 4-6, 5-1, 5-8, 6-3.

Fracture – It is a break in rock due to mechanical failure under stress. It may or may not have displacement, including crack, joint, and fault.

Fracking – is an abbreviation for hydraulic fracturing. It is an artificial process to dislodge oil and gas from tightly held underground shale formation.

Fractal – denotes geometric form of a part that is the same statistically as the whole in shape and properties. For example, a rhombohedral calcite crystal can disintegrate into several smaller but geometrically alike crystals. Each is a fractal to others. Fractal is often used in the design of small-scale experiment for the large, natural, real application. 2-12.

Franklinite – Zinc-iron oxide. 2-13.

Frictional heating – Heating originated from friction during displacement along a fault.

Fused silica – It is a compound of silica that has been artificially fused and solidified. It does not have crystalline structure. 1-4B.

Geode – A nodule with hollow or filled spherical or sub-spherical cavity. Typically, it is walled by chalcedony with its cavity filled or partially filled with quartz or calcite crystals. I1-11, I1-15, I1-18; 1-4, 1-9, 1-12, 4-10, 5-2, 6-9, 6-12, 6-13.

Gneiss – High grade metamorphic rock, foliated or banded. I3-10, I3-13, I5-3, I5-14, I5-18; 3-3, 3-19.

Graded bedding – A sequence of bedding of which an individual bed starts with coarse grain at the base and gradually reduces its grain size to the top; the cycle is typically repeated to have a sequence or repetition of graded bedding. A reverse grading from fine to coarse grains can happen too.

Granite – A light-colored, coarse-grained plutonic igneous rock (formed at depths) of which the quartz content ranges from 20 to 60 percent of the light components and the ratio of alkaline (sodium or potassium) feldspar to the total feldspar ranges between 35 and 90 percent. I3-5, I3-6, I3-9, I3-10, I5-14, I5-17; 3-1, 3-5, 3-22.

Granodiorite – A coarse-grained plutonic rock with composition between granite and diorite. I5-7.

Graphite – A grey, black, soft mineral of carbon. Unlike anthracite (coal), it is not combustible. 3-18.

Gravel – An aggregate of unconsolidated, round rock fragments with grain diameter greater than 2 mm, including different proportions of granules, pebbles, cobbles, and boulders. It consolidates to become conglomerate.

Groundmass – is the matrix part of a porphyritic igneous rock. It is very-fine grained without visible crystals, in contrast to the visible phenocrysts – big crystals. 6-2.

Groundwater – 4-19, 5-3, 5-5.

Gypsum – A hydrous calcium sulfate ($CaSO_4 \cdot 2H_2O$). It is an evaporite and can appear in various crystal forms, for example, selenite. I4-1, I5-4; 4-8.

Hanksite – A greenish yellow hexagonal evaporite. I5-4.

Hematite – Ferric oxide, Fe_2O_3. 3-8.

Hiatus – A break or interruption in the continuity of sedimentation caused either by no deposition or by erosional removals before newer sediments were deposited again.

Igneous – Related to rock or mineral that solidifies from magma (molten rock). Ch 3.

Illuvium – is the residual after the rock has been weathered and leached. In soil sciences, it means the redeposited leachates. 4-18.

Ilmenite – is an iron-black, opaque mineral with rhombohedral crystal form. It is a mineral made of ferrous oxide and titanium dioxide, $FeO\,TiO_2$. It is the principal source mineral for titanium, Ti. 1-8.

Inclusion – A fragment of rock that was formed earlier and included in the newer igneous rock. It is also known as xenolith or enclave. I3-1; 1-5, 3-6.

Intermittent – A spring or a stream that discharges only during certain period, but it is dry most of the time.

Jasper – It is an opaque chalcedony – cryptocrystalline silica formed with volcanic rocks, like lava. Usually, it is reddish brown and irregularly shaped. I5-13, I5-20; 1-3, 1-11, 4-3, 4-12, 4-13, 6-1.

Joint – A potential or actual fracture in minerals or rocks without displacement across it.

Karst – A type of topography that develops by dissolution of limestone, dolomite, or gypsum. It is characterized with sink holes, caves, depressions, stalactite, stalagmite, and subsurface streams.

Kyanite – a greenish blue, columnar aluminosilicate, a metamorphic mineral. $Al_2O_3SiO_2$. 3-13.

Labradorite – A plagioclase with greater calcium than sodium content, which often displays bluish iridescence. 3-21.

Lamina – Very fine, thin layering in sediments or sedimentary rocks. 4-1, 4-2, 4-5, 4-15.

Lava – Magma (molten rock) that oozes to the Earth's surface. It also refers to rock that has solidified from lava flow, such as rhyolite, andesite, and basalt. I5-22; 2-14, 3-7, 3-17.

LD – It is an abbreviation of 'Long Dimension', used only in this book for sizing a specimen.

Lepidolite – See mica. I5-11; 3-9.

Liesegang rings (banding) – Secondary, color rings or curved bands which precipitate from fluids that enter porous host rocks, notable in sandstone, lithified volcanic ash, and weathered granite. I5-6; 4-4, 5-5.

Lichen – Symbiotic assembly of algae and fungi on rock surface in dry climate. Algae extract moisture and nutrients through photosynthesis and supply food to fungi; and in return, fungi provide protection to algae. Depending on species variety, lichen can show various colors and forms. I1-12, I5-1; 1-2.

Limestone – A sedimentary rock that consists mainly of calcite. It is aggregate of organic debris or inorganic deposition from calcium-carbonate bearing solution. Ch I2, I2-4, I2-5, I2-6, I2-8, I2-9, I5-1, I5-2; Ch 2, 2-5, 2-6, 2-10, 2-14, 5-4, 6-5.

Liquefaction – Refer to the state of transforming weak, incoherent, unconsolidated layers into liquid form that can pierce overlying layers, as induced by strong seismic shaking or excessive overburden pressure. I4-3.

Lithification – The process of transforming unconsolidated sediments into cemented and consolidated sedimentary rocks.

Lithostatic pressure – The pressure exerted by a column or stack of rocks, analogous to hydrostatic pressure by a column of water.

Mafic – It refers to rock with dark minerals, usually silicates with high magnesium, calcium, and iron content. Its counterpart is light or felsic rock.

Magma – Molten rocks.

Magnetite & **Lodestone**. 3-22.

Malachite – A bright, green hydrous copper carbonate mineral. $Cu_2CO_3(OH)_2$. I1-17; 3-10.

Mantle – The layer or shell between the crust and outer core of Earth. It is about 2,900 km thick.

Marble – Recrystallized limestone through metamorphism without going through melting. I2-3, I2-7, I2-15, I2-16, I2-18, I3-7, I5-19, I5-22; 2-1, 2-2, 2-4, 2-9, 2-14, 6-5.

Martian blueberries – are nickname for small pebbles on Mars for their sizes and bluish false color. 5-9.

Matrix – The fine-grained material that fills the interstices of coarse-grained crystals in igneous rocks. It also refers the fine-grained part of conglomerate. 2-10, 3-7, 5-6, 5-8, 6-3, 6-6.

Metamorphism – Transformation of existing minerals and rocks into assemblage of rocks in new temperature, pressure, and chemical conditions at depths far below surficial weathering and cementation zones. It is a solid-to-solid transformation.

Meteorite – Rock originates naturally outside but falls on our Earth. 5-10.

Meteofalse – A rock falsely identified as meteorite. Also nicknamed meteowrong. 5-11.

Mica – A group of silicates with complex chemical formula and sheet-like structure. It can be readily split into fine laminae with luster on the surface. It can be transparent or translucent tinted with white (muscovite), black (biotite), golden (phlogopite), pink/purple (lepidolite), or sericite (small, flaky). 3-9.

Migmatite – A rock mixture of igneous (granite) and metamorphic (gneiss) rocks. It results from partial melting of metamorphic rock and recrystallization of the melt into igneous rock. I5-14, I5-18.

Monzonite – A rock with composition between syenite and diorite, with equal amount of orthoclase and plagioclase but with little or no quartz. I5-7.

Moqui ball – is a sandstone ball (nodule or concretion) with hematite rind. Their individual sizes can range from one to ten centimeters in diameter. It comes from Navajo sandstone formation, originally from Jurassic sand dunes. 5-3, 5-9.

Mudstone – Rock equivalent to shale but lacking the fine lamination or fissuring. I4-2, I4-3, I4-4, I4-6.

Mylonite – Rocks formed through extreme brecciation and pulverization under steady shear stress. The less competent components may show ductile flow that engulfs more competent fragments. Mylonite is named for texture and it can have various mineral compositions. I2-1, I2-2; 3-15.

Nodule – A rounded or irregular shaped body that forms and embeds in sedimentary rocks. It is usually an aggregate of mineral grains and is harder than its surrounding rocks. See also concretion. I2-3, I2-11, I2-13, I5-21; 1-1, 2-10, 4-10, 4-14, 4-17, 4-18, 6-9.

Obelisk – is a stone pillar with rectangular cross section and a pyramidal top. 3-7.

Oblate – A spheroid of which one axis is shorter than the other two of equal length.

Obsidian – A glassy volcanic rock, dark colored with conchoidal fracture. I5-14; 3-17.

Offset –The displacement between two geologic units that used to be contiguous before faulting.

Onlapping – An overlap of sedimentary layers with the overlying layer extending or pinching out more than the underlain layer. I4-5.

Onyx – Straight, color-banded chalcedony. A Mexican onyx is a carbonate (calcite), not silica. 1-12, 2-15.

Oolitic – It is a texture of fish-egg like aggregates. It can grow from oolith (eggs of fish or shellfish). I2-9.

Opal – It is solid, hydrous silica jell. It can occur in various low-temperature conditions in veins or nodules. It can appear in volcanic or sedimentary terrain. The best of it shows opalescent luster. Most are white tinted with other hues. If heated, its value as a gemstone can decrease through dehydration. 1-1C, 1-12, 4-18, 6-4.

Orbicular granite – Granite or gneiss with internal ball-shape (orbicular) texture. I5-17.

Orthoclase – A potassium feldspar or K-feldspar in granitic rocks. It is white or reddish. 3-4, 3-5.

Overburden – The material above a layer of interest.

Oxygenation – Production of oxygen by nature, through photosynthesis by plants or some bacteria.

Parallelepiped – A six-sided solid with each side being a parallelogram. 3-12.

Parallelogram – A plane geometry enclosed by two pairs of parallel line segments. 3-12.

Parent rock – It is the source rock from which another younger rock has originated.

Patina – A thin, weathered coating on the surface of metals or stones. It differs from desert varnish in that the patina originates from weathering of the object itself, not external addition as in varnish.

Pegmatite – is a dike-like granitic intrusion, standing for the last stage of magma evolution. Its crystals are typically larger than the equivalents in granite. 3-4, 3-9.

Peridotite – An ultrabasic igneous rock, primarily composed of olivine. I5-18; 3-2, 3-6.

Pebble – A rock fragment having a diameter between 4 and 64 mm.

Petrified wood – It is a fossil wood that has been chemically replaced by silica. Usually, the silicification happens to woody part only; rarely the bark is silicified. I5-8, I5-9, I5-10; 4-10, 4-11, 4-16, 6-4, 6-8.

Phenocryst – refers to big crystals in contrast to finely grained ground mass (background matrix) in porphyritic igneous rocks. 3-5, 6-2.

Phonolite – A fine grained extrusive volcanic rock, composed of silica-deficient feldspathoid which is one category in QAPF classification. 1-13H.

Phosphorescent – Short-time light emission after the causative light source is turned off.

Phylogenetic tree – is a scheme of classification for organisms according to evolutionary development and diversification, expressed in a diagram of tree-like branches. 5-8, 5-10.

Playa – A dry lake in the desert. Most of the time, it is dry.

Post-depositional – Something happened after a depositional event.

Prokaryote – is a microscopic, uni-cellular organism without clearly defined nucleus and cell membrane and absent of some organelles, which are organized or specialized cell structures.

Pumice – rock formed from volcanic ash. It is porous but impermeable and can float in water. 3-17.

Pyrite – An iron sulfide, FeS_2. It is usually yellow with cubic or octahedral crystalline form. It is nicknamed fool's gold. I5-15.

Pyroclastic – Clastic rocks formed through volcanic eruption, characterized by a mix of big and tiny fragments. I5-20; 3-7.

Pyroxene – A group of dark rock-forming minerals consisting of magnesium, calcium, aluminous silicates. Unlike the amphibole, it lacks the hydroxyl component and its cleavages, if seen, often intersect near 90 degrees, rather than 56 or 124 degrees. Jadeite (hard jade) belongs to pyroxene group. Pyroxenite is a rock consisting of pyroxene.

QAP – is a classification scheme (Streckeisen diagram) for felsic igneous rocks, based on the volumetric ratios of Q (quartz), A (alkaline feldspar), and P (calcium plagioclase). In addition, the diagram has a fourth component, foid, which is opposite to the Q apex (QAPF). The triangle FAP is used to classify silica-deficient rocks.

Quartz – see index under quartzite.

Quartzite – A metamorphic rock that has been transformed from sandstone at high temperature and pressure without going through melting. Ch I1, I1-3 to I1-10, I1-12, I1-13, I1-17, I1-18; Ch 1, 1-5, 1-6, 1-7, 1-8, 1-10.

Rare earth elements – A group of metallic elements with atomic number from 57 to 71 (the lanthanide series). As a group, each rare earth element is not rare, but they occur together in minute concentrations and are difficult to segregate them apart. They are important trace constituents for special metallurgy.

Redox – An abbreviation for reduction and oxidization processes. 5-3.

Rutile – An elongate prismatic, acicular, or needle-like mineral of titanium dioxide (TiO_2). I2-13; 1-8.

Sand/sandstone – Sand is a rock fragment of which the diameter lies between 1/16 and 2 mm. I3-10, I4-5; 4-5, 4-7, 4-17, 6-5.

Saturated – Depending on context, 'saturated' has two different connotations. 1) In groundwater, it means water has fully filled the porous space. 2) In solution chemistry, it means a solute has dissolved to the full extent in solvent. The chemical saturation depends on temperature and pressure as well as the presence or absence of other solutes. A solution can be over-saturated, which is at unstable state, and a solute can settle out of the solution due to mechanical disturbance or addition of a seeding solute. 5-3.

Schistosity – foliation that is formed by parallel arrangement of minerals, for example, mica.

Sedimentary rocks – see Ch I2, I4; Ch2, 4.

Semi-conductor – A solid substance that acts like an electrical insulator or conductor, depending on the direction of electric current flow.

Schist – A medium grade, foliated metamorphic rock, which can be split into thin flakes or slabs. I5-16; 3-3.

Schorl, tourmaline – Schorl is a common dark, black tourmaline. Big tourmaline crystal makes good museum display, and some can be of gem quality. 1-5.

Septarium – A spheroidal concretion made of mud or marl (calcareous mud), which dehydrates to yield interior inter-connected cracks and the cracks are filled with calcite or aragonite. I5-21; 4-14, 4-19.

Sericite – A short, flaky, white mica. 1-5, 5-8.

Serpentine – A hydrous, iron-magnesium silicate. It is green with greasy, silky luster and, when touched, soapy feeling. It can be knife scratchable, as distinguishable from jade. 3-2.

Shale – A sedimentary rock consisting chiefly of clay. It is finely layered and splintery. I4-7.

Silica – Silicon dioxide. Ch I1; Ch 1.

Silicate – A mineral consisting of anion SiO4 (or other forms) and metallic ions. Ch I3; Ch 3.

Silt – A rock fragment with size ranging from 1/256 to 1/16 mm in diameter.

Sink hole – A hole resulted from dissolution of limestone, salt, or gypsum. See also karst.

Simulation – A computer modeling that is purported to explain or simulate a physical system.

Solid solution – is a solid of which the chemical composition lies between two end members.

Sorting – A measure of the uniformity in grain size distribution of sediments.

Slickenside – is a surface with striations caused by breakage or friction on a fault plane. The striations are asymmetric. You can use your fingers to feel the relative direction of fault movement. 1-10.

Snowball (global) theory – stipulates the entire Earth had been covered with snow or ice for certain periods of time in the Pre-Cambrian era. 5-8.

Solubility – the extent that a solute can be dissolved in a solvent (e.g., water).

Speleology – denotes exploration or study of caves. A secondary mineral that forms in the caves through interaction with water is called speleothem. 2-6, 2-7, 2-8, 2-11.

Sphalerite – Zinc sulfide, (Zn, Fe)S. 2-13, 3-20.

Spheroid – It is like a sphere with one axial length greater (prolate) or shorter (oblate) than the other two.

Stalactite – is a cave deposit that hangs downward from cave ceiling. 2-6, 2-15, 6-12, 6-13.

Stalagmite – is a cave deposit that rises above cave ground. 2-6, 2-15, 6-12, 6-13.

Stratigraphy – study of rock strata – its correlation, condition of formation, and evolution.

Streak – Long, narrow lines on the surface of rocks, distinctive with different colors. It also means the color of powdered or pulverized mineral, used sometimes to help mineral identification of hand specimen.

Streckeisen – see QAP.

Striae – Linear, parallel, short, slight ridges or grooves on a flat surface. (Singular: stria.)

Stromatolite – is a term attributable to shallow-water carbonate deposits or sedimentary structures constructed by cyanobacteria and other organisms. Stromatolite also incorporates some non-carbonaceous sediments. It shapes like a mound and appears laminated and columnar. It is the fossil building but is not the fossil builders. Stromatolites are the oldest biogenic products known on Earth; however, stromatolites appear sporadically through the geologic time to the present. Oncolite is a variety with spherule nodules and thrombolite is another variety with clogged mass without lamination. 4-12, 5-8.

Suiseki – The art of stone appreciation in Japanese.

Talc – the defining mineral for Mohs scale of 1. It is whitish, greenish, or greyish hydrous silicate. It has greasy, soapy feel. I5-19.

Tektite – rock that was melted from rocks at a meteor impact site, catapulted into the air, shaped aerodynamically, and fallen back to Earth as a solid glassy rock. 5-12.

Thulite – A manganese-bearing variety of zoisite. It is purplish with shades of pink or red. I2-16.

Tourmaline – A group of hydrous silicate with a variety of metallic elements. It occurs as 3-, 6-, or 9- sided prismatic crystal with striations across the faces. Some are of gem quality, but most appear as common, black schorl. I1-13; 3-9.

Trachyte – A group of porphyritic, extrusive volcanic rocks with alkaline feldspar and minor mafic minerals. 1-3H.

Travertine – is a thinly bedded carbonate deposit (calcite/aragonite) with various colors of white, yellow, or orange. It forms through surface (hot springs) or subsurface evaporation (caves). I2-11; 2-3, 2-6, 2-7, 2-8, 2-11, 5-4.

Tufa – A calcareous incrustation over rocks around hot or warm springs. Formed through evaporation, it is spongy and porous. See dripstone. I2-10; 2-6.

Turbidite – is sediment or rock formed by turbidity currents. It is characterized by graded bedding (bottom to top, coarse to fine grained or vice versus) and moderate sorting.

Ulexite – A boron-bearing evaporite in the desert. It is nicknamed, TV rock, for its optical fiber-like behavior. I5-15.

Ultima Thule – is a gaseous, bi-spherical space object in the post-Pluto belt. Figuratively it means beyond the known world. Officially it has been renamed Arrokoth – an American tribal name. 5-2.

Unconformity – It is a stratigraphic boundary that separate rocks of different ages, but it should not be a fault contact surface. I1-10, I4-2, I4-3.

Varnish, desert varnish – It is a thin film cover of rock (a few micrometers). It is hard, shining, or glazed iridescent with various colors. It is a coating mix of clay, iron & manganese oxides, with some microbial. It is an add-on to stable, hard rocks in dry desert environment.

Vein – A thin, sheet-like intrusion into crevices in rocks. Veinlet refers to small, thin vein.

Ventifact – A stone shaped, worn, faceted, cut, or polished by wind blasting in the desert or other very windy environment. I3-4, I3-5; 1-3F.

Vermiculate – An adjective to describe a stone that has the appearance of being 'gnawed by worm'. I2-6.

Volcanic bombs/rocks – I3-1, I3-2, I3-3, I3-7, I3-11, I3-12, I5-14, I5-22; 3-6, 3-7, 3-12, 3-14, 3-17, 6-2.

Volcanic ash – An ash-like rock that has been spewed into the air by volcanic eruption before its falling to the ground and cemented. I3-8, I5-3; 3-7, 3-12, 3-14, 3-17, 5-5.

Vug – Cavity. 6-9.

Wonder rock – Nevada wonder rock – a lithified volcanic ash (rhyolite) with multiple bands of diffusion relics (Liesegang bands). It does not have to originate from Wonder, Nevada. I5-6, I5-7; 4-4.

Wash, desert wash – A broad, dry gravely bed along an intermittent gully or stream in the desert.

Weathering rind – A rind of weather product over a piece of individual rock, e.g., cobble. It often masks the identity of its enclosing rock. It differs from 'spheroidal weathering' in that the latter refers to bedrocks. I5-6.

Willemite – Zinc silicate, Zn_2SiO_4. It has intense green florescence under UV light. 2-13

Xenolith – An 'alien rock' or inclusion in an igneous rock. It was transported as solid in a moving magma. The xenolith and the host rock do not share the same mineralogical or chemical constituent or composition. It is texturally distinct from the host. I3-1; 3-6.

Zoisite – It is a hydrous calcium aluminosilicate, a green metamorphic mineral, altered from calcium rich mineral such as epidote. I2-16.